DIARY METHODS

SERIES IN UNDERSTANDING STATISTICS

S. NATASHA BERETVAS   Series Editor

SERIES IN UNDERSTANDING MEASUREMENT

S. NATASHA BERETVAS   Series Editor

SERIES IN UNDERSTANDING QUALITATIVE RESEARCH

PATRICIA LEAVY   Series Editor

Understanding Statistics
Exploratory Factor Analysis
Leandre R. Fabrigar and
Duane T. Wegener

Validity and Validation
Catherine S. Taylor

Understanding Measurement
Item Response Theory
Christine DeMars

Reliability
Patrick Meyer

Understanding Qualitative Research
Autoethnography
Tony E. Adams, Stacy Holman Jones,
and Carolyn Ellis

Qualitative Interviewing
Svend Brinkmann

*Evaluating Qualitative
Research: Concepts, Practices, and
Ongoing Debates*
Jeasik Cho

Video as Method
Anne M. Harris

Focus Group Discussions
Monique M. Hennink

The Internet
Christine Hine

Diary Methods
Lauri L. Hyers

Oral History
Patricia Leavy

*Using Think-Aloud Interviews and
Cognitive Labs in Educational Research*
Jacqueline P. Leighton

Qualitative Disaster Research
Brenda D. Phillips

Fundamentals of Qualitative Research
Johnny Saldaña

Duoethnography
Richard D. Sawyer and Joe Norris

*Analysis of the Cognitive Interview in
Questionnaire Design*
Gordon B. Willis

LAURI L. HYERS

DIARY METHODS

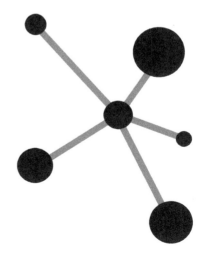

Oxford University Press is a department of the University of Oxford. It furthers
the University's objective of excellence in research, scholarship, and education
by publishing worldwide. Oxford is a registered trade mark of Oxford University
Press in the UK and certain other countries.

Published in the United States of America by Oxford University Press
198 Madison Avenue, New York, NY 10016, United States of America.

© Oxford University Press 2018

Library of Congress Cataloging-in-Publication Data
Names: Hyers, Lauri L., author.
Title: Diary methods / Lauri L. Hyers.
Description: New York : Oxford University Press, [2018] |
Includes bibliographical references and index.
Identifiers: LCCN 2017023281 | ISBN 9780190256692 (pbk. : alk. paper)
Subjects: LCSH: Qualitative research—Methodology. | Diaries. |
Narrative inquiry (Research method) | Social sciences—Methodology.
Classification: LCC H62.H895 2018 | DDC 001.4/2—dc23
LC record available at https://lccn.loc.gov/2017023281

9 8 7 6 5 4 3 2 1

Printed by Webcom Inc., Canada

CONTENTS

Preface vii

Acknowledgments xi

CHAPTER 1   Introduction: The Emergence of the Diary as a Research Tool 1

CHAPTER 2   Diary Data Collection as a Qualitative Research Method 27

CHAPTER 3   Qualitative Diary Research Design 61

CHAPTER 4   Analyzing and Writing a Report on Qualitative Diary Research 103

CHAPTER 5   Putting It All Together: Planning, Evaluation, and Ethics of Qualitative Diary Research 139

References 169

Index 199

PREFACE

Among the many choices of methods available to qualitative researchers, the diary method is distinct for its capacity to capture phenomena of interest on a regular basis, in context, and over time. Apart from that, the method is as flexible as other qualitative methods and can be adapted to suit a variety research questions, diarists (a.k.a. "participants"), data formats, epistemological assumptions, and styles of analysis. Whether the diaries are located in preexisting archives or solicited from participant recruits, the resulting data can be rich and compelling. However, a qualitative diary study is usually not the first choice of research design when one is considering a new line of research. In addition to sounding like a whole lot of work, the diary method is somewhat *off the beaten path*, a bit mysterious, and even kitschy. Researchers typically view the very possibility of conducting a diary study with great reticence, perhaps peering skeptically at the method from the corner of one eye. Despite such resistance, many qualitative researchers have adopted the diary method with great success. With a little better understanding of what is involved, those who are hesitantly considering the method may also come to find that a diary study is well worth their while.

There are several contemporary trends in the sensibilities of the popular culture and human science discourse that quite nicely overlie the perspective offered in many diary studies. In fact, we are living in an era that not only speaks to but depends on the very data that a diary creates—an immediate snapshot of a moment. First, with new social media and digital technology, there has been an explosion of attention to the online, in the moment, "live" individuals, and their everyday lives. This new technologically assisted self-focus is evident in the popularity of obsessively documenting our thoughts, behaviors, and social engagements. Web-based electronic scrapbooking on social media and wireless lifestyle tracking devices have engendered "digital narcissism" and the cyber-tethered self (Tanner, Maher, & Fraser, 2013). Privacy is replaced with welcomed intrusion by others into our daily lives. We invite others to monitor it all. It now seems somewhat quaint that diary researchers in decades past worried that solicited diary participants would be encumbered by reporting on their lives while they were trying to live them. This has now become a cultural norm.

Second, society is more concerned than ever about records. In the 1985 movie *Brazil,* directed by Terry Gilliam, bureaucracy has engulfed citizens in piles of churning paperwork. Although much of our documentation is in electronic rather than paper form today, we have expanded the amount and frequency of what we document *exponentially*—in our personal lives, in the workplace, and in educational settings. This is partly fueled by our markedly litigious and fact-checking culture. The scientific method and the ease of accessing data have led us to become very meticulous about keeping track of our sources and employing only evidenced-based solutions to life's questions. With cyber documentation (Jones, 2016), we generate records that not only store the past but make it available to change the future. Diary researchers stand to gain when regular citizens are not only amenable to, but even perhaps psychologically addicted to, chronic documentation, as they wind up doing much of the work for us, and with pleasure.

Third, the scientific method has become more precise than ever. Even with social-scientific phenomena, we are able to examine microphenomena, eyeblinks, response time, covert cognitions, and brain waves to the millisecond. We can literally freeze time to break down all sorts of implicit and unconscious processes. Computer assisted statistics, fine-tuned measurements, and carefully crafted operational definitions help isolate cause-and-effect relationships and frame rigorous conclusions. This kind of thinking is useful for diary researchers, as the diary method offers a more precise snapshot of events in context—state phenomena—that cross-sectional trait measurements just cannot reveal. This, in fact, has motivated my own use of the diary in research. As a feminist social constructionist, I have been compelled to devote the better part of my academic scholarship thus far working with colleagues to document everyday incidents of discrimination that one would typically forget (e.g., Hyers, 2010; Hyers & Hyers, 2008; Hyers, Swim, & Mallet, 2006; Swim, Cohen, & Hyers, 1998). At times, the diarists and the readers themselves have dismissed daily discrimination as trivial or harmless, but the chronic nature of these events, written in endless diary entries by diligent research participants, reveals the frequency and therefore the sociopsychological gravity of everyday prejudice and its weight in reifying social stratification.

Fourth, and perhaps in response to each of these aforementioned trends, there is a countercultural resistance in the form of the "slow knowledge" or "slow science" movements (Orr, 2002). There is a desire to retreat, to unplug, and to become more contemplative. A nostalgic return to simpler times makes the good old-fashioned diary seem like a welcome means to a more holistic understanding of the self and others.

Considering these cultural forces, it seems like diary research will continue to be used as it has in the past by a steady minority of researchers. It may, in fact, even increase in popularity. Technology will continue to change the significance of the diary in daily life and as a tool of social science research. In this volume, the diary as a cultural phenomenon will first be explored, as well as how it came to be used by researchers. Following this will be a discussion of the archival and solicited diary in qualitative research in particular. Next, the basics of designing an archival and solicited qualitative diary study will be reviewed. Analyzing and writing (. . . and analyzing and writing and analyzing and writing and analyzing and writing . . .) will be discussed next. Finally, the strengths, weaknesses, and ethical considerations of qualitative diary research will be explored.

ACKNOWLEDGMENTS

I must first thank my wonderful advisor and friend, Janet Swim, who got me into this line of work when I was a graduate student at Penn State. Together we witnessed how qualitative diaries can be a powerful tool for social justice research. I am grateful to Patricia Leavy, Abby Gross, Courtney McCarroll, and the helpful production staff at Oxford University Press for conceiving of this project and bringing me on board. I also want to convey sincere appreciation to my supportive colleagues at West Chester University of Pennsylvania who regularly reached out to provide encouragement. I especially want to thank the many mentors, friends, and assistants who were in the trenches with me, helping with scholarly resources, copyedits, and writing advice, including Bill Cross, Samantha Fernandez, Karen Kohn, Debbie Mahlstedt, Shane Martin, Richard Minuti, and Akemi Nishida. Finally, I want to thank my mom and dad for their inspiration and my Philly friends for their patience during my many writing retreats at the Hollow. I dedicate this book to my son, Shannon, who's first diary at the age of two was full of nothing but scribbles mimicking grown-up writing, a memento of days gone by and a vivid reminder of how time flies.

DIARY METHODS

INTRODUCTION

The Emergence of the Diary as a Research Tool

> Diaries are among our most precious items of heritage. No other kind of document offers such a wealth of information about daily life and the ups and downs of human existence.
>
> —The Great Diary Project

OVER THE last several centuries, diary keeping has evolved into a popular medium through which diarists can bear witness to their experiences and the events of the world. The diary is a treasure trove, containing the riches of first-hand testimony on a wealth of subjects: from the adventures of travel to the despairs of prison, from the mundane ruminations of adolescence to the horrors of the battlefield. Langford and West (1999) have noted how the diary resides in the personal life space of the writer, uniquely balancing "between the spontaneity of reportage and the reflectiveness of crafted text, between selfhood and events, between subjectivity and objectivity, between the private and the public" (p. 8). Once adopted as an instrument for research, the diary provides researchers access to what Sheble and Wildemuth (2009) describe as the "places they might not otherwise be able to go: personal homes, the minds of individuals, and geographically dispersed locations"

(p. 16). The embedded and contextualized nature of diary data appeals to those in the humanities and social sciences who are seeking the "thick description" that is the hallmark of qualitative research (Geertz, 2003).

From Literary Device to Research Tool: A Brief History of Role of the Diary and Diary Research in the Social Sciences

To appreciate the current uses of the diary as a qualitative research tool in the human sciences, it is helpful to understand the interrelated history of the diary as it migrated from its survivalist origins, to the privileged pens of the aristocracy, and on to become a part of popular culture. From ancient times to the present, "citizen scientists" have maintained diary logs of their observations of natural phenomena, ranging from spectacular astronomical events to the appearance of garden hedgehogs, with little attention to the diarists' personal thoughts and life events (Irwin, 1995; Russell, 2014; Silvertown, 2009). Typical of this style is the quaint diary of naturalist and citizen scientist Edith Holden, who only hints at personal reflection in her year-long horticultural record, as in this entry about a springtime morning (1906):

> April 1: Very still, grey day. I went to a little spinney to see a large bunch of the Great Round-Leaved Willow, which is a perfect picture just now, covered all over with great golden catkins, that light up the copse like hundreds of little fairy lamps. The bees were humming all round it, busy gathering pollen (p. 39).

The regular recording of observations in a diary format by botanists, farmers, hunters, explorers, and astronomers has served practical purposes, and was easily taken into the purview of modern positivist science (Aono & Kazui, 2008; British Ecological Society [BES], 2014). At the same time, there was a somewhat limited use of diary-style documents for the recording of everyday life, such as public deeds, financial logs, and church records; however, private confessional writing was relatively nonexistent (Smyth, 2013). It is only relatively recently that diary keeping emerged as a literary and contemplative possibility, most perceptibly around the beginning of the seventeenth century (Moran, 2013). During the

Victorian era, the diary was brought into the social-psychological realm. Growing interest in this new genre of private confessional diary writing eventuated in the publishing of various diaries for public consumption. Whether released during the writer's lifetime or posthumously, personal diaries became increasingly more available, attracting the interest of the general public and scholars alike (Carter, 1997). The diary became a familiar medium of expression and a convenient means to record (and subsequently read) about everyday life. Scholars began delving into extant diaries as source material and soliciting participants to keep specially tailored diaries; thus diary keeping as a social scientific research tool developed out of this larger cultural practice of private diary keeping.

The Diary Emerges in the Literature of Popular Culture

Innumerable cultural transformations have contributed to the accessibility of (and the inspiration for) the diary as a medium of self-expression: the printing press, the Industrial Revolution, institutionalized public schooling, the rise of a middle class, emerging widespread public literacy, the Protestant Reformation, and social pluralism (Boerner, 1969; Seelig, 2006). Diary writing as a religious practice has been variously employed by a range of religious clergy—Catholic monastics, Zen Buddhists, and Islamic Sufis—though, historically, this spiritual aid was unavailable to lay practitioners who could not read and write (Legeune, 2009; Makdisi, 1986; Terzioglu, 2002). A perceptible boon to the diary as a personal tool for the common layperson came from the spiritual contemplations of Protestants who wrote "journals of conscience" (an adjunct to prayer and an alternative to the Catholic confessional) documenting their daily deeds and misdeeds as part of their personal spiritual development (Fothergill, 1974; Kupky, 1928; Todd, 1992). One finds such guilty ruminations in the diary writings from the late 1500s by Puritan Samuel Ward (Cressy and Ferrell, 2005):

26 May
How God gave this morning, being Sunday, before thou rise, some good meditation against wearisomeness in God's service. Thy dullness this day in hearing God's word. Thy carelessness and impotency in exhorting thy Christian brethren.

Thy unwillingness to pray. The little affection I had in praying in S.J.'s study. Remember thy promise now, when thou are not well, how if God restore thee to health thou wilt be careful to perform all Christian duties. Remember this.

27 May
Thy overmuch delight in these transitory pleasures of this world.

. . .

June 14
My negligence is not calling upon God before I went to the chapel, and the little desire I had there to call on God, and my drowsiness in God's service. My sins even through the whole day [17 enumerated in great detail] . . . and thus sin I daily against thee, O Lord. (p. 34)

Eventually, schoolchildren were encouraged to keep diaries as a (secular) form of righteous character-building. For instance, a children's magazine from the late 1800s advised readers (Jerome, 1878):

What is the good of a journal? There is very much. In the first place, it teaches habits of order and regularity. The boy or girl who every evening arranges the proceedings of the day in systematic order, and regularly writes them out, is not likely to be careless in other matters. (p. 790)

Thus, there developed an association of diary keeping with personal dedication, prudence, and a well-planned life that has stuck with the journal ever since (Pelish, 2016).

In addition, dramatic increases in travel (whether by choice or under duress) sparked one of the most influential diary forms—the travel diary (Abdelouahab, 2005; Monga, 1998). Personal travel diaries were kept by every type of sojourner imaginable, from devout religious pilgrims, to political emissaries, to trail-blazing solo women tourists (Howard, 1980; Keyserling, 1923; Roy, 1960; Schlissel, 2011). Some explorers documented daily danger and impending death, such as Antarctic adventurer Ernest Shackleton (published by Wild in 1923) who registered his life's last entry:

4 January

At last after 16 days of turmoil and anxiety on a peaceful sun-shining day we came to anchor in Grytvitken. How famil-iar the coast seemed as we passed down. We saw with full interest the places we struggled over after the boat journey. Now we must speed all we can but the prospect is not too bright for labour is scarce. The old smell of dead whale per-meates everything. It is a strange and curious place. A won-derful evening. In the darkening twilight I saw a lone star hover: gemlike above the bay. (p. 1)

Once connected with travel, diary writing came to be viewed as a necessity on one's literal journey and a poetic metaphor for one's figurative journey through life. This synergy is depicted in Hesse's fictional journal *Wanderung: Aufzeichnungen* (*Wandering: Notes and Sketches, 1920/1972*) where the protagonist's journey and journal commence simultaneously:

I love deeply everything at home, because I have to leave it. Tomorrow I will love other roofs, other cottages. I won't leave my heart behind me, as they say in love letters. No, I am going to carry it with me over the mountains, because I need it, always. (p. 3)

Plentiful amongst the religious and literary elite and the growing middle class, the diary was unavailable to some who had a story to tell but lacked the luxury to write—due either to illiteracy, scarcity of time, or lack of security to leave traces of their private observations. Therefore, we are less likely to find represented in the archives very many diaries of the indentured, enslaved, and politically displaced at the time that diaries were coming into vogue. Their subjective experiences would be underrepresented in both the private and the public logs, regrettably; at a time of such cultural upheaval, they would have likely been quite compelling. Often sympathetic allies used their diaries to document the expe-riences of those unable to. An example is found in the detailed diary of William Still, son of an African American freedwoman and Underground Railroad leader who used his diary to keep detailed records of the humanity and character of each of the peo-ple he was assisting to freedom (Still & Finseth, 2007). Similarly, Reverend Butrick accompanied the Cherokee on their "Trail of

Tears" to Oklahoma in 1838 and used a diary to detail the terrifying hardship of their forced displacement (Musgrave, 1998):

Thursday.
As several waggons and some sick persons are still behind, we wait today for them. This morning a little child about 10 years old died. Previous to starting on this journey, I determined to let it be a journey of prayer, and to devote much time every day to that sacred duty, but instead of this, I have very strangely neglected prayer.

. . .

Friday & Saturday
Afflicted with a fever afternoons and a cough during the night. So also on the Sabbath was unable to attend meeting. Our dear Wloska had a meeting. It is disturbing to reflect on the situation of the nation. One detachment stopped at the Ohio River, two at the Mississippi, one four miles this side, one 16 miles this side, one 18 miles, and one 13 miles behind us. In all these detachments, comprising about 8,000 souls, there is now a vast amount of sickness, and many deaths. Six have died within a short time in Maj. Brown's company, and in this detachment of Mr. Taylors there are more or less afflicted with sickness in almost every tent; and yet all are houseless & homeless in a strange land, and in a cold region, exposed to weather almost unknown in their native country. But they are prisoners. True their own chiefs have directly hold of their hands, yet the U. States officers hold the chiefs with an iron grasp, so that they are obliged to lead the people according to their directions in executing effectually that Schermerhorn treaty. (p. 1)

Among the precious few of the first-hand antebellum diaries of an African-American writer is one by the Rev. Dr. Benjamin Tucker Tanner, a nineteenth-century editor, African Methodist Episcopal (AME) minister, bishop and founder of freedmen's schools, who, living in the North, had penned his anxieties (Woodson, 2010):

Friday Nov 23, 1860
I attended a wedding last night . . . It is a cold rainy day and I calculated upon visiting today but it is so disagreeable that

I concluded not. So I studied my regular hours. This political and financial condition of the country is terrible—rumors of secession, war, trouble.

. . .

December 24, 1860
Received a letter from Bishop Payne who is at home, also one from my sister Nancy. I spent about four hours in my study today. The country seems to be bordering on a civil war all on account of slavery. I pray God to rule and overrule all to his own glory and the good of man. (p. 1736)

Diary keeping did not contradict the feminine role, although the nature and weight given to women's diaries has not equaled that of men's (Gannett, 1992). Private diary keeping was an accessible form of expression for women and girls, though generally the earliest surviving "faithful friends" (Bunkers, 1987; Hunter, 1992) are the journals of women from the upper classes who had the ability and time to read and write (Brereton, 1998; Crane, 1983; Steinitz, 2011). One of the first documented diaries in history was actually written by a young woman, Sei Shogagon, who served as attendant to a court empress at the turn of the last millennium, in what is now Kyoto, Japan. She used her diary to record musings on nature and the goings-on of the court (Washburn, 2011). Due to their oft-restricted sphere of existence, women's diaries tended to focus more on domestic life, as is true of one the most voluminous of women's diaries at this time, the 2,000-page diary of eighteenth-century Quaker Elizabeth Drinker, which begins simply and ends poignantly, 49 years later—a life's work (Drinker and Crane, 1991):

1758, October 8
First day. Drank tea at Jos. Howell's; called to see M. Foulk.

. . .

1807, Nov. 3
Our old friend and acquaintance Sam Pleasants departed this life last night about 10 or 12 o'clock. I was much surprised, as well as shocked when I heard it, tho' he had been ill for a week past. He and wife have been married between 45 and

46 years. Sam Pleasants was about 71 years of age. Little did
I think last sixth day week, when he was talking with us in
this parlor, that I should never see him again. How uncertain
is Life! (p. 411)

Thus, as it evolved, private diary keeping connected one's life course
to an ongoing narrative, to an uneditable story the writer (and
possibly others) could refer to for reflection on what had passed,
sometimes on things having never been spoken. Writing created
a historical record, a tangible trace of small moments and fleeting
thoughts. The historical, psychological, and sensory record left in
the thousands of diaries produced in the centuries past was like no
other time before.

The Diary Stirs a Self-Reflective Self-Consciousness

The significant shift from oral traditions to widespread literacy in
Western culture made possible (or at least hastened) the sort of
self-reflective, contemplative writing common in diaries, thereby
impacting our very experience of our humanity. The technology of
private reflective writing and the potential for printing and publishing of autobiographical testimony encouraged—if not required—
self-consciousness, self-awareness, and self-objectification. As
Moran (2013) explained:

> Diaries can serve as a useful corrective, in showing the
> confusing randomness and singularity of everyday experi-
> ence as it is lived through. They help us to see the recent
> past as an era of still-to-be-decided tensions and contin-
> gent moments, instead of a story to which we already think
> we know the ending. Diaries show us that daily lives are
> experienced corporeally, as a series of sensual pleasures or
> discomforts. (p. 4)

Schlaeger (1999) has described how the "new preoccupation with
the inner self" and the spread of literacy led to "the printed word's
takeover of the mind" (p. 22). For Sorapure (2003), the more
recent act of online diary writing becomes a display of the self,
"a screening moment" of a "scrolling life." Ong (1982) describes
this relationship of the experience—written and then read—as one
that "touches the depths of the psyche," and further:

> The fuller reflective discovery of the self . . . is the result not only of writing but also of print: without these technologies the modern privatization of the self and the modern acute, doubly reflexive self-awareness are impossible. The evolution of consciousness through human history is marked by growth in articulate attention to the interior of the individual person as distanced . . . a consciousness [one] would never reach without writing. (p. 174)

Once written in a diary, our thoughts become a mirror, allowing for reflection and self-objectification. In the hands of others, the written diary becomes a window into a psychological moment, an opportunity to understand another's perspective and to reflect on our common humanity.

The Diary Contributes to New Disciplines of Human Inquiry

It may be more than mere coincidence that the popularizing of the autobiographical style of writing found in the diary preceded emerging scholarship of the humanities and the social sciences—some suggest that the diary hastened their emergence. The diary's introspective style may have actually encouraged the kind of self-consciousness that was a necessary precondition to the emergence of the self-reflective lens required in these academic disciplines (Ong, 1982). The mechanics of recorded self-reflection—of making a permanent record, of documenting memories that might otherwise be misremembered, and of the potential for the private self to be publicly revealed—opened up the possibility of a social scientific study of ourselves. On one hand, the private narration of the self may have increased our knowledge of human nature, according to Ong (1982):

> By separating the knower from the known, writing makes possible increasingly articulate introspectivity, opening the psyche as never before not only to the external objective world quite distinct from itself but also to the interior self against whom the objective world is set. (p. 105)

On the other hand, the permanent time-stamped record of the self may have actually changed human nature, creating a more empirical view of the self. The type of writing in the diary was quite consistent with the Renaissance ideal of empiricism, encouraging a view of the human experience that is no different from the scientist's or a historian's view of the world. As Moran (2013) notes, "There was a growing acceptance by the middle of the century of the significance of ordinary experience, how this might be articulated through diary writing, and even how this information might be useful to future historians" (p. 4). This is quite clear in Jerome (1878):

> A person who keeps a journal naturally tries during the day to remember things he sees, until he can write them down. Then the act of writing helps to still further fix the facts in his memory. Keeping a journal cultivates habits of observation. A well-kept journal furnishes a continuous and complete family history. It is sometimes very convenient to have a daily record of the year, and the young journalist will often have occasion to refer to his account of things gone by, a daily record of the year . . . and of his own progress. It is pleasant to exercise the faculty of writing history. (p. 790)

Thus Jerome suggests the diary helps one to better observe, remember, and revisit events to explore the progression of one's own life.

The Diary Becomes a Researcher's Tool

Scholars gradually began to pull diaries into their discourse in the fields of literature, history, geography, the humanities, sociology, and psychology. Diaries offered a subjective perspective on events in a way that historical documents could not, revealing the "intimate history of the recent past full of vivid detail and human interest" (Moran, 2013, p. 1). Several groundbreaking publications in the fledgling field of psychology incorporated diaries for illustrative purposes, as case studies, and as data sets. Psychologist William James (1902) included diaries among his prized *"documents humains"* in his descriptive survey of subjective religious experience—even excerpting from what was a best-selling read at his time, the diary of Ukrainian artist Marie Bashkirtseff. James quotes her:

[Monday, September 6]
I cry, I grieve, and at the same time I am pleased—no, not exactly that—I know not how to express it. But everything in life pleases me. I find everything agreeable, and in the very midst of my prayers for happiness, I find myself happy at being miserable. It is not I who undergo all this—my body weeps and cries; but something inside of me which is above me is glad of it all. (p. 96)

Interestingly, psychologist G. Stanley Hall (1904), also referred to Bashkirtseff's renowned diary, amongst many other diaries quoted in his multivolume study on adolescence. Occasionally, sets of diaries were published expressly for the use of select academic audiences. For example, the anonymous collection *A Young Girl's Diary* (Hug-Hellmuth, 1922) was intended by the editor "for parents, educators, and members of the medical and legal professions only," and earned a commendation by Sigmund Freud in the preface:

> This diary is a gem. Never before, I believe, has anything been written enabling us to see so clearly into the soul of a young girl during the years of pubertal development .... A description at once so charming, so serious, and so artless, that it cannot fail to be of supreme interest to educationists and psychologists. (Freud in Hug-Hellmuth, 1922, p. 7)

Clinicians in training used diaries as studies of mental illness, such as Squires' (1937) "psychopathographical sketch" of Dostoevsky in *Psychanalytic Review* and Wildermuth's study of two schizophrenic diarists in *Schizophrenia from the Inside* (1932). Diaries were also used for therapeutic purposes, such as anger diaries (Meltzer, 1937) and to understand dreaming in dream diaries (Calkins, 1893; Jewell, 1905; Van Eeden, 1913). Author Vernon Lee's interest in the psychology of aesthetics led her to collect and make available unedited diaries of responses to works of art in galleries "because I wanted to place my materials unspoilt at the disposal of other students" (Lee & Anstruther-Thomson, 1914, p. 365).

In line with the mindset that one's journal represents one's life journey, diaries were particularly useful in providing evidence of stage-progressed maturation and child development. Charles Darwin used his own diary of his children's maturational milestones in *A Biographical Sketch of an Infant* (1882) to document the psycholinguistics of infant development. In this case, the entries include a mix of Darwin's objective description of events, with a touch of his own subjective impressions and reactions as well:

April 11th
It appeared to me that the Baby decidedly looked at my finger, which it took in its Hand.

April 16th
The Baby can now put any object into its mouth with some skill. I observe when taken out of doors, & being annoyed by light *frowned* very much & almost closed its eyelids. Some weeks ago, when sucking some coldish milk, which it disliked, kept little frown on forehead, just like old person, when doing something disagreeable. Say 50–60 days old 7 or 8 weeks old. Continues occasionally to roll his eyes in drunken manner, whilst sucking.

April 16th
Was exceedingly amused by his pinnafore being put over his face & then withdrawn.—I think for some weeks pinching his nose & cheeks was a joke— How can he find bo-peep amusing? (p. none indicated)

Similarly, early child development expert and pioneering qualitative research methodologist Charlotte Bühler included diaries in her study of the inner experiences of child development as part of her "definite material from which we could learn whether expressions of well-being, complaint, hope, desire or resignation, ambition, or plans occurred in any definite, regular period of life" (1935, p. 405). Even early comparative developmental psychologists employed the diary to study animals, as in such Stanley's (1897) and Mill's (1896) series of observational diaries of the "earliest psychic life" of dogs, cats, rabbits, guinea pigs, pigeons, and domestic fowls. Gilman's (1921) developmental rendering of *A Dog's Diary* was amusingly published in the *Journal of Comparative Psychology*:

I am a black-and-white cocker spaniel, and, now being three years old, I feel that my experience may be understood by others.

On February 11th, I had a great disappointment, I thought one of my little brothers had arrived, for I suddenly saw something that looked very much like him, and I barked very loudly to show him that I was there too, but it turned out to be only my reflection in a stupid piece of furniture. I won't be fooled by that again, nor had I been before, when my mistress held me up in front of a mirror. Of course, there were new discoveries every day.

On the 14th I was much startled by an open fire on the hearth, and when I found that the house wasn't burning down, I decided to enjoy it instead of barking. (p. 312)

In the fields of sociology and economics, there were notable advocates of diary methods. In a 1925 methodological manual for students of sociology, sociologist Vivian Palmer (1928) advocated the use of diaries because they provide the "advantage of having been written by the individual whose experiences are being recorded, thus eliminating the filter of a second person," which in her view was well worthwhile, despite the cost that "details in which a sociologist is interested will be omitted by the person who writes the diary" (p. 181). Palmer was part of the "Chicago School," a group of interdisciplinary social scientists organized in the 1920s and 1930s that came to welcome the use of diaries as part of their larger effort toward methodological openness and gathering holistic data (Blumer, 1969; Cortese, 1995; Mowrer, 1927; Zimmerman & Wieder, 1977). For example, an early scholarly article in the *Journal of Applied Sociology* by Krueger (1925) focused on methods for soliciting life-history documents rather than using preexisting diaries. In it, Krueger made the case for solicited and unsolicited materials to provide a complete picture of the subject:

The life-history in distinction from the diary . . . requires a technique not only for securing documents already written but for getting persons to write them . . . . It indicates to the writer what information is desired. It eliminates the problems of taboo and irrelevancy. (p. 290)

Because there was a divide developing in sociology between quantitative and qualitative approaches to data collection, there were also early advocates (including the American Sociological Association president, Ernest Burgess, 1927) for the two to be combined in a mixed-method approach. Converse noted (1984):

> The quantitative side of sociology was at this time being tended for the most part by demographers and statisticians who worked with grouped data of the census and other governmental statistics, or ecologists who studied physical-cultural distributions. Sociologists interested in attitudes were not generally as well trained in quantitative techniques. They tended to work intuitively with interviews of an unstructured sort . . . using life histories, written or recounted, letters, diaries, and personal documents on the qualitative side of life . . . . Real integration of the two methods required case studies in greater number and standardization than could usually be had. (p. 8)

In the same pre–World War II decade, but across the ocean, an unusual collective of researchers commenced the (still ongoing) "Mass Observation" project, with the mission to document minute details of the daily lives of working class residents of a British industrial town (Sheridan, 1993; Summerfield, 1998). Many of their approximately 500 volunteers were asked to keep diaries about their everyday lives, documenting their personal affairs to such a degree that some viewed the study as an invasion of privacy (Black & Crann, 2002). As used in the Mass Observation study, the solicited diary eventually became more common than the unsolicited, preexisting one. Why not make use of this unique form of documentation to target certain people of interest and ask them to write deliberately about topics of special interest to a researcher?

What was emerging was the solicited or commissioned diary as a *primary* research tool, which lent itself for use in the collection of both quantitative and qualitative data. Fields as disparate as education, business, nursing, and geography also began to variously incorporate solicited diaries. Relying on secondhand (unsolicited) diaries was not the most precise for these fields that valued very specific and specialized sorts of data. As an example of this complaint, one geographer rejected secondary diary data as "fragmentary" and even "fugitive" because it was riddled with "an ill-assorted miscellany of irrelevant observations" (Anderson, 1971, p. 209). Business and industrial-research use of specialized diaries would eventually take off in the form of efficiency and time-use diaries, consistent with values of workers as manipulatable "machines" to be socially engineered for optimal performance. Medical diary research was largely born through the field of nursing scholarship. The holistic approach to health care through documenting the patient's round-the-clock condition, so central to nursing care, led to the early adoption of charting and daily record-keeping (though not usually in the first-person voice of the client). Psychology began to use solicited diaries, such as a diary study published in the eclectic *American Journal of Psychology,* in which Kambouropoulou (1926) explored different senses of humor in a one week's worth of college student participants' diaries:

[Laughter without humor] I had to tell my room-mate that her uncle died; it was the first time I did such a thing. I practiced different ways of telling her, but every time I came to the door, I giggled and could not go in.

[Laughter caused by physical event] At luncheon-table several of the girls nearly upset dishes, —one the bread plate, another, a glass of water, and still another something else. Finally, when the third thing happened, we all began to laugh, wondering what would happen next.

[Laughter at inferiority] I was amused by a story I heard of a girl here and her prejudices. She was discussing sectarian and non-sectarian schools with some friends. "Oh," she said, "you see I am a Unitarian and Mother wouldn't let me go to that school because it was so narrow. There were no Unitarians there, and Unitarians are the most broad-minded people there are."

[Laughter caused by a non-physical mental event] Girls trying to sing a song made up on the spur of the moment. They were laughing themselves, were off the key, and almost broke down in places. Of course, the rest of us laughed. (p. 271)

Kambouropoulou describes the methods, category labels, and examples very meticulously, in this contemporary-styled report.

The Diary Conflicts with Positivism

By the early twentieth century, self-report and narrative methods, especially introspective and reflective ones, began to be devalued. Positivist and empiricist philosophers had already been expressing doubt as to whether a thinker can be both the observer and the observed, or whether an event can be observed without distortion while it is occurring (Scharff, 2002). The emerging hegemony of positivist and post-positivist quantitative science began to solidify the marginalization of qualitative, subjective accounts of the human experience (Popper, 1959). As Costall (2004) notes, even some social scientists who were originally famous for employing subjective observation methods expressed conflicting allegiances and eventually began calling them into question.

Psychologists fairly quickly shifted their self-report standards to highly structured "retrospection" (basically, the delayed retrospective self-report, characteristic of the standard survey design), marginalizing the type of ongoing introspection characteristic of the diary. This communicated two new values that infused the new human science in America: (1) theoretically, the individual becomes viewed as a set of constant traits rather than as fluctuating states, and (2) methodologically, the individual is best understood, not through his or her own free-form, sloppy self-expression, but through structured poking and prodding. Wundt, who has been heralded as a founder of psychology and of introspective methods, himself doubted the scientific value of observation, introspection, and immediate self-report because the participant becomes "lost in self-absorption," providing observations that are "arbitrary" (Blumenthal, 2001). As the personal narrative was being marginalized, William James (1902) expressed dismay:

> Plenty of persons today—"scientists" or "positivists," they are fond of calling themselves [rely on] the strict use of the method of experimental verification . . . elementary forces, physical, chemical, physiological, psycho-physical, which are all impersonal and general in character. (p. 134)

Yet James was also concerned with the empiricist's dilemma over introspective accounts of experience, himself likening attempts at narrating one's own experience to "seizing a spinning top to catch its motion, or trying to turn up the gas quickly enough to see how the darkness looks" (James, 1884, p. 14). American behaviorists embraced observation, yet they were resistant to self-report and subjectivity (Costall, 2006). In his 1913 treatise, *Psychology as a Behaviorist Views It*, Watson declared, "Psychology . . . is a purely objective, experimental branch of natural science which needs introspection as little as do the sciences of chemistry and physics." A decade later, in his revised edition, Watson (1924) balked at qualitative self-report, chiding, "You are supposed somehow to halt from moment to moment your ordinary daily activities and to analyze the accompanying 'mental states' in terms of 'sensations,' 'images,' and 'the affective tones' present" (p. 33).

Sociology had grown to neglect the personal self-report of life experiences as well, but not solely to shore up and standardize the scientific method in deference to positivistic methodological pressures. Instead, for sociologists, the additional theoretically driven tendency to devalue diary data was due to a field-specific valuing of socio-structural influences on individuals. This led to what Plummer (2001) referred to as "the rejection of the human subject." He characterized this as an "interminable tension" between subjective experience and objective external forces:

> Dissolve the subject! Although such statements are supported by very sophisticated arguments, they do bring with them the spectre of a dehumanized collectivist idealism which can kill of any concern for the concrete joys and suffering of active, breathing, bodily human beings; they bring with them a denial of the root tension that has existed within sociology since its earliest days by co-opting "the subject" into an ideology; they harbor a myopia which can deny insights of other approaches and contrary discipline. In short, they encourage a premature theoretical closure and a tottering towards sure, safe absolutism, denying the role of active human beings and their lived experiences. (p. 5)

With the advent of "objective" structured-response scales, self-report data-collection was most likely to survive through more convenient responses to a set of standardized and normed closed-ended response scales (e.g., responses restricted to Likert agreement scales, Semantic Differentials, etc.; Peabody, 1962). Life experiences are expressed as ratings that are converted to averages within an individual's set of responses and then across groups, until each individual and group can be represented by a single numerical mean and standard deviation. Reductionist quantitative measures began to be used to portray everything, from personal traits and attitudes to relationships to major life events, replacing concrete narrative details. As Gergen (2015) lamented, the search for universals in the social sciences have so trumped efforts to "illuminate the life of a single individual" that, overall, "case studies, biographical research, and life-history research occupy but a minor and typically neglected niche in disciplinary structure" (p. 95).

The Diary Is Reinvigorated by the Narrative Movement

A growth in interest in the qualitative diary and in the unsolicited diary occurred after what has been called the "narrative turn" in the social sciences (e.g., Kreiswirth, 1992; Polkinghorne, 1988). As part of this movement, the self-reflexive stories and unique personal life narratives of both individuals and groups were given new credence. The narrative turn renewed interest in diary research across a range of subfields of sociology, psychology, linguistics, hermeneutics, feminist theory, cultural studies, phenomenology, symbolic interactionism, and queer theory, to name just a few. Although this development was marked as a late twentieth-century event, an exact starting point is hard to pinpoint (as is the case with many social and intellectual movements), and there were important early stirrings. Really, one could argue that the narrative turn was a "narrative turning back," because there are many early– and middle–twentieth-century examples of the narrative being embraced and advocated (e.g., Allport, 1942; Shaw, 1930).

According to Goodson and Gill (2011), there had been an early–twentieth-century peak of narrative research that had long passed when major figures in psychology and sociology made their case for the narrative. For example, in 1942, Allport declared the diary nothing short of the "personal document *par excellence*" in social science research (p. 95), and he made this pronouncement at a time when his contemporaries had been moving steadily away from qualitative and narrative data-collection methods that were

beginning to be deemed pseudo-scientific. Rejecting quantitativ-
ists' simplified representations of human experience as distortions
of the complexity of reality and the concrete nature of individual
experience, a strong defense of diary data was offered by Allport
(1942), who saw diary documents as a preferred (if not required)
alternative:

> Acquaintance with particulars is the beginning of all knowl-
> edge scientific or otherwise. In psychology the font and ori-
> gin of our curiosity in, and knowledge of, human nature
> lies in our acquaintance with concrete individuals. To know
> them in their natural complexity is an essential first step.
> Starting too soon with analysis and classification, we run the
> risk of tearing mental life into fragments and beginning with
> false cleavages that misrepresent the salient organizations
> and natural integrations in personal life. In order to avoid
> such hasty preoccupation with unnatural segments and false
> abstractions, psychology needs to concern itself with life as
> it is lived, with significant total-processes of the sort revealed
> in consecutive and complete life documents. (p. 44)

Similarly, in sociology, long before the arrival of the narrative turn
that was decades to come, Dollard (1949) chastised sociologists for
looking at the human experience cross-sectionally. He argued that
"detailed studies of the lives of individuals will reveal new perspectives on a culture as a whole" (p. 4) and rejected the "formal cross
sectional" approach sociologists normally took to explore groups.

The later twentieth-century defense of the human experience
as narrative grew out of a range of feminist, emancipatory, social
constructionist, multicultural, and post-colonial critical theory
movements (e.g., Barthes, 1987; Collins, 2000; Fanon, 1994; Fine,
1992; Geertz, 1974; Harding, 1987; Said, 1979). Scholarly stature
began to be accorded to the diary by scholars such as Philippe
Lejeune, who helped found the Association for Autobiography
and Autobiographical Heritage in Paris (LeJeune, 1992). As
Popkin noted (2009), "Thanks in good part to his initiative, the
domain of the autobiography became more heavily populated
and acquired the characteristics of civilization: scholarly conferences, learned journals, contesting interpretative schools" (p. 1).
Similarly, in defense of the narrative as an alternative to quantitative reductionism, French theorist Roland Barthes declared that

narrative expression is "like life itself," emphasizing that "the narratives of the world are numberless" (1966, p. 79). Anthropologist Clifford Geertz (1986) advocated paying more attention to "the most local of local detail" or "experience-near" aspects because, "Whatever sense we have of how things stand with someone else's inner life, we gain it through their expressions, not through some magical intrusion into their consciousness" (p. 373). The rise of attention to social cognition, self-theory, and the rise of the cognitive revolution in psychology also sparked interest in the narrative (Kreiswirth, 1992).

Qualitative diary research challenges the very concept of the fixed or concrete personality in the person–situation debate, favoring social- and self-construction (Hogan, 2009; Lewin, 1939; Reis, 2008). Qualitative diary researchers lean closer to conceptions of human personality as a reflection of *state* rather than *trait*, and of human behavior as a function of a person-by-situation interaction (Lewin, 1939). In this respect, diary research is more consistent with the contextualized and fluid view of individual experience advocated by social constructionist and symbolic interactionist theorists (e.g., Berger & Luckmann, 1966; Blumer, 1969; Cooley, 1902; Foucault, 1978; Gergen, 1985, 2009; Goffman, 1959; Mead, 1934).

Wheeler and Reis (1991) offered diary research as a viable and preferable alternative to the dominant use of "one time measures such as personality and attitude questionnaires and projective tests, meant to measure enduring characteristics" and "personal interpretations of past experience" (p. 339). Diary research enables a more direct study of our social world. Blumer (1954) favored the naturalistic values inherent in qualitative diary research:

> [E]mpirical instances are accepted in their concrete and distinctive form . . . . Its success depends on patient, careful and imaginative life study, not on quick shortcuts or technical instruments. While its progress may be slow and tedious, it has the virtue of remaining in close and continuing relations with the natural social world. (p. 10)

The new field of symbolic interactionism in sociology (Blumer, 1969; Goffman, 1963; Hochschild, 1983; Messinger et al., 1962) also brought renewed focus on the immediate social situation and daily interactions. The reductionism of positivistic quantitative empiricism is resisted when phenomena are studied in diaries, because they are contextualized and interconnected across time and within the individual's own life narrative. Agnew (1999), acknowledged this special value that is evident in diary observations:

> Ongoing, open-ended, and written without the benefit of hindsight, it is through the absence of retrospection that the diary lays claim to immediacy. This immediacy conveys to the reader a direct and apparently unmediated insight into the life and times of its author and hinges on what has been called the "autopsy principle," the claim to truth based on the assertion: I was there and I saw it with my own eyes. (p. 50)

Just as the use of solicited qualitative diaries was consistent with the narrative turn, so, too, was the familiar use of preexisting unsolicited diaries. Unsolicited and unstructured diaries offer a special sort of witness to the human experience. For example, examining soldiers' diaries, Hill (2014) explored the construction of masculinity during wartime:

> The jolting of the wagon affected the wounds and half suppressed shrieks issued from our lips at every jolt. One poor fellow next to me has his leg splintered by a shell, big tears streamed down his face with the agony he was undergoing, but never a word of complaint passed his lips. (p. 217)

A diary written during a particular sociopolitical crisis is like a time capsule, revealing the lived experience of an historical epoch, such as one of the most famous diaries of the twentieth century, the heartrending diary of the young captive Anne Frank. Across the centuries of writers, the accumulated stock of extant diaries, whether posthumously published, unpublished, or in private collections, is something quite precious. One of the longest running columns in the *New York Times* is called the "Metropolitan Diary," in which residents write "Dear Diary" entries that capture some vivid element of the human condition. As Millim (2010) declares, diaries are "indispensable documents that allow us to further our understanding of persons and periods" (p. 281). There are several diary archives and research centers, such as the *World Diary Project*, founded in 2012 from an original collection of more than

1,500 private diaries amassed by Irving Finkel, otherwise known as "the man who saves life stories."[1]

The Diary Moves into the Twenty-first Century

Diary research is certainly not the most common research method used in the social sciences, but it has maintained a steady, small presence. The scholarly research continues to be peppered with research involving diaries. As a rough guide to its prevalence moving into the twenty-first century, a simple search of the scholarly research in psychology and sociology is quite revealing (see Figure 1.1).

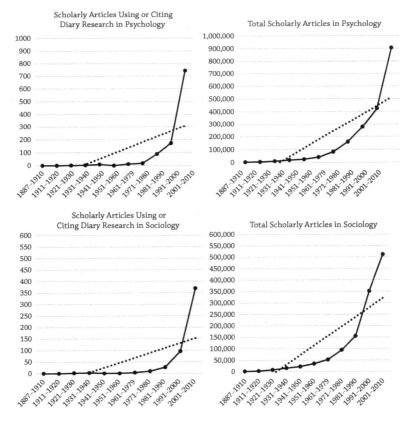

Figure 1.1 Scholarly diary articles by discipline and over time.

Figure 1.1 shows the frequency of diary research being either employed or discussed in the scholarly research in the fields of psychology and sociology. The two right-hand charts depict over-all scholarly research articles from major, field-specific search engines for *psychology* (*Psych Info* and *Psych Abstracts*) and for *sociology* (*Sociology Abstracts*). The two left-hand columns depict scholarly articles within those larger sets that mention diary research (either citing them in literature reviews or actually using them as data or source material). Before 1950, a handful of stud-ies was published in either field. During the narrative turn around the 1980s–1990s, diary research in both psychology and sociology jumps up a little steeper than the increase in research overall. One can also see that overall research is increasing at a steeper growth rate than diary research. The diary method has now been used to document everything from daily laughter (Kambouropoulou, 1926) to time use (James & Moore, 1940), and in regard to such diverse topics as education (LaPalio, 1981), pain (Schumacher et al., 2002), and multi-media engagement (Black & Crann, 2002). There are examples on an ambitious international scale, such as Szalai's (1966) International Time-Use study, in which 2,000 par-ticipants recorded what they did and how they spent their time in one 24-hour period (Szalai, 1972). Travers (2011) has also used the diary method to examine stressors. Diaries have proved useful to industrial organizational psychologists to study work-place communication, productivity, and engagement with work (Csikszentmihalyi & Larson, 2014). Marketing researchers have used diaries to development advertising strategy (Zarantonello & Luomala, 2011). Social psychological phenomena have been examined using diaries on social comparison (Wheeler & Miyake, 1992), language acquisition (Bailey & Ochsner, 1983), and every-day prejudice (Swim, Hyers, Cohen, & Fergusen, 2001), as well as more general studies on time use throughout the day (Cooper & Schindler, 2003; Szalai, 1966).

With a strong sense of the scientific, factual form of thinking about our experiences, scientists and popular culture continue to turn to the diary, though it is clear that the diary has evolved from what it was a century ago. Positivistic sensibilities have shaped the nature of the most typical diary research studies in several obvi-ous ways. First, diary research is primarily based on solicited, not archival, diaries. One finds that, in the social sciences, "solicited" is synonymous with "controlled" in diary research. The most typical diary study will involve purposive sampling of participants who are asked to write in diaries about a very specific experience for a time period that is structured and supervised, typically with the *a priori* understanding that the diary will later be analyzed by researchers and perhaps even the participant themselves. Studies using preexisting archival diaries as source material are less common and viewed as providing potentially sloppy data (Allport, 1942). The fields of the humanities, history, and anthropology have been more willing to embrace secondary analyses of unsolicited diaries for the rich data they can provide (see Langford & West, 1999; Paperno, 2004), with psychology and sociology preferring to solicit new diary documentation of phenomena.

Second, diary research is often conducted when researchers are attempting to get "more accurate" renditions of a human experience. One finds that diary studies are justified by researchers as producing more "accurate" data; the immediacy of documentation allowing the researcher to get closer to the "truth" of a phenomenon. For example, to capture this unbiased immediacy through diary entries, Shiffman and colleagues (Shiffman, Stone, & Hufford, 2008; Stone & Shiffman, 1994) randomly timed their participants' entries using their method of "ecological momentary assessment" to "minimize recall bias, maximize ecological validity with random time sampling" (p. 1), reducing the "bias" of the individual's own post-hoc experiential reconstruction.

Third, diary studies are more often used to collect quantitative rather than qualitative data. Many contemporary "diary" studies are so quantitative they bear no resemblance to the poetic prose of their unsolicited predecessors. One can find a larger number of quantitative diary studies in the social sciences than qualitative ones, pointing to what seems to be an altogether misleading application of the term "diary" in the first place. All of the top most-cited social scientific diary studies in the scholarly search engines, with topics ranging from *daily stress* (Bolger & Schilling, 1991) to *time use* (Szalai, 1972) to *interpersonal relationships* (Laurenceau, Barrett, & Pietromonaco, 1998), produce quantitative data from diaries. This is partly due to the favoring of standardized survey instruments and what has become a quantification of the study of human experience, where people are described with respect to statistics and in relation to averages and norms (O'Keefe, 2005).

Diaries tend to have a solid structure, often incorporating survey design, quantitative or mixed-method analyses, and standardized forms. Examples include Lazarus and Cohen's (1977) Hassles Scale and Uplifts scale, the Holmes and Rahe scale (Kanner, Coyne, Schaefer, & Lazarus, 1981), and Wheeler and Reis's (1991) Rochester Interaction Record.

One of the most amazing changes to diary writing in popular culture is the technologically pervasive "diary style" of thinking about one's life as a story to document. Early researchers so concerned that participants could not simultaneously experience and document life events would be shocked to discover that the two are obsessively intertwined in our modern lifestyle—with selfies, blog posts, and other *online and in the moment* technologies. In the last couple of decades, there has been a cultural shift for people to document their lives more than ever before (Scannella, 2009; Van Dijck, 2004). People who have access to the Web regularly update their status in social media (e.g., on Facebook, Instagram, etc.), often while engaged in the event they are documenting. Even fleeting momentary impressions of daily life are being immediately documented (e.g., on Snapchat, Twitter, etc.). Through the Internet, "Dear Diary" has become a very public "Dear Everyone," and once-private thoughts are aired on a public soapbox (e.g., Rettberg, 2008; Kaun, 2010). "Private" became "public" became "purposely public." The subtle hybrid act of communication that Van Dijck (2004) described of a diarist whose writing is supposedly intended for private use, but who often betrays an awareness of its potential to be read by others—that is out the window in social media diarying. Diary advocates of a hundred years ago who pressed young children to keep up with their life documentation would be quite surprised.

In Conclusion, and Looking Ahead

The diary in research is as diverse as the experiences of those who record their experiences within them. The general public continues to embrace diary keeping as a form of personal self-discovery. The humanities and social sciences have continued to show interest in examining preexisting diaries and solicited diary data as a window into the human experience. Diary methods are flexible and offer many advantages for researchers of all philosophies and in all fields. It seems that, now more than ever, the public is receptive to diary keeping and recognizes the value in the regular documentation of the human experience.

Note

1. For information on secondary analysis of diaries, see A. Chassanoff (2013), Historians and the use of primary source materials in the digital age, *The American Archivist, 76*(2), 458–480; C. Seale (2011), Secondary analysis of qualitative data, in D. Silverman (Ed.), *Qualitative Research* (3rd ed., pp. 347–365), Los Angeles, CA: Sage; and Corti and Bishop, 2005, http://www.qualitative-research.net/index.php/fqs/article/view/509/1098. There are a few ambitious efforts at archiving the world's available diaries; for a list of existing diary source material online, see http://historymatters.gmu.edu/mse/letters/ldonline.html.

For the last two cites:

L. Corti and L. Bishop (2005), Strategies in Teaching Secondary Analysis of Qualitative Data, Forum: Qualitative Social Research, Volume 6, No. 1, Art. 47 – January 2005.

And

History matters (2017), The US Survey Course on the Web, Letters and Diaries online, Produced in association with the Visible knowledge project.

2

DIARY DATA COLLECTION AS A QUALITATIVE RESEARCH METHOD

THE DIARY method is distinguished in the qualitative methodological canon for its unparalleled potential to capture the details of otherwise time-sensitive and context-specific phenomena. The diary has always been among the options in the qualitative methodological repertoire, and as a secondary source material, it predates other common methods for data collection, such as semi-structured interviews, focus groups, and ethnography. Every qualitative method has its own approach and unique strengths. Just as the one-on-one interview harnesses the intimacy of conversation and the focus group harnesses the energy of interaction, the diary harnesses the power of immediate personal witness.

The Qualitative Diary Project in a Nutshell

Completing a qualitative research project using diaries is no small undertaking. There are the standard tasks of any research project: reviewing the literature and identifying the research questions; designing and carrying out the data collection protocol; and analyzing and discussing the data. For archival diary studies, the researcher must locate diaries that will address their question of interest, even though originally, the diarists probably had a different purpose for keeping a diary. For solicited diary studies, the researcher faces the challenge of recruiting participants who will commit to the regular observation and reporting of certain phenomena over an extended period of time, all at the behest of a researcher who ultimately retains their diaries. The active data collection phase of a diary study involves consistent effort from the researcher. If all goes well, and ample data are collected, the researcher then faces the painstaking task of generating a succinct yet comprehensive report from what can be quite an expansive data set.

Diary Researchers

Diary researchers are responsible for designing the diary project around the research questions they pose, then scouring the archives or orchestrating a solicited diary collection for answers. If there is one trait that diary researchers tend to share, it is simply that they are interested in studying the ephemera embedded in daily life. No doubt diary researchers also share a certain amount of patience in order to coordinate diaries and then work through complex data sets. Apart from these qualities, however, there is little else linking diary researchers themselves as a cohesive group of social scientists. Some are guided more by positivistic, quantitative, realist assumptions, and some are guided more by constructivist, qualitative, and relativist values. Some are doing basic research; some, applied. Their expertise and fields of inquiry are as varied as their subject matter.

Diary Participants

The success of any diary study depends on the efforts of the diarists and the relevance of their entries for the research questions posed by the researcher. Diarists are sought as experts on some unique life experience rather than for any particular literary skill or fame. Nonetheless, archival diarists—whether they are famous or not—should be held in high regard because their cherished extant writings could not be recreated in any other way. More often than not, the writers of archival diaries could not have anticipated their entries would be the subject of a particular researcher's analytical attentions. In contrast, the writers of solicited diaries knowingly keep a diary in the service of a research protocol. They, too, should be regarded with much appreciation for their dedication and vigilance in the service of a larger research project. As Milligan, Bingley, and Gatrell (2005) warn, some people are "more predisposed to be diarists than others, and will use the opportunity to reflect on and record events in their everyday lives, whilst others will view the task as a more boring and repetitive activity—a chore to be completed" (p. 1888). The identities of participants solicited to write diaries for research are typically withheld, their entries anonymized, and their observations aggregated across a group of other diarists participating in the same study, which can help balance out the variations in diary entry quality and quantity.

Diary Entries

For the researcher using archival diaries, there is no control over the format the diaries are in. Entry content, frequency, length, style, and duration are all beyond the control of the archival diary researcher. Archives may contain actual handwritten diaries, facsimiles, or diaries reprinted in type. If they are in a foreign language they may be or may not be translated. As Watson (2016) described, it can be a powerful experience to interact with the pages of diaries themselves:

> Considered as a cultural object, the diary becomes sacred by virtue of its age and proximity to the past. Thus materiality and temporality are inseparable in relation to the authenticity embodied in these yellowing pages, the old-fashioned writing and faded ink, which signify the past. To handle the volumes is to be connected directly to the past, the moving hand as witness to history. (p. 115)

Diaries written for personal use but left to posterity through publication, donation, or archeological fortune may be written in all ranges of form and content. Researchers can find archives of diaries based on specific demographics, topics, geographical regions, and historical epochs through research centers and libraries; however, they should be prepared to find frustrating inconsistencies in the types of details provided and even in the legibility of writing. With contemporary electronic communication and the Internet, the nature of diary and journal writing through blogging provides more access to diary writers of all kinds and around the globe. In the case of electronic and Web-based diaries, they will be typewritten and often include photographs and other visual images, as well. As Cardell (2014) declares, with social media and personal technologies, "The diary now is a performative space, a print genre, a digital platform, a behavior regime, a smartphone app" (p. 3).

In solicited diary studies, the diarists themselves are not ordinarily responsible for figuring out what to write about in a freeform way; rather, they are guided about what aspects of their daily life the researcher would like them to document and how to record them with diary entries. Entries may focus on any combination phenomena: micro-level cognitions, emotions, or behaviors (e.g., expatriates' emotional adjustment and culture shock; Wechtler, 2015); meso-level interactions in the immediate environment (e.g., caregivers challenges caring for an ill family member; Hughes & Callery, 2004); and macro-level sociopolitical events and institutions (e.g., Jews' and Arabs' daily stressful and uplifting experiences living at the epicenter of the Israeli–Palestinian conflict; Ben-Ari & Lavee, 2007). Soliciting diary entries from participants *in situ*, the diary researcher can obtain information that is more immediate and contextualized than with other, more retrospective research methods such as interviews or surveys. If entries are electronically recorded, then date and time stamps, time spent on task, and even global positioning data can be embedded in each entry. Entries are made episodically and accumulate chronologically throughout the duration of the study, on a preset schedule (e.g., morning and evening), when signaled by the researcher who follows a predetermined schedule (e.g., fixed or random), or after a certain event of interest occurs (usually as close in time to the event as possible). The active data-collection phase may last a day, a week, a month, or longer. The mode for making diary entries is increasingly diversifying from the conventional "paper-and-pencil" handwritten diary, with diary entries being made with computer, cell phone, wearable technology, pagers, emails and social media, photography, videography, and audio recording. Multimodal diary data can include written, oral, and even video entries. Entries may incorporate quantitative checklists and fixed-response items alongside qualitative short-answer and open-ended response prompts in mixed-methods designs.

Epistemological Orientations of Diary Studies

The design of any diary study is contingent upon researchers' epistemological orientations and their research questions, although, as Patterson (2005) points out, participants may be independent from these matters:

> Qualitative diary research does genuinely merit the label "thick description," if for nothing more than the fact that there are sustained passages where the text of the diaries is left to speak for itself without the imposition of any explicit theoretical frameworks or hypotheses that need tested or generalisations that need to be drawn other than those which are mediated by . . . disciplinary bias, choice of language and personal decisions about what to include and not to include. (p. 154)

So, while entries may stand alone, the researcher faces some decisions. There is no single method for analyzing diary data. There are choices about whether to collect archival or new diaries, to include one or many diarists, and to examine whole diaries or just a selection of entries. It is suitable to choose *emic* (inductive) approaches to data analysis in which the themes emerge from participant's own voice, or to choose *etic* (deductive) approaches, in which the themes are imposed from existing theory. Diary researchers may use diary data to provide causal or descriptive accounts, using realist or constructivist data analysis, and for the purpose of basic or applied research agendas. Given that qualitative research tends to be the latter of each—more descriptive, constructivist, and applied—the uses of diaries for these types of projects will be examined in the remainder of this chapter. Each is described separately; however, one can find studies that may contain elements of all three.

Descriptive Diary Research

Descriptive diary studies are especially useful for exploratory research and to provide documentation of phenomena, events, or the lives of groups or individuals for a permanent record (Sandelowski, 2000, 2010). Certainly, all qualitative research is inherently descriptive; however, descriptive studies are designed with ostensibly modest goals to "merely" describe a person, situation, or event in everyday terms, not to fit any elaborate theoretical, critical, or interpretive frameworks. Akin to naturalistic inquiry, descriptive research tends to be conducted (either implicitly or explicitly) from a realist perspective, with the researcher simply relaying patterns observed.

These realist assumptions are revealed when descriptive researchers use methodological strategies to substantiate the representational accuracy of their observations (Madill, Jordan, & Shirley, 2000). For example, one strategy for validating the accuracy of descriptive observations is to present ample data, through large sample sizes or over longer time periods. In this way, the observations are substantiated because they are frequent or recurring. Another strategy is to use triangulation, combining observations from diary data with other data sources (e.g., letters, surveys, or interviews); incorporating varied participant voices and perspectives (e.g., first- and third-person voice or demographically diverse standpoints); or gathering data through a mix of quantitative and qualitative methods. Researchers may develop a precise codebook with operational definitions of codes or employ multiple data coders to corroborate observations. All of these strategies are indicative of a realist perspective, with an assumption that the *careful* researcher can objectively describe the phenomena. Archival diaries that were written purely for the diarists' own purposes do add an additional layer of naturalistic validity. Passing the "dead social scientist" test for which one asks, "Would the data be the same, or be there at all" (Potter, 2010, p. 667), yes, if it weren't for the researcher—yes, archival diaries would still be there, as they are naturally occurring data. While it is quite the opposite for a solicited diary, which can be quite intrusive, the commonplace nature of diary writing can be less contrived than responding to a survey or sitting for an interview. Three common types of descriptive diary methods discussed here are content analysis and historical and biographical research.

Content Analysis of Diaries

One of the most widely used systematic means for describing patterns in data, content analysis was developed in the social sciences by middle of last century (Berelson, 1952; Bernard, 1952). It is a systematic means to categorize or summarize patterns of content, in media, visual, and textual data (Hsieh & Shannon, 2005). The researcher observes the data and reports *as objectively as possible* what is there. In emic content analyses, the researcher will not impose *a priori* coding categories, but rather will summarize what emerges from the data themselves. For example, Schlagman, Schulz, and Kvavilashvili (2006) conducted a content analysis of over 200 spontaneously occurring autobiographical memories that were documented in a week of diaries to explore age differences in reminiscences. Multiple raters classified the memories into 17 emerging content categories (see Table 2.1): Their content analysis revealed that older people experienced happier spontaneous memories more frequently than did youth, in what appeared to be a maturational phenomenon.

In etic content analyses, categories are derived from existing theories, past research, or from very specific *a priori* research questions. For example, Duncan and Grazzani-Gavazzi (2004) used an etic coding scheme to content-analyze over 1,000 positive events recorded in participant diaries from a multinational sample. While they found that happy times occurred more in groups for Italians and in solitude for Scots, the researchers were prevented from thoroughly coding participants' descriptions of the accompanying emotions because such details were not a part of their *a priori* coding scheme. They described this as "unfortunate since the nuances associated with positive incidents under our present convention could not be investigated further . . . . This does however illustrate that perhaps we need to do more to account for the variability in describing positive emotion states" (p. 375). In some etic designs, shortcuts such as computer-assisted key word searches or simple word counts are employed to content-analyze diary content; however, such strategies can similarly limit the potential richness that diary documents are prized for (Tov, Ng, Lin, & Qiu, 2013). As Duncan and Grazzani-Gavazzi (2004) conclude, using a mix of etic and emic coding in content analysis may be the best way to tackle the richness of diary data. Although the research questions will ultimately guide the approach taken in a project, those working with the contextualized richness of diary data should be open to the possibility of incorporating some emic coding in a content analysis.

Table 2.1

Percentages (Frequencies) of Memories by Content Category and Age Group

Content category	Percentages (frequencies)			
	Young group (n = 11)		Old group (n = 10)	
Person (i.e., primarily about other people)	17%	(21)	14%	(14)
Accidents, including injuries and illnesses	13%	(16)	1%	(1)
Stressful events	12%	(15)	2%	(2)
Holidays	11%	(14)	6%	(6)
Conversations	8%	(10)	0%	(0)
Leisure/sports activities (including hobbies & games)	6%	(8)	12%	(12)
Objects/places	5%	(6)	10%	(10)
Going out (e.g., going to the pub/dancing)	5%	(6)	5%	(5)
Work/university	5%	(7)	9%	(9)
Romantic involvement (e.g., being intimate, romantic dinners, receiving gifts for Valentine's Day)	4%	(5)	3%	(3)
School	5%	(6)	6%	(6)
Deaths/funerals	4%		4%	(4)
Miscellaneous	2%	(3)	5%	(5)
Special occasions (birthdays, weddings, engagements, parties)	2%	(2)	6%	(6)
Births	1%	(1)	3%	(3)
Traveling/journeys	0%	(0)	4%	(4)
War/army	-		9%	(9)
Total memories	100%	(125)	100%	(99)

Schlagman, S., Schulz, J., & Kvavilashvili, L. (2006). A content analysis of involuntary autobiographical memories: Examining the positivity effect in old age. *Memory, 14*(2), 161–175.

Diaries in Historical Research

Historians use systematic methods to tell a story about a person, community, event, or era from the past, making use of a range of artifactual, oral, and textual source material. Diaries are especially useful to historians for getting multiple perspectives, personal observations, and off-the-record information on historical events. Critical historiographers, who revisit and call into question formally presented historical interpretations and representations of past events, benefit from the unofficial voices found in archival diary sources. Diaries can also be used to construct an account of an historical event when other materials are unavailable. As Tuchman (1998) said, "Most simply, we all live history, and not merely in the grand sense of wars, recessions, and political transformation. Rather, we live out the assumptions of our *epoque* in the most mundane aspects of our daily lives" (p. 313). Thus, diaries can round out historical investigations with personal meanings and interpretations of events (Plummer, 1983, 2001; Thies, 2002). However, for Schoppa (2010), they are as much "slippery slopes" as they are "goldmines," because questions will remain regarding whether the entries depict "what indeed happened; what the writer perceived happened; what the diarist truly thought; and what his motives and reactions were" (p. 1). The American Social History Project (2017) recommends that historians using archival diaries read them as if they held a great work of literature, carefully deciphering the cast of characters, central plots, and symbolism:

> Keep an eye out for language that puzzles you . . . for instance, many modern readers are puzzled by some correspondents' interjection of "D.V." in the midst of certain sentences expressing hope ("by now, D.V., you are safely at home") . . . . Then, finally, one writer solves the puzzle for us by spelling it out: *Deo Volente*, God willing. Such puzzles will help you to be alert to the fact that the meaning of certain words or phrases is coded (to say in the mid-nineteenth-century that a woman had "taken a cold" almost always meant that she was pregnant). (p. 1)

Diaries in historical research may be the sole source of data, but more often they supplement other public and private documents of life, including letters, photos, prescriptions, subscriptions, receipts, tattoos, and any of a range of other "naturally occurring" human artifacts (Stanley, 2013). Historians may refer to the diaries of officials who were charged with documenting daily events as part of an occupational or religious responsibility (Smyth, 2013). If the diaries are not the writings of famous dignitaries, artists, or religious figures, they are typically the personal diaries of laypersons (as in the collection at the World Diary Project). Historians also conduct secondary studies of diaries archived by other researchers from past studies. Long-running or longitudinal diary studies that are being run by other researchers, such as the Mass Observation Study, can be fruitful sources for historians (Chassanoof, 2013).

Diaries in Biographical Research

Falling under the umbrella of "biographical research," there is a range of ideographical studies of the particular life, including the biography, memoir, and case study. Diaries help biographers who have taken on this task of "recreating a life" (Edel, 1978) to achieve a richer retelling of an individual's experiences in some chronological order. Biography often involves representing the life and times of someone alive or deceased who hails from outside of the researcher's close associations, so diaries would of course be a useful source material to promote understanding. "Memoirs" can include private diaries, since they are written from more of an insider's perspective, telling about a period of an individual's life, about their career pursuits or another significant quest or saga, or about associations with family and friends. In the case of biography and memoir, the subject may not be aware of the research. In contrast, life-history is a collaborative research method that involves an extensive accounting and are typically written by a non-acquaintance who works with a subject-participant. Case studies focus on a particular life, group, community, or specific geographical space. As the name implies, they may be clinical in nature, as in Deuchar and Quay's (2001) case study on one bilingual child that included a diary of the child's vocabulary development, kept by her mother (see Table 2.2).

At the time of the "narrative turn" in the social sciences, a related "biographical turn" was motivated by a stewing discomfort with the social-scientific tendency to represent the human condition as completely determined by broader sociostructural

Table 2.2

Diary Entry at Age 1year 4 months and 11 days

Situation	Word	Gloss	Pronunciation	Additional information	Language of adult
breakfast at home	gone		[gɔ:]	on finishing her cereal and juice	Spanish
breakfast at home	bajar	get down	[ba]	wanting to get down from her highchair	Spanish
at home after breakfast	panda		[pa]	bringing mother a book showing a panda	Spanish
leaving the house	casa	house	[ka]	pointing at the house from outside	Spanish
lunchtime at university	zapato	shoe	[pa]	referring to her shoe	Spanish
arriving home	casa	house	[ka]	outside the house	Spanish
at home	más	more	[ma]	wanting more of something	Spanish
at home	bajar	get down	[ba]	wanting to get down	Spanish

Vocabulary Coded in Deuchar & Quay's Case Study (2001). By permission of Oxford University Press.

forces, removing human agency and perspective, and thus inadvertently marginalizing the voice of the individual (Caine, 2010; Chamberlayne, Bornat, & Wengraf, 2000; Possing, 2001; Renders, de Haan, & Harmsma, 2016). Furthermore, when biography gave voice, it was often primarily focused on famous or privileged individuals at the expense of perspectives from everyday people and marginalized groups. Thus, the use of the diary in biographical research served as a particularly useful way to represent personal and private perspectives and everyday human experience.

Constructionist Diary Research

Qualitative researchers often lean toward epistemological constructivism. Consequently, they tend to share several key assumptions (Gergen, 1985). They tend to reject naïve realism, the idea of a singular reality of the world existing apart from the one perceiving it. Instead, they argue that one's "reality" is shaped by the language one uses to describe the world, which is culturally and historically situated. Moreover, what counts as valid knowledge is socially negotiated and sustained via social interchange. Therefore, the act of naming and explaining the world holds great weight, as it can fundamentally affect people's experience of themselves and their sense of reality in tangible ways. A range of qualitative research techniques has emerged from these basic principles as an antidote to traditional positivist and post-positivist research methods. Assumptions about the fluidity of reality and the situated nature of knowledge lead to more "voice" from the standpoint of the participant, more emic coding methods, researcher reflexivity, and with all of that, more elaborate theoretical schemes necessary for basic descriptive diary research. Examples include ethnography, phenomenology, hermeneutics, semiotics, and narrative inquiry.

Ethnographic Diary Studies

Among the very oldest of the qualitative methods, ethnography is distinctive in its focus on understanding a group, community, or culture from an insider's perspective. Ethnography emerged within the early fields of anthropology and sociology, and thus it originally characterized groups in the form of ethnicity, tribe, and culture. Over time, ethnography has been transformed, today characterizing a range of other types of groups, large and small, perpetual and temporary. Ethnography originally was more naturalistic and aimed to be objective; ethnographers spent ample time immersed in a local cultural context to find what "others" could learn about this group. Researchers turned to insider "informants" who explained their group's activities on their own terms and through their own worldview. As Bruner (1993) explained, "The distancing of ethnographic subject from native object was essential to an older model of ethnography, for how else could we be the impersonal authoritative voice empowered to represent the Other? . . . Traditional ethnography required a sharp separation between subject and object if it was to retain its authoritative voice" (p. 5). Today, ethnographic work encourages constructionist, relativist, and emic representations of both individuals and groups. Ethnographers are known for their use of participant observation, which in extreme cases can involve overt immersion into the group of interest and even undercover observation (which is now less common). The immersion of the ethnographer's self and perspective into co-creating the account of the group of interest has become more acceptable with the emergence of critical anthropological accounts (Turner, 1993). This has led to more interest in a wider array of solicited and archival documents, including surveys, public records, and diaries, to help round out material from an ethnography, although such materials are typically only part of a whole research project. Solicited diaries have worked particularly well in educational and medical settings because writing, documentation, and evaluation are often part of regular professional duties (e.g., Ball, 1981). Archival diaries can be useful for certain cultural groups studied over a long period of time or that are no longer convening. Integral to ethnographies are the researchers' exhaustive field notes or "research diaries"—not to be confused with participant diaries. Ethnographers often rely on these field notes for recording all they come to learn from their participants and also for reflexivity and self-care as they navigate new methods or unfamiliar phenomena (Browne, 2013).

In the evolution toward a field of "digital anthropology" and the "digital humanities" (Griffin & Hayler, 2016), ethnographic research has gradually moved to embrace the virtual and digital "fieldspace" of groups convening on the Web (Murthy, 2008). There are many ways that technology has contributed to the possibilities of diary-style digital ethnography in the twenty-first century, according to Murthy (2013):

> The continued growth of ubiquitous computing, the presence of unobtrusive and relatively high-powered computing

> devices in our everyday lives, will profoundly affect the ways in which social research will be conducted. Many of our potential respondents have laptops or mobile devices with integrated web cams, enabling us to conduct interviews via free video conferencing software . . . [E]thnographers need not be lumbered by a backpack full of digital devices . . . digital audio recorder, a video camera, laptop computer, digital camera, and, of course, article notebook . . . . (p. 29)

Materials exchanged in an online ethnography may include solicited and self-initiated diaries that are textual, oral, visual, mixed-media video, and even the researcher's own field notes and conclusions (Pettersen, 2013; Pink, 2003). The digital age has changed the scope and practice of ethnography. The ethnographic studies of the past often involved elaborate travel to access localized resource documents. More such documents are becoming digitized and globally accessible. Furthermore, the very concept of what constitutes the space of a localized demarcated field in ethnography is challenged with the increasingly mobile and virtual nature of Web-based communities (Berg & Düvel, 2012). Virtual spaces allow (and necessitate) the opening up of ethnography to more "fields." These virtual networking spaces are not simply connecting researchers to more geographical fields, but the virtual spaces become the fields (e.g., Madianou & Miller, 2011 & 2013). Some of the special features of a diary study—the frequent, self-expressive, personal updates—have become part and parcel of Web life, and in many cases providing new forms of "diary entries" accessible to ethnographers. This more, everyday self-initiated online documentation (e.g., through social media) contributes the immediate temporal feature so valued in diaries, even though this "diary" may be nothing like its paper-bound predecessor. For example, Sampanes et al. (2011) conducted an ethnography of mobile workers through the use of photo diaries. Many respondents submitted photographs taken by their mobile devices and provided researchers with short responses that described each picture and its context. The digital nature of their ethnographic data enabled more direct and immediate access to participant voice and often through diary-like records. Referring to this as "auto-ethnography," Clark and Gruba (2010) asked foreign-language learners to document their experiences while engaged in a language practice website.

The researchers described the approach as "auto-ethnographic" because participants were asked to "record their own experiences and interpret data reflexively to better understand an experience" (p. 166). There is actually an interesting irony here, if one looks back to earlier researchers' almost apologetic use of "intrusive" Palm Pilot and pager technology (Csikszentmihalyi & Larson, 2014; Larson, 1989; Le, Choi, & Beal, 2006) as essentially "pulling teeth" to get participants to record their immediate thoughts and feelings and behaviors (Harding, 1997):

> When a person is beeped or otherwise notified to record their experience and other evaluative measures, he or she completes an Experience Sampling Form (ESF), which is usually designed to take less than two minutes to complete. . . . Subjects do not feel the method is intrusive and feel that the method accurately records their time use. (p. 27)

Now they would do such logging without thinking with cell phones, Twitter, and fitness-tracking technology. In fact, one would have to physically take away many contemporary technology users' devices in order to keep them from their willful and habitual capturing of the immediate moment.

Phenomenologal/Hermeneutic/Semiotics Diary Studies

The three unique approaches of phenomenology, hermeneutics, and semiotics share a similar premise that all meaning is contextualized and interpretation necessarily honors "situated meaning" (Constas 1992; Ricoeur, 1975; Shank, 1995). From that common viewpoint, however, the approaches diverge. A typical phenomenological study focuses on discourse and interaction, often through semi-structured interviews, to explore the active construction of meaning. A typical hermeneutic study would involve the interpretation of linguistic texts and motifs, often archival or archaeological ones, from the worldview of those who generated them. And semiotics typically focuses on identifying and interpreting linguistic *and* non-linguistic systems of representation or signals, including symbolic representations, visual data, and all forms of media.

In the compendium of qualitative research, there are various crossovers of these methodologies, both in theoretical development and in research practice. In fact, they may be all be employed within the same study, as in one archival study of the early nineteenth-century diary of Catholic mystic Saint Faustine Kowalska (Kandler, 2003). In it, Kandler simultaneously used a "semiotic, phenomenological, and hermeneutic approach" to focus on how flowers are connected with religious experiences. Kandler explored the context and meaning surrounding flowers mentioned in Saint Kowalska's diary, as in this entry in which the Saint relays a miracle she experienced in the convent kitchen:

> I took up the pot with ease and poured off the water perfectly. But when I took off the cover to let the potatoes steam off, I saw there in the pot, in the place of the potatoes, whole bunches of red roses, beautiful beyond description. I had never seen such roses before. Greatly astonished and unable to understand the meaning of this, I heard a voice within me saying, I change such hard work of yours into bouquets of most beautiful flowers, and their perfume rises up to My throne. (p. 259)

Throughout the paper, Kandler discusses the meanings of roses in Christianity as well as for the devout diarist. Such studies involve some analytical coding, most typically by the researchers themselves, who explore meaning within the diarist's own worldview. It is not always easy to identify the precise aspect of a diary study that is phenomenological versus hermeneutic versus semiotic. In fact, the methods of a study that proclaims to be phenomenological, hermeneutic, or semiotic may be identical; however, researchers will aim to be theoretically consistent, orienting their papers within the bounds of one or another of their chosen epistemological orientations throughout manuscripts.

Phenomenologists attend to the ways individuals make sense of the world through their immediate lived experience and their interactions (Giorgi, 1975; Husserl, 1983; Spiegelberg, 1975). They focus on experience as described, and they can find plenty of such content in diary writing. For example, in a phenomenological diary study of the experience of work–life balance (Montgomery, Panagopoulou, Peeters, & Schaufeli, 2009), participants were asked to write in diaries at the day's end about (1) occasions when they experienced work thoughts or issues occuring in their personal life or vice versa; and (2) how they construed any such crossovers. The nature and emotional valence of work–life overlap were then coded in an emic fashion to represent participants' experience of each occasion. Phenomenological researchers commit to representing the life experience of participants in their own words, though they also recognize a certain level of co-creation. While co-creation might seem more apparent in an exchange during a one-on-one interview, it can certainly occur in solicited and even archival diary studies. In a solicited diary study, the researcher co-creates when designing the diary instrument (deciding who shares, and framing how) and when coding (organizing what is shared). In an archival diary study, the researcher co-creates during the process of selecting the diaries (deciding who shares) and again when coding the diary content.

"Hermeneutics" refers to the "art of interpretation" and originally centered on interpreting or translating sacred and legal texts from the point of view at the time of their creation. It has evolved in its application in the social sciences to be about interpreting another's world view and interpreting meaning from their perspective, and "texts" have expanded to include written as well as aesthetic human creations (Angenot, 2014; Dilthey, 1977; Kinsella, 2006). The focus of a hermeneutic diary study will be on construals and expression of meaning, language, and definition. For example, in a hermeneutic diary study of women's experience of their pregnancies, Lundgren and Wahlberg (1999) asked women to keep diaries throughout their pregnancies, with the express purpose "to understand, interpret, and uniquely describe as a whole." They described their process:

In this method, understanding the relationships between the whole and the parts can be done only in relation to the whole—a process known as *the hermeneutic circle. . . .* The diaries were analyzed according to the hermeneutical/phenomenological method. Each diary was first read to bring out a sense of the whole and, after that, subsets called "meaning units" were marked. Then, the meaning of the text was organized into different themes by relating the meaning units to each other. In this process, each diary was first analyzed. Next, the different diaries were analyzed together, going from the part to the whole (the hermeneutic circle). In the final operation of transformation, a description and interpretation meaningful for midwifery was developed. (p. 14)

Ultimately they interpreted the essential structure of women's experience of pregnancy to be expressed as the concept of "transition to the unknown." There were three themes that coincided with stages of pregnancy: the first trimester meant meeting one's life situation; the second trimester meant meeting something inevitable; and the third trimester meant preparing for the unknown. The researchers then explored these construals of pregnancy in relation to midwifery and childbirth education.

Semiotics grew out of linguistics and involves the study of signs and symbols—anything that is coded or patterned or that represents something else (Angenot, 2014; Cullum-Swan & Manning, 1994; Manning, 1987). Semiotics uncovers or "breaks" the codes of all sorts of symbolic systems, including written and verbal speech, and nonverbal expressions, drawings, performances, photos, advertisements, symbols, arrangements and positioning of symbols and text, visual data in general, and media of all sorts. A semiotic approach to studying traditional written diaries might be indistinguishable from a phenomenological or hermeneutic approach; however, a semiotic approach is adaptable to other non-traditional types of diaries. Therefore, semiotics is less likely than phenomenological and hermeneutic methodologies to employ purely textual diaries, and in the case of solicited diaries in contemporary times, is more likely to solicit video diaries, photography, or drawings from participants (Buckingham, 2009). For example, Markwell (2000) explored online diaries with photos and text that he "subjected to semiotic analysis . . . in order to understand better the ways in which nature was constructed and represented through tourists' photography" (p. 93). Of the themes that emerged, one was nature depicted as wild yet tamable. One visual example was found in a photo that depicted a mountaintop view with both natural landscape and formal garden beds and pathways. A textual example of the theme was also offered:

> I did something fantastic today, I climbed the summit of Mt. Kinabalu. We got up at 3.00 am after a horrendous night's sleep. It took my group 3 hours to reach the summit. It was physically exhausting. Half the time we were pulling

ourselves up bare rock by a rope! It was dark, tiring and scary. When I finally got to Low's Peak it was all worth it. The view blew me away—it was stunning!!! I was so happy when I got to the top. I conquered the highest mountain in SE Asia! (Markwell, 2000, p. 95)

Semiotics encourages diverse approaches to both solicited and archival data in the spirit of decoding anything that serves to stand for something else.

Narrative Inquiry with Diaries

A method that goes by such names as *narrative inquiry, narrative analysis,* and *narratology,* the goal of this type of research is to explore the story as a metaphor for human experience. We construct our realities through narrating our lives, thus stories play a crucial role in self-understanding, in mutual understanding, and in almost every human activity. By the last couple of decades of the nineteenth century, narrative inquiry or narrative analysis evolved into a multidisciplinary method "which cuts across such areas as literary theory, history, anthropology, drama, art, film, theology, philosophy, psychology, linguistics, education, and even aspects of evolutionary biological science" (Connelly & Clandinin, 1990, p. 2). Narrative researchers focus on stories as they are spoken, but they also embrace stories "told" in textual sources, one of which may be diaries. They may take varied approaches to exploring narrative data (Bruner, 1985 & 1991; Connelly & Clandinin, 1990; Gee, 1989; Polkinghorne, 1988; Wells, 2011). Some may focus on the type of narrative (which varies in relation to the content) and to aspects of the narrative such as the relevant social interactions; or some may focus on the connections of past, present, and future that create continuity; or others may focus on the settings or situations (Dewey, 1938; Connelly & Clandinin, 1990). Some researchers may also focus on unraveling the purposes that participants' stories serve for the participant narrators (Polkinghorne, 1995).

In some cases, the researcher analyzes the story as a sequence, looking within or across participant narratives and identifying patterns of storied elements (such as chronology, plot, crisis, or resolution). For instance, the plot is integral to weaving connections between disparate events to make causal intimations, to make meaning, or to put temporal boundaries around an event (Bruner,

1990; Polkinghorne, 1995; Wood, 1991). As Polkinghorne (1995) points out, there can be a plot in as little as two sentences:

> To illustrate the operation of emplotment, I will use a simple story. "The king died. The prince cried." In isolation the two events are simply propositions describing two independent happenings. When composed into a story, a new level of relational significance appears. The relational significance is a display of the meaning-producing operation of the plot. Within the storied production, the prince's crying appears as a response to his father's death. The story provides a context for understanding the crying. (p. 7)

Many individual diary entries will contain plot elements. However, the larger plot of a diary is unlike more conventional storied narratives, or what Fincher (2013) refers to as a "non-storied narrative":

> As a life-document, a diary has certain features. Typically a diary is written from the author's point of view and in the present tense. A diarist may reflect on the past but does not inhabit it, and the diarist (unlike the biographer or oral historian) *cannot* know what happens in the future. That means the author cannot know what "the ending" is going to be, or where it will fall. In this way, common features of "story," such as suspense, climax and denouement, are devices unavailable to the diarist, and overall the plot isn't going anywhere, isn't leading to anything (although, of course, there may be stories *inside* diaries, my comment here is about a diary as a whole). A diary preserves a narrative structure, in that it is sequenced by time, but is unable to exploit the story sequence of causality. (p. 84)

Part of the appeal of studying archival diaries with regard to a plot is that they offer a perspective on history that is locked in time, with an embedded sociohistorical knowledge that the diarist knows and the researcher doesn't, and vice versa. For example, a European diarist writing before World War I knows what it is like to feel the foreboding of an approaching world war, yet only the contemporary reader knows the extent of the war that came.

Some narrative researchers, rather than deconstructing elements of diarists' stories, will instead aim to construct their own unified story out of disparate narrative segments. They take bits and pieces of life stories and weave them together into a tale of a single person's experience or of many people's experience of a single event. Those concerned with the dialogic or co-constructed nature of reality may focus on how the participant and the researcher themselves together construct the narrative if they are involved in an active exchange. In the case of solicited diaries, co-construction cannot be denied with regard to the researcher's serving first as an audience of the diarists and then later as the re-teller. Conducting narrative research with solicited diaries, Fincher (2013) candidly states, "the ironic fact is that (whatever they imagined) I was, quite literally, the diarists' audience. Over the year, I was the only person to read every diary entry . . . . Unlike ordinary diaries, they were written to be read, and they demanded to be read . . ." (p. 79). Fincher's diarists at times wrote their diaries as if to an imagined audience, as if their narratives were a virtual soapbox for social change.

As an example of an archival narrative diary analysis, one study explored nurses' diaries of critical care patients (Egerod & Christensen, 2009). In this unusual set of archival diaries, the diarists were nurses who had been following an occupational practice in some European countries of keeping diaries about progress through rehabilitation for patients who might not have remembered their experiences. The researcher's goal in their narrative analysis was to describe typical patterns across the nurses in the content and organization of their patient diaries. Consistent with more constructivist values, the researchers included a form of reflexivity called "Preconceptions of the Researchers" in which one researcher describes her own involvement in nursing but no involvement in this critical care diary keeping practice, and the other indicates involvement in nursing and openness to bringing this practice to her unit. The researchers described various elements of the diary narratives: "main characters," "behind the scenes," and the plot in "the dramaturgical metaphor":

> [T]he stage evolves around the hospital bed, occasionally expanding its radius to include wheel chairs and expeditions out of the unit to surgery or the outdoors. The props include the patient lift, the television, the ventilator and the dialysis equipment. The nurse is in the spotlight as the constant companion of the patient, while the doctors move silently in the shadows. (p. 271)

Often missing from the diary narrative is a planned ending, especially in unsolicited diaries. As Lejeune (2009) pondered:

> What is the end of a diary? The beginning of a diary is almost always indicated: it is rare to begin one without saying so. In one way or another you mark off this new territory of writing—with a name, a title, an epigraph, a commitment, a self-presentation. (p. 187)

Fincher (2013) describes the trailing off or sudden end of diaries and their narratives, noting that "few plan to finish keeping a diary" (p. 84). Nonetheless, the narrative analyst will find much of the traditional story in diaries to explore, and depending on the type—solicited or archival—and they will have many options for analytical strategies.

Applied Diary Research

Applied qualitative researchers exploit the strengths of systematic research methods to address practical issues. The values of positivistic science emphasize control and objectivity, often reinforcing a segregation between basic research and applied intervention; however, qualitative researchers have pushed back against this norm, often designing their studies so that making social change is an essential part of the research itself. Diaries are an excellent way to explore situations of concern; to design policy, programs, and products; and to evaluate the effectiveness of interventions. In addition, the everyday and personal nature of diary writing, logging one's experiences and behaviors day by day, can increase awareness. Diaries can be used for both research and intervention, simultaneously making a change and informing theory, hence Lewin's famous adage, "If you truly want to understand something, try to change it."

Social Justice Diary Research

Social justice research is distinctive in that it aims to serve as a catalyst. Social justice researchers recognize that bias and values are an inevitable part of science; they emphasize the common good and well-being for all, and they aim to make a change to society as well as to academic and scholarly endeavors. Activist research projects can carry as much stigma among positivistic science as an "activist judge" in the courtroom—for it is thought that they should not make social change, only reflect it. Some academics argue that activist research is an ethical imperative in the social sciences (Speed, 2006) and that activists should put social change above their individual academic careers (e.g., Epstein, 2001).

Activist qualitative research has perhaps the longest history in sociology, where academics have from the beginning directed their gaze to social problems embedded in the social structure. As part of Washington Gladden's (1908) "social gospel," activist efforts can be seen in the work of Goodwin Watson and Gynnar Myrdal (Hyers, Brown, & Sullivan, 2015). Although one can find examples of the social constructivism and intercultural acceptance promoted at the same time by early anthropologists, their research agenda tended to be more non-interventionist, following a naturalistic science perspective. Because psychologists have focused on the individual and are under the heavy influence of the medical model, they have come to social change from a difficult position—often promoting clinical solutions rather than activist ones, although an early exception was evident in the founding of the Society for the Social Psychological Study of Social Issues and in the works of such activist theorists as Gordan Allport and Kurt Lewin. Today, activist researchers are found in nearly every branch of the human sciences (Cancian, 1993; Fine & Gordon, 1991).

Feminism and queer theory have had a strong influence on social justice research efforts in the human sciences. They offer a politically justified alternative to conventional science, bringing a perspective that is non-hierarchical, more subjective and contextualizing of experience (Naples, 2003). Feminist empiricists and feministstandpoint theorists have called for more accessible research design and criticized value-free, "objective" science as a myth because all knowledge must be understood as socially, historically, and politically context-bound. They argue that knowledge creation and ownership has been associated with patriarchal power. Similarly, Queer theorists criticize normative assumptions and argue that all identities (e.g., gender, sexual, social class) are not fixed or intrinsic but are culturally constructed, fluid, and unstable/changing, and they reject the power dynamics behind assuming otherwise. For example, in an archival diary project exploring dimensions of privacy in Midwestern American women's diaries from the nineteenth century, Bunkers (1990) works with diaries of women focusing "on the ways in which the diarists' experiences of race, class, ethnicity, geographical setting and gender identity might have shaped the form and content of their text" (p. 18). The research questions are informed by feminist theory and the methodology by feminist values:

> Initially, I had envisioned approaching these texts as an "objective observer." I soon ascertained, however, that such a stance was neither possible nor desirable for me as a reader and scholar. My own experiences, attitudes and beliefs would inevitably shape my reading and interpretation of another woman's diary or journal. How could it be otherwise? I needed to remember that I owed it to each diarist, as well as to myself and the individuals who would eventually read the results of my research, to be as scrupulous as I could in defining the ways in which my own perceptions have influenced my reading of the diaries and journals in my sample. By so doing, I work within a self-reflexive paradigm. This shift in paradigm has undermined everything I had ever been taught about how to conduct academic research. I certainly could no longer pretend to lay claim to the title of Universal Scholar. Yet I liked looking at women's diaries and journals from an involved, empathetic perspective. So that is how I have gone forward. My new perspective necessitates the acknowledgment that, although I am the person conducting the research, I do not "own" its results, any more than I "own" the texts which I am studying. In fact, I have a responsibility not to attempt to assert a false "ownership" over my source materials but to understand my work as a collaborative process.
>
> I learn how to be reflexive about my research and writing processes, asking why I study these texts, how my own predispositions and biases affect my responses to individual women's texts and what I can give back in exchange for what I've received. Most importantly, I grow to respect the women whose lives I study, and I willingly take on the responsibility of doing all that I can to keep their texts from again being devalued, lost or forgotten. (p. 18)

Bunkers' research goals that are certainly reflective of feminist standpoint theory (Harding, 2004). One can find examples of feminist diary studies that focus on women's agency and empowerment (as opposed to victimization). For example, my own research using diaries has taken a feminist approach to exploring women's experience with everyday prejudice, with an emphasis on how women actively confront oppression in their daily lives (Hyers, 2007). Following a diary-keeping period, students met in small focus groups to discuss ways to address the prejudicial experiences they had documented the week before, emphasizing their agency.

Emancipatory, post-colonial, and anti-racist efforts in the social sciences value the experiences of marginalized groups in society and in academia. This type of work tackles social inequity and asymmetrical power relationships, and uses research to make direct links to political and social action (Brown & Stega, 2005; Potts & Brown, 2005; Smith, 1999). This type of work centers on voices that have been on the margins and empowers individuals and groups to create their own knowledge in order to contribute to intellectual and political liberation. The diary method is useful in emancipatory work for two reasons. First, diary studies offer ways to engage others' personal experiences for taking back "voice." For example, in a two-week solicited diary study of young adult black Americans by Strauss and Cross (2005), the theory of dynamic and self-initiated black identity as an active everyday negotiation or "transaction" both within the black community and in intergroup interactions was explored. Focus groups within the community were first conducted to help inform the diary format. Then the diary study followed with a new sample reporting race-sensitive situations and how they contended with them. A second way diary studies can be emancipatory is that they offer a means to mobilize participants. In an example from education, Reichmann (2001) describes language teaching and the teacher's own reflexive professional development through a fifteen month-long dialogic journal exchanged between herself and another teacher. She describes "jointly constructed" themes that emerged in their exchange with regard to obligations, power relations, and information shared. In this respect, the present study highlights the importance of sustaining long-term, critical, discursive practices in teaching to enhance emancipatory discourse so that "teachers (and teacher educators) can develop their own voice and learn more about themselves and their work—in other words, they can rearticulate who they are, what they do, and why they do what they do as teachers (p. 6)."

Participative inquiry, or participatory action research (PAR), has been described as a democratic or cooperative way to "break the monopoly" on the generation of knowledge through community action (Fals-Borda & Rahman, 1991). Combined with the principles of action research (Fine, 1992), the already well-documented benefit of diary writing has begun to be incorporated for social change and consciousness raising efforts in community settings (Foster, 2009). Diaries can be turned into community engagement activities rather than mere personal documentation. In PAR studies, participation is a strategy of cooperative inquiry, involving as many stakeholders as possible in as many aspects of the project as possible. For example, de la Rue (2003) explored ageism in a nursing context, with the goal of ageism reduction in nursing students. Through a combination of focus groups and reflective diaries, they conducted a PAR study in which data collection, analysis, and the application were collaborative. The clinical journals revealed critical reflection by the participants on their experiences of ageism:

> Once you are aware of the biases you hold, you can more consciously control them. . . . I have learnt a valuable lesson on how the individual elderly folk are . . . what it is like for them . . . it has been valuable to me, from a nursing and civilian viewpoint. (p. 13)

The transcribed data were shared with the study participants in a collective, self-reflective inquiry so that they could establish a course of action and evaluation. The nurse participants became involved in all stages—designing, acting, observing, reflecting, and planning a subsequent intervention.

Cook and Ledger (2004) described a similar PAR method of a "user-led research project" with those who have faced mental health service needs. They were inspired by Beresford and Wallcraft's (1997) "Psychiatric System Survivors and Emancipatory Research," which involves "survivors speaking and acting for themselves; improving their lives and liberating themselves from an oppressive psychiatric system; changing and equalizing relationships between research and research subjects, and developing survivors' own knowledge collectively" (p. 10). Taking this mental patients' rights perspective, Cook and Ledger (2004) describe "users" to include those who have used or currently use mental health services, who consider themselves to be survivors of the psychiatric system, or who have had significant experience of mental or emotional distress. They then "invited anyone with experience of mental distress and/or using services to select their research question and submit a proposal. No standard of formal education or research experience was specified, as full training was to be given." The researcher then provided support for projects, such one project exploring the effects of a dance therapy project called "Dancing for Living" on participants' emotional well-being:

> My role in terms of support is to provide and deliver a training programme as well as to work alongside all the research projects to their completion. This can mean giving advice on all aspects of the research, sometimes working with researchers on the research, and also sometimes providing emotional support. . . . This is done by building the capacity of survivor-researchers, and by sharing their research findings about alternatives to mainstream treatments extensively with survivors and users. The methods used were: Peer pair interviews: dancers paired up and asked each other six qualitative questions about the dancing. Writing and drawing: all dancers were encouraged to keep a diary, or write poetry, or use pictures to depict feelings/experiences of dancing. Group discussions: the three researchers ran three focus groups. (p. 68)

As is often the case in the very interdisciplinary methods of PAR, diaries were one part of the data collection, but not necessarily the only data used to inform the project.

Diaries in Educational Research

One of the most obvious uses of diaries is in education, especially when entries are written, open-ended, biographical, and reflective narratives typical of a writing assignment. The method is useful for teachers to understand the learning process, for learners to "vent" frustrations and develop self-awareness of their own learning, and for communication between teachers and learners, including providing a means for students to provide teachers with evidence of their learning and a means for teachers to provide feedback (Bailey, 1991). Teachers themselves have long kept diaries to document lesson plans and outcomes, and to provide daily evaluations of their teaching growth (Wightman, 1936). Published academic articles in education mention diaries in primary, secondary, and higher education, using them as a means to evaluate student reading, learning, time use, and even prospective students' selection of schools (Beckers, van der Voordt, & Dewulf, 2016; Cowell, 1937; Douglas, Lawson, Cooper, & Cooper, 1968; LaPalio, 1981; Long & Henderson, 1973; Wragg, 1968). For instance, diaries have been used to encourage reflexivity in learning a foreign language (Turzańska, 2014). The self-reflective and longitudinal style of documentation can help students and teachers identify points of struggle in a more evidenced-based manner and help those who study education to better understand the learning process (Sá, 2002). Noyes (2004) used video diaries, "a process developed into a kind of personal diary, 'written' to videotape," to explore the learning dispositions of children. For example, one child goes before the video camera and logs her entry:

> I don't know what to say . . . now maths . . . I hate it, I hate it, I hate it . . . (pause) . . . three things about maths . . . boring, boring, boring. . . . The thing that makes maths hard for me is that I don't think I'm really good at it . . . erm . . . I have to say this prufully, I mean trufully, erm . . . I know what everyone's thinking, that . . . I'm the dumbest kid in the class . . . and me and Sophie really need desperate help. I'm not saying that she's bad or anything but me and Sophie need really desperate help. (p. 199)

The entries can be quite raw, and as Noyes pointed out, "the data produced are unashamedly complex but therein lies an advantage . . . " (p. 207).

Diaries in Clinical Research

Because clinicians practice involves the evaluation and treatment of patients, they are accustomed to the regularity of observation and log-keeping that is characteristic of diary research. The medical and health profession is one of the oldest professions to practice detailed daily diary keeping for the management of symptoms, treatments, hygiene, and nutrition of patients (Guly, 1996; Hawkins, Ralley, & Young, 2014). Nurses recognize the benefit of narrative diary accounts as a means to bridge the gap of under-standing between the impersonal nature of epidemiological stud-ies and the nuanced realities of treatment in an individual patient's life. The field of psychology had adopted the medical model very early on, publishing clinical case studies of human social and men-tal health phenomena using their own logs and sometimes clients' diaries to demonstrate symptomology. Psychotherapists studying the manifestation of mental health challenges and their treatment can examine the nature of clients' daily activities through what Mackrill (2008) refers to as the "porthole . . . to extra-therapeutic aspects that are central to psychotherapeutic practice" (p. 16).

In a paper advocating for solicited and unsolicited diary meth-ods in clinical research, Jones (2000) describes a very personal analysis of a 350-page archival diary of one cancer patient. During a health interview, the patient revealed that he kept a private diary of his battle with cancer, which he then allowed Jones to include in his study. Jones coded the diary for various themes along points in the patient's health and treatment trajectory. Rich excerpts were revealing of several dimensions of the patient's experience of can-cer, from symptoms, to communication, to treatment. One theme Jones identified was a "breakdown of professional interaction," as in this patient's diary framed:

> Mr Abdul, using a wooden spatula, examined my throat, and said, "Nothing wrong with your throat." Actually Mr Abdul distressed me, saying, "You can go now," but a nurse, female, in the room said, "But Mr Abdul, Mr P is here about his throat, and you haven't examined it yet," whereupon he therefore did so. (p. 562)

Research on health promotion and risk reduction often takes a holistic contextualized approach, soliciting diary logs from client participants on diet, exercise, pain, thirst, sleep, and an assort-ment of other daily events in "health diaries" (Gregory, 1990; Rosner, Namaji, & Wyke, 1992; Verbrugge, 1980). Health diaries can provide a more patient-centered approach to understanding health care and well-being, including "social aspects of a person's day-to-day health, which are important for a holistic appreciation of health" according to Freer (1980, p. 281). As an example of a drug use risk-reduction diary study, Singer and colleagues (2000) included solicited diaries amongst a half-dozen other methods, including interview and ethnographic observation, to explore intravenous drug use (IDU) and hepatitis risk.

> We ask IDUs to keep diaries so that we can learn about issues that might not otherwise be remembered or reported by participants on standardized 30-day-recall survey questionnaires . . . day-to-day variations in syringe acquisition and drug use patterns, social and contextual influences on these patterns . . . [and] coping strategies. (p. 1052)

Their diary method helped them identify very specific challenges to interventions that drug users faced in the field so they could make recommendations for program adjustments accordingly. The personal nature of diaries can be beneficial to health researchers aiming to explore an array of risky behaviors that are infused in daily living, such as sexual behavior and alcohol consumption (Coxon, Davies, & McManus, 1990; Davies, Hunt, Macourt, & Weatherburn, 1990; Hilton, 1989).

Clinical researchers have noticed that keeping a diary can affect patients, and thus be used as an intervention itself, for everything from consciousness raising to pain management. Cognitive behaviorists have noticed the potential of diary keeping for behavioral modification, as Wheeler and Reis (1991) explain: "The mere act of recording the behavior changes its frequency in a desirable direction" (p. 341). In a study by Duncan (1969), diaries were used as a part of a behavior modification intervention with youth: "Would you like to lose weight? Stop swearing and being sarcastic? Have beautiful fingernails? Teenagers in this study reported they wanted to, and did" (p. 541). Applications of diary writing have also been made to coping with stress in daily living, which seems to be alleviated in part simply by documenting everyday stressors and engaging in appraisals of them in the diary (Lazarus & Folkman, 1987). It can even stave off existential ennui, as noted by Langford and West (1999), who see the diary as a "daily affirmation of resistance to the assertion of one's non-existence." Highlighting other potentially clinically advantageous effects of diary keeping, including spiritual (devotion) and cognitive (remembering), Mackrill (2008) cautions that such interventions do change the nature of the data one collects:

> In psychotherapy studies, the diary is not merely a method that records data about the client's ongoing therapy. The

diary is a secondary form of intervention that affects and, some would argue, contaminates the data concerning the psychotherapy. Research has suggested that writing about emotional experiences and thereby confronting emotionally upsetting events may be associated with improved mental health. (p. 15)

Singer et al. (2000) also reported that the diaries were a catalyst for self-awareness and help-seeking, "influencing some participants to reconsider their risk and drug use behaviors and [have] led to several requests for assistance in lowering risk and entering into drug treatment" (p. 1052). The diary requires deliberate focus, discipline, mindful meta-cognitions about the self, and serves as a reminder of therapeutic goals outside the clinic (Schmitz & Wiese, 2006). Given the potential for therapeutic amplification, clinical diary research that is not intended as an intervention study should keep these potential side effects in mind.

Diaries in Industrial, Organizational, and Consumer Research

Solicited and unsolicited diaries have made valuable contributions in the fields of industrial and organizational development and in consumer-related research. Diaries are useful at nearly all points of industrial and organizational scholarship, as Fisher and To (2012) detail:

There is an increasing realization that there is meaningful within-person variation over short periods of time on a number of constructs of interest to organizational researchers. These include thoughts and feelings such as job satisfaction, goals, recovery, moods, emotions, and intrinsic motivation/ engagement/flow; behaviors and outcomes including coping behavior, effort, creativity, performance, emotional expression/emotional labor, citizenship behavior, and counterproductive work behavior; and fluctuating environmental situations and demands such as social interactions, workload, task characteristics, work–family conflicts, and other stressors. (p. 866)

Solicited diaries can contribute to the contemporary "evidence-based" movement in organizations, since the solicited diary is an excellent means to get useful data. Diaries have been used to study weekly creativity and flow (Csikszentmihalyi, Larson,

& Prescott, 1977; Frederiks, Ehrenhard, & Groen, 2013). Beal and Weiss (2003) refer to diaries as one of a group of "methods of ecological momentary assessment" useful in organizational research. Zundel, MacIntosh, and Mackay (2016) aver that, "For researchers of practice, video diaries can add participants' intense reflections on organizational affairs, access to dispersed communities of practice, and as 'unselective' recording devices, they offer audio-visual glimpses into the wider work-world of the participants" (p. 2). Their data included textual comments and visual images. Archival unsolicited diaries can be useful, too; for example, in studies of the historical workplace like Blewett's (1984) study of the diary of Susan Brown, a factory mill worker from the late 1800s. Diaries can also help measure subtly unfair aspects of work life and be used to evaluate organizational programs and policies. For example, my colleagues and I have used diaries to explore difficult-to-witness workplace equality issues with regard to professional development, revealing disparities faced by minority groups in higher education (Hyers, Syphan, Cochran, & Brown, 2012). Time-use or time-budget diaries collected across the last century (Anderson, 1971; Fisher, Egerton, Gershuny, & Robinson, 2007; Gersbuny & Sullivan, 1998; Sorokin & Berger, 1938) have been useful for quantifying gender disparities and convergences in work–life balance across time and over large samples (Berk, 1988; Grønmo & Lingsom, 1986).

Diaries are also useful for consumer behavior and marketing research (McIntyre, 2013). Although a qualitative approach is only one route in consumer research (Hirschman, 1986), attention to narrative methods has grown. Diary panel market research has been used to explore people's use of products and reactions to advertisements, purchase histories, and a range of other consumer related information (Lee, Hu, & Toh, 2000; Parfitt, 1967). Patterson (2005) described a diary exploring the appeal of text messaging or SMS (short message service) on cell phones. In diary entries, after receiving texts, participants in his study described the "kick" they got from this type of communication, which was then still so new to many, as one diarist wrote:

It's funny how two little beeps can bring such excitement as you wait in anticipation to find out who the message is from and what it is they have to say to you. Then again those same two little bleeps can totally destroy you if the message is bad news. In this particular instance the message sound brought reasonably good news. Phew! (p. 156)

Patterson's study was of texts usage, but of course, now Web and cell technology have become increasingly common ways to collect consumer diary records. More elaborate consumer and design research methods have also been developed. For instance, a creative multimodal diary technique (using written diaries, cameras, and other materials) to encourage culturally relevant design, a "cultural probe" is an interactive diary method that originated in work by Gaver, Dunner, and Pacenti (1999) to explore ways to integrate senior citizens into community activities.

Conclusion

As should be apparent, there is a great deal of flexibility in the diary method. It is important to reiterate that these types of diary studies, described separately, can and do overlap in practice as the rule rather than as the exception. Furthermore, diary studies are often combined with some amount of quantitative data. My assumptions moving forward, in describing a basic diary design, will follow most closely with my own epistemological assumptions, that of a moderate social constructivism.

3

QUALITATIVE DIARY RESEARCH DESIGN

THE WIDESPREAD cultural familiarity of the diary as a form of self-expression may give a false impression that a diary study is a simple undertaking. Qualitative methods are often misperceived as non-technical and requiring little in the way of preplanning. Although it is true that diaries are a comfortably intuitive tool for researchers and participants alike, there is much involved in running a successful diary study. Any diary research project will go much more smoothly with a systematic approach, a strong design, effective data management, coherent analysis, and a clear understanding of what one is getting into. Researchers should consider whether the nature of diary data is the best fit for their research questions. There are also considerations to be made about participant selection and recruitment, and diary entry format.

The Nature of Data One Can Obtain from a Diary Study

There are several types of data a diary study can generate. Diary studies involve data that are somewhat unique, and in some instances, it is the most sensible means of answering certain types of research questions. Diary studies do not involve as much interaction between the researcher and the diary writer, who is often in a private location remote from the researcher, which sets it apart from many other, more interactive types of qualitative methods (e.g., interviewing). If a researcher is interested in any of the following types of data, a diary may be a good choice:

- *Personal testimonies*, as the firsthand witness to a historic time period or to contemporary issues and current events: Diaries may be the only means of understanding an event or they may supplement official characterizations of historical epochs. For example, Hyne's (1998) included soldiers' diaries as part of a more personal portrait of 20th-century wartime: "Historians tell the big stories, of campaigns and battles, of the great victories and the disastrous defeats . . . . The stories that soldiers tell are small-scale" (p. 11). Similarly, Garfield (2006) found value in studying war from the civilian perspective through the diaries of "Five Ordinary People in Extraordinary Times," admitting, "It is the personal accounts that will always fascinate us most" (p. 3). One of his archival diarists, a British mother of three, Tilly Rice, wrote in her August 1939 diary about how " The Germans have now started leaflet raids" and how she was "hoping they would do something like that; I thought it would be interesting to see if their stuff was any good." She then laments "But to my disappointment all they've dropped is extracts from Hitler's speech. We don't want our streets littered up with stale news. Can't they think up something more amusing than that? And they are supposed to be an efficient race" (Garfield, 2006, p. 323).

  Solicited diaries can be used for testimonies as well, when participants are needed to provide personal witness to a current situation of social concern. As an example, Gill and Liamputtong (2009) asked women to write diaries about what it is like to parent children with autism spectrum disorder, an increasingly more common diagnosis in contemporary times, so that "their stories are made more visible and readily accessible to a wider audience in our society" (p. 313).

- *Everyday events*, to include nearly any part of daily living that can be logged, listed, checked off, or commented upon:

this varies from the most mundane detail to the most vivid episode occurring in diarists' own lives. Archival diaries often contain mundane details on everyday life due to the way the diary has evolved as a medium for self-documentation in modern culture. No matter the situation or purpose of the archival diarist, often their diaries contain everyday information about their social engagements, chores, diet, and sometimes even their sexual exploits or spiritual experiences (Drinker & Crane, 1758/1991; Rosefield, 2015). A common starting point for many diaries is the weather, as a diary writing advocate recommended at the turn of last century (Jerome, 1878):

But what are you to write about? First, the weather. Don't forget this. Write, "Cold and windy," or "Warm and bright," as the case may be. It takes but a moment, and in a few years you will have a complete record of the weather, which will be found not only curious, but useful. (p. 32)

There will, of course, be many inconsistencies in diaries due to the idiosyncrasies of what particular diarists find important about their everyday lives to document. For example, in a study of the impact of everyday activities and community gardening on healthy aging (Milligan, Bingley, & Gatrell, 2005), seniors completed pre- and post-measures of well-being along with end-of-day activity diary entries, such as these from a participant:

Mon: Fine day so I varnished two garden seats and the conservatory.
Tues: Wet. Ironed for myself and family. Walked to shops for paper.
Wed: Varnished garage door and started painting fences.
Thurs: Quiet day, had hair permed, shopped, cut grass.
Fri: Finished painting fences. (p. 1887)

Everyday events can be so familiar and mundane that they might go easily unnoticed in the "mindlessness" of daily living unless one is asked to log them in a diary. Even volatile events, if a regular occurrence, may be paid little heed over time; so, for instance, Radcliffe and Cassell (2014) asked couples to use diaries to describe their everyday work-life conflicts that might be swiftly forgotten.

- *Longitudinal or chronological details,* so as to explore the order or timing of events: If multiple diary entries are examined by one diarist, by definition, they are longitudinal data. Often diary studies will include dozens of dated and sequentially logged diary entries. Archival diaries have long aided historians in reconstructing the timing of events, both in individual biography and in major historical accounts (e.g., Friedman, 2004; Gera & Horowitz, 1997). Diary entries can help provide information on the weekly, daily, or even hourly timing of events, and also on the monthly, seasonal, or yearly timing, as well. Solicited diary studies may be used to explore the ordinal timing of psychosocial events in order to better understand them. For example, early work on stress and coping employed solicited diaries to disentangle whether negative mood precedes (and thereby leads to) negative appraisals of life events, or whether a series of negative life events precede (and thereby cause) negative mood (e.g., Bolger et al., 1989; Caspi, Bolger, Eckenrode, 1987).

- *Processes, systems, or phases,* to explore more holistically events that occur in a progressive, systematic manner: In a fascinating archival study using the diary of Hellyer to retrospectively presage his untimely death by suicide, Baddeley, Daniel, and Pennebaker (2011) assessed changes in Hellyer's writing of various written documents (including his diaries) in the seven years preceding his death. Their analysis showed a tragic intrapsychic process evidenced by increases in first-person singular and decreases in first-person plural pronouns and increases in negative emotion words, indicating an increase in self-focus, isolation, and negativity. They theorized that this process of increasing depression and suicidal ideation could be identified via computerized text analysis to "decode" and potentially prevent suicide in others. In a solicited diary study of the process of coping with fibromyalgia, Affleck et al. (1998) conducted what they referred to as a "daily process study" of a sample of women who wrote diaries about the complex process of coping with pain, fatigue, mood, and sleep deprivation (recorded within-day, momentary, on handheld computer devices) on achievement of daily social and health-related goals (recorded in end-of-the-day diaries). In another solicited diary study on process, Travers, Morisano, and Locke (2015) explored students' progress in five phases of goal-setting over a six-month period. Their study helped them understand the complexity of "each individual's learning and development experience (e.g., the intervening psychological processes) as well as the specific strategies they used (e.g., improved planning and timetabling of their studies). They were able to identify the "active ingredients" that were perceived to lead to academic growth (p. 230). Sometimes researchers discover a process they did not expect to find, after it is revealed across multiple diary entries. For instance, in my own research on women's experiences with everyday prejudice (sexism, heterosexism, anti-black racism, and antisemitism), diaries collected over time revealed that those who did not respond assertively to a perpetrator carried the incident with them days later, ruminating about future responses they could make and talking about the incident more with others for social support (Hyers, 2007).

- *Frequencies or counts* that are totaled, checked, or tallied: Phenomena may be counted either directly by participants who are reflecting on their day, automatically by a technological device, or manually by the researcher. Although counts or percentages are not typically the goal of a qualitative study, they are often included anyway in diary study reports for descriptive purposes. Archival databases such as the *World Diary Project* have electronically searchable diaries if researchers are interested in doing word or subject counts. Through careful counting of the intersection of different types of activities reported in solicited time use diaries, Mattingly and Blanchi (2003) found gender differences in nuanced aspects of daily activity. Specifically, they found women's "free" leisure time was more likely to be contaminated and fragmented by non-leisure activities than was men's leisure time.

- *Contextual details* surrounding phenomena of interest: These may include details about the immediate social setting, associated feelings, or the ongoing day-to-day storyline surrounding an event. Archival studies may pull contextual details from diaries, along with letters and other supporting documents. For some solicited diary studies, the express goal is to explore the context surrounding certain events (rather than the events themselves), often to make causal connections. For example, Zarantonello and Luomala (2011) asked participants to keep diaries on chocolate consumption to explore the "sensations, feelings, thoughts, and behaviors" related to various "chocolate consumption contexts," such as the "context of escapism":

> It's the perfect time for a movie and a sweet. I chose Troy [movie] . . . and a delicious Magnum [chocolate]. (Male)
>
> Tonight, I watched some TV from my comfy sofa, munching Pavesi Gocciole extra dark. (Female)
>
> I have just got home. The kitchen light is still on and my dad is still up. Damn! Right in the kitchen. Nothing doing, Nutella [chocolate] must be tasted in solitude. (Female) (p. 67)

Another instance of a context-focused solicited diary study, Poppleton and colleagues (2008) used diaries to explore the "spillover effect" of work concerns into home life and home concerns into work life, to determine where such cognitions are more burdensome and how the context of the diarists' workplace's organizational culture influenced feelings about spillover. As is the case of frequency information, researchers may wish to report rich contextual information that is often available in a diary, even if it is not the focus, for descriptive purposes. It is notable that such "thick description" is less common in mixed-method studies that tend to leave context out of the report, or reduce context to numbers. For example, in a study by Conway and Briner (2002) on the emotional impact of workplace trust and broken contracts, participants recorded "every explicit and implicit promise the organization had broken that day . . . in detail"; however, their descriptions were stripped from the data, ultimately converted into a dichotomy of zero (no promise broken) versus one (at least one or more promises broken).

- *Dynamic amorphous phenomena,* marked by frequent change and transformation: What Radcliffe (2016) referred to as the "dynamism" of daily experience, variability is the truest state of affairs for most phenomena. Diaries can help reveal evolving and fluid phenomena in ways that cross-sectional, one-time measures cannot. Often diary studies that focus on unstable indicators lean toward a mix of quantitative and qualitative methods, such as the aforementioned Conway and Briner's (2002) study of organizational trust. In another study of the effects of variations in work context on emotions, Kiffin-Petersen, Murphy, and Soutar (2012) used solicited diaries to explore the effects of customer interactions on service industry employees. They preferred a qualitative diary method "because it can provide a deeper understanding of the occurrence of affective events, employees' appraisal of those events, and of the possible fluctuations in the positive emotions that are generated" (p. 1181). Their study revealed subtle fluctuations due to within-person variation and to emotional contagion from friendly customers:

> **The customer told a joke to me and her friends. It was at the end of the day and I was starting to feel a bit flat. Laughter is always an uplifting experience. (F, retail, 46 yrs)**
>
> **A customer who had a great sense of humour. It was refreshing to talk to someone who enjoyed a good laugh, and it was contagious. Happy. (F, telemarketing, 47 yrs). (p. 1196)**

- *Ambiguous, subtle, or covert phenomena,* not likely to be in the immediate awareness of diarists: In archival diary studies, entries may be analyzed in a technical or clinical manner not pertinent or familiar to the writer at the time. For example, Richardson (2012) reread women's archival World War II diaries from a contemporary trauma theory perspective, also looking for signs of depression—all of which is clinical diagnostic terminology not likely to be in the lexicon of the diarists in the era they lived in. Diaries from social groups who were stigmatized or engaged in socially deviant behaviors may require a contemporary rereading to identify (perhaps intentionally) ambiguous references made by diarists, as Carmichael (1998) made the case for identifying queer perspectives in the archives. At times, the act of diary writing for a solicited diary study can bring attention and awareness of a phenomenon to the diarist who was not very conscious of it before, as described, for example, by an oncology patient in a diary study on pain and pain management (Schumacher et al., 2002) who reported, "It made me more aware. It helped me better judge my pain." Similarly, food diaries have helped people be more aware of their eating habits (Hardy & Gray, 2012; Zepeda & Deal, 2008). Sometimes diary participants describe phenomena that are hard to articulate so they are somewhat obscure to them and perhaps entirely misunderstood by those around them. For example, Plowman (2010) uses diaries to explore the "gendered organization" or the subtle sexism that is often "hidden and silenced" from other coworkers, as these two entries illustrate:

> I suspect that gender, and maybe more specifically sexuality plus the tricky domain of masculinity/ femininity and propriety play a strange role in this all . . . mmmmm. It is complicated. . . .
>
> [I find] it hard to cope with it's when I start to raise issues about how I am feeling especially if I am uncomfortable about something. Those are too personal issues, which shouldn't be raised in the work environment. But I am not sure if it is a gendered thing. . . . But I am worried that it can too easily become "my personal issue" as opposed to seeing that those feelings do impact on one's work performance, as well as relationships at work. How should these be managed? (p. 32)

Sometimes collecting diaries from different types of diarists can reveal overlooked differences in their experiences, as

I found in work with Swim and colleagues (Swim, Hyers, Cohen, & Fergusen, 2001) that revealed women's different experiences of everyday sexism compared to men's.

- *Private ruminations, introspections, and reflections* of the diarist reflecting upon life experiences: This really is the quintessential nature of the diary, an homage to the legacy of the diary as the place wherein individuals do their mental work. Any solicited or archival diary study that includes open-ended narrative and "wrapping up" of the days' events has the potential to provide this rich introspective data. A most famous archival diary unveiling private ruminations is found in the diary entries of Kierkegaard (1938). Despite evidence that he anticipated— as famous diarists often do—that his entries could one day go public—nonetheless Kierkegaard's entries are rife with intimate, personal, psycho-philosophical ruminations and resolutions, as in this one from 1845 (Rhode, 1988):

> And so with us human beings. Our whole earthly existence is a sort of indisposition; with some the cause for it is that they make too great an effort; in others too little effort, and if one inquires into the cause, the man you ask will first say: "Do you make a great effort?" If you answer yes, he will say: "The cause is that you work too strenuously." If you answer no, he will say the opposite, put his tail between his legs and slink off. Even if somebody offered me 10 rixdollars I would not take it upon myself to explain the enigma of life. And, anyway, why should I? If life is an enigma, a puzzle, he who has posed it probably will come forth in the end and offer the solution when he feels that nobody is too eager to make a guess any longer. (p. 22)

The diary has become the multigenerational, cross-cultural site for processing and introspection. For example, evacuated Japanese children living outside dangerous urban centers during World War II were encouraged by teachers to use the diary as a private place for self-expression:

> You must faithfully write down your thoughts and feelings just as they are (*ari no mama no kokoro, ari no mama no*

kansō). A diary that gives form to your true heart will be of great value . . . . Write down, day-by-day, the problems you need to reflect on (*hansei*) and other issues you might be feeling. (p. 3)

Moore (2016) uses those archival diaries to explore how children struggled with their situation in a manner different from adults', but no less legitimate an account. Contemporary stress and coping researchers have unsurprisingly latched onto the diary method as a very useful means for soliciting access to private ruminations. For example, Szabó and Lovibond (2006) asked participants to record naturally occurring worries in diaries, and not unlike the Kierkegaard's self-correcting rumination just quoted—about one-third of participants' entries about internal worries were accompanied by internal resolutions, as well.

- *Ephemera,* or the fleeting or short-lived events that if not quickly recorded could be lost track of or forgotten: The regularity of diary writing can help gather data on phenomena that are so quick (e.g., exposure to advertisements, rapid decisions) that they are nearly automatic and often quickly forgotten. Many archival personal diaries will include events of a day that, if not written in the diary, would not have been remembered. Similarly, in a solicited daily study of injection drug users' daily risk-related decisions in their communities (Singer et al., 2000), a researcher asked, "Would you remember this in 6 months?" to which the participant responded with the proverbial lament, "No way, I can barely remember what I did last week" (p. 1052). Even more fleeting, task shifts (or interruptions) are perhaps the ultimate example of short-lived events, captured in a diary study by Czerwinski, Horvitz, and Wilhite (2004). In their study, an average of 50 task shifts was documented by information workers:

  Their diaries demonstrated that returned-to projects were more complex, on average, than shorter-term activities. These key projects were significantly lengthier in duration, required significantly more documents, were interrupted more, and experienced more revisits by the user after interludes. These critical projects were also rated significantly harder to return to than shorter-term projects. Returned-to tasks were over twice as long as other tasks. . . . Overall, we found that information workers switch among tasks a significant number of times during their work week. (p. 179)

Therefore, diaries can help to document short-lived events that are both intentional and unintentional.

The Participants in a Diary Study

In order to have diary entries to work with, the researcher typically needs either to locate a source of relevant archival diaries or to recruit diary writers and then work with the entries that are acquired. There is a distinct disciplinary divide in the use of archival diaries, such that the humanities have taken far more advantage of them than the social sciences have. Obviously, historians turn to archival diaries because of the information they provide about the past. Scholars in literature, philosophy, and anthropology study archival diaries of famous writers or historical figures—in some cases, it is the diary itself that has brought the writer fame. Social scientists favor new diaries that they collect from anonymous volunteers because this is more consistent with the post-positivistic value of researcher "control" that dominates the sciences. The use of unsolicited diaries in the social sciences is only found in the very early days of the human sciences. As quantitative scientific methods took over, archival diaries, with their imprecision and unaccounted for "confounding" encumbrances, were the stuff of literature, not science. The narrative turn (Goodson & Gill, 2011) opened the social sciences up to narrative methods in general, but the research potential of the archival diary has remained regrettably untapped by social scientists. Solicited diarists have been more typical.

Depending on the type of diary project, a diary study will include two categories of participants—the diarists themselves who have written or will write the entries, and the diary researcher who will work with the entries. Both deserve some attention. The diarists' and the diary researchers' roles are quite different in an archival diary study from what they are in a solicited diary study.

Archival Diary Study "Participants"

For an archival study, "participants" is a misleading label for the diarists, because they were not directly solicited for participation in the *present* researcher's study. There are not usually participants whom the present researcher is corresponding with. As is the case with other types of secondary research studies (e.g., secondary survey analysis), in archival diary studies, the researcher locates preexisting data, and any difficulties they have in identifying and accessing relevant diary source material depend on the research project. Often, the more specific the question, the harder it is to find the answer. Similarly, the more specific the context and content of the entry, the more challenging it may be to find usable diary data. It is a challenge to find the specific treasure one is seeking, and the hunt may involve some inevitable roadblocks and distractions along the way, as part of the process that Toms and Duff (2002) characterize in the telling title of their methodological article: "'*I Spent 1½ Hours Sifting Through One Large Box . . . .* ': Diaries as information behavior of the archives user: Lessons learned." There are two types of "participants" in archival research: those who kept diaries of their own volition and have left them to posterity, and those who kept diaries as part of a research project which the researchers have retained and made available to researchers.

Archival Personal Diaries

Over the last several centuries, due to widespread cultural changes, such as increasing literacy, access to the means for producing long-lasting diary documents, and popularity of personal diary-keeping, the number of surviving diaries is incalculable. There are national and local archives all over the world that house unpublished diaries of the ordinary and the famous. Published anthologies abound, offering collections of ordinary diarists who have shared a similar experience, station in life, or period in history. Published diaries of significant cultural figures are becoming more and more common, often with either overt or covert intimations that they assumed their diary would eventually come before an audience. There are also uncountable unpublished personal diaries that are in the public domain, in places such as the Creative Commons. Archivists are struggling to keep up with transitioning paper documents to searchable databases (Yakel, Shaw, & Reynolds, 2007).

Archival Research Diaries

In some cases, archival diaries exist from prior research studies. Often these diary participants completed structured entries for a research study, a clinical case study, or an educational assessment. For archival studies of previously solicited research diaries, researchers may gain access via small- or large-scale collections at universities, published case studies, and in some cases, online research archives. One of the most famous storehouses is the Mass Observation Project. In 1937, the Mass Observation Project invited people from all parts of the United Kingdom to record everything they did, from when they woke up in the morning to when they went to sleep at night, on May 12—the day of King George VI's coronation. These diaries provided a glimpse into the everyday lives of all sorts of people in Britain on this particular day. The diaries are now held as part of the University of Sussex's Special Collections at "The Keep." Interest in this unusual study has waxed and waned over the years, but it continues, with the solicited documents perpetually stored at a research center that has continued calls for participants well into the 21st century:

> Would you like to keep a one-day diary? The Mass Observation Archive is calling on staff and students (as well as individuals throughout the UK) to chart their opinions, feelings, and experiences in a one-day electronic diary. (http://www.sussex.ac.uk/internal/bulletin/staff/2014-15/080515/12maydiary)

All the entries are conveniently computer-searchable by code word. Another great source of archival diaries, also in the United Kingdom, is stored at the *World Diary Project*, founded in 2012 from the collection of Irving Finkel. There are efforts worldwide to electronically transfer local holdings of diaries at historical societies, archives, and libraries around the world, to provide more access to researchers no matter where they are. Similar to old-fashioned ethnographic methods, in some cases, diary researchers must travel to access diaries in archives that do not circulate and for which there is no electronic reproduction available.

In the contemporary information age, digital diaries abound as well (Chassanoff, 2013). One can find diary source material on Internet blogs, curated websites, Facebook, Twitter, and even on sites dedicated to electronic diary writing and journaling. Even though such diary entries may not be ancient—some could be as old as a day—they are, by definition archival, unsolicited diary entries, and reading them would not be entirely dissimilar to reading a diary of a Victorian writer penning entries with an inkwell and a feather quill.

Solicited Diary Study Participants

Participant recruitment in a solicited diary study is similar to the active recruitment for any other social science study. The researcher will identify a research question that will determine the type of diary participants who will be the best for generating the diary entries. Then the researchers will need to develop a plan to locate and recruit the participants.

Participant Selection Criteria for Solicited Diary Studies

There are many considerations in participant selection. Participants solicited for a diary study are selected because they will contribute in essential or at least desirable ways:

- They will have the *experience of interest* while taking part in the study (e.g., pregnancy, chronic pain, television viewing) to be able to write about it.
- They will need the basic *capacity to self-reflect* on that experience, sometimes after time has passed, although this can be addressed by having only short answers throughout the day as an alternative to end-of-day or end-of-week retrospective reflection.
- In general, they need the *ability to thoughtfully write about their experiences*, although creative researchers can find a way to work around this as well by using drawings, audio, or video entries as alternatives to writing.
- It is also essential that the participants have an *openness to and trust in* the researchers and their process, especially when entries are about personal or controversial subjects (e.g., about drug use or intimate partner violence).

- All things being equal, a diary participant with *interest in the subject matter* will provide stronger data than a participant who is disinterested.
- Researchers also need to carefully consider if they want to aim for a sample that is *diverse versus homogeneous,* not just on the criterion of interest but demographically, as well. A diverse sample will go beyond "the usual suspects" (i.e., the most common participant demographic, who Braun and Clarke, 2006, identify as the straight white male); however, some research questions will be best addressed with a very narrowly defined sample.

Roles of Participants in Solicted Diary Studies

It is important to consider the participants' roles in the study, which will vary depending upon the epistemological orientation of the project. In most cases, the participants are characterized as *informants,* who report on their experience to the researcher who commenced the study. In some cases, they are viewed more as *co-investigators,* serving as research assistants or participant observers, even collaborating on research design, analysis, and reporting. In rare cases, one can find diary studies with just one participant, the *researcher-diarist,* who participates in an introspective self-study, as in auto-ethnography (Humphreys, 2005), not unlike the introspection techniques of early psychology. A *recipient of an intervention* (e.g., receiving a treatment, engaging in a new activity, or participating in a program) may document the effects in their diary so that researchers can evaluate the effectiveness of the intervention. There are also participants who are *diary writing as an intervention* in and of itself, making revelations about goal setting, learning educational material, or recognizing keys to their mental health (Mackrill, 2008). As Klein, Boman, and Prince (2007) note, a "striking aspect of writing is that it can be a way of 'telling ourselves something that we never knew before'" (p. 229). Sometimes in educational or therapeutic settings a feedback group interchanges diaries with one another. There may be a dyad in which only one person writes and the other responds, tandem pairs both writing and exchanging, and round-robin diary-keeping groups in which everyone writes and responds to each other's entries. For example, Morawski and Rottmann (2016) conducted an intervention study in which teachers reflected on their practice of teaching:

> [W]orking in two groups of three, each teacher engaged in a round robin journal response by first responding in her or his own journal for two minutes to the sentence stem, "A teacher is . . . ." Then, passing her or his entry to the teacher on the right, each teacher then read the received entry and responded in writing to this entry for three minutes. The latter process repeated itself until each teacher receives her or his original response back. (p. 9)

In action research studies, diary participants may be *stakeholders* and will take the results from their own diaries as a means of consciousness raising and subsequently develop a plan for a policy or program change.

Sampling Solicited Diary Participants

In most qualitative research, participants represent a non-probability sample. It is usually less important that they are randomly selected from a representative population or randomly assigned to conditions of an experimental variable as in quantitative studies. This is not to say that a qualitative diary study cannot be used in a traditional experimental or quasi-experimental design. Nonetheless, most typically, convenience sampling methods are used. There are several common sampling strategies that a diary researcher could consider:

- *Convenience sampling*, also called "opportunity sampling," involves recruitment not so much for representativeness or for diversity, but simply because the people are in the researcher's social networks. The researcher makes use of their own workplace and social networks.
- *Snowball sampling or friendship pyramid sampling* relies on the participants' social networks rather than of the researcher's networks. Participants recruit their associates to participate. Often after being in a diary study, participants develop a comfortable interest in the study and may have a better idea of other people who would fit the selection criteria. If the study does not have to be done

at a particular time for all participants, snowball sampling can work very well.

- *Quota or stratified sampling* involves careful selection of just the right ratio of participant characteristics, often to reflect a cross-sectional sample of a community on demographic variables (mirroring ethnic or gender distribution) or on phenomenon-related characteristics (e.g., in a study of depression, selecting participants who experience differing types of depression).
- *Case study* incorporates diary entries, often along with a range of other documents, as part of a holistic study of an individual person or organization. Diaries are an excellent choice for a case study because case studies usually welcome rich and involved data sets. With a limited sample, it is easier to work with the kind of involved and rich data set that a diary can produce.
- *Theoretical sampling* may be used if one is doing a Grounded Theory study (Glaser & Strauss, 1986, 1975) and they are engaged in a semi–open-ended window of data collection, seeking new angles, new perspectives, and new voices. With this strategy, new targeted sampling that varies from one's initial set of selection criteria may occur after data collection has commenced.
- *Random selection* and *random assignment*, when probability sampling is used to select a sample from a larger population or when assigning a participant to a condition at random, can also be used in a diary study if the goals are to represent a larger population or to compare two or more groups in an experimental mixed-method design.
- *Rolling* or ongoing *recruitment* can be used if there is no particular time frame for when the study can be started. Participants can be started on the study and finish at varying times.

Recruiting, Rewarding, and Retaining Solicited Diary Participants

Recruitment and advertisement strategies for diary studies will depend on the topic of one's study and its design. An easy way to recruit is via word of mouth, special-interest websites, fliers, and in-person announcements at organizations and community centers. If the individuals of interest are from "hidden" (e.g., undocumented immigrants) or "hard to reach" populations (e.g., drug users), then it may be helpful to locate support groups or service providers, community agencies, or liaisons to a community. Sometimes asking participants to join in a pre-diary focus group or survey study can help engender interest and later commitment to a diary study. If the diary data must be collected from all participants during one specific time window due to staffing limitations or a time-sensitive event (e.g., preceding a national election or during a holiday season), researchers can drum up interest in the study over several weeks leading up to the diary start date, with announcements, informational meetings, and pretesting so that recruits can be gathered into a list well before the study is due to begin.

Because diary studies can be labor intensive, incentivizing participation is important. The hefty commitment of time and the need for bringing research materials or correspondence into one's everyday space warrants fair compensation. Sufficient incentives for participation may include cash payments (e.g., for every diary entry), the chance to win a lottery (where legal), a focus on important social issues, or gaining skills or therapeutic benefits that come from diary keeping. If the subject matter is of interest to the participant (e.g., devout meditators writing about the benefits of their practice; a student writing about study abroad), the incentive is sometimes the journaling itself.

Retaining dedicated diary writers requires regular follow-up and careful applications of incentives. Budget for more participants than the initial goal, since attrition can be high due to the labor-intensive nature of diary research. As LePage (2016) notes in a review of diary-styled cell phone-based studies that collect "real-time data," it is easy to recruit volunteers to download diary apps, but retaining them with no follow-up has resulted in samples' dropping from higher than 100,000 to only about 500 remaining, and "pestering" them can increase dropout rates. It is a good idea to follow up but also to reward participants as they go along in the study, such as halfway through and then at the end, to encourage involvement and show appreciation for their commitment. Rewarding continued participation helps keep diary writers motivated, although incentives cannot be so great as to seem coercive.

Solicited Diary Participants Sample Size

As with many qualitative studies, the diary research samples are not usually randomly selected to be representative of a population, but rather are purposively or conceptually selected due to their prospects for documenting certain experiences. Diary studies tend to be small, but remember that even one diarist can generate quite a lot of data. Diary participants may start as a group at a set time, or they may start on a rolling basis, with the final sample size not predetermined. Longitudinal diary studies can involve an initial recruitment followed by ongoing retention efforts, including replacements in the case of attrition. In some cases, the sample will need to be larger than desired, or participants may keep diaries over a longer period of time, in order to capture a particular event of interest in an event-contingent design (Curtis, Gesler, Smith, & Washburn, 2000).

The Researcher as an Overlooked Participant in Solicited Diary Studies

The researcher's role varies as a function of the epistemological assumptions informing the design of the diary study. In quantitative studies, the role of the researcher is downplayed; the objective and systematic data-collection methods are assumed to make the characteristics of the researcher superfluous. In most qualitative research, the researcher is recognized as a participant in the project, too, so it is useful to put some thought and intention into the role one is playing in one's own diary study. The qualitative researcher typically has a more active role. Even the most hands-off researcher can be construed as a participant, both instigating the project and, many times, shaping the conclusions that are drawn.

Qualitative research is usually very interactive, though diary studies tend to be less so. The researchers are often remote from their participants once data collection (diary writing) begins, because the diarists must be immersed in their own personal context and their own observations. This is an aspect of diary writing that sets it apart from most other qualitative designs. Unless diaries are collected daily through interaction with the researcher, participants often "go away" for days or weeks on end, submitting their entries to a remote researcher. The diary researcher can be a facilitator (of observation, thoughtfulness, and insight in participations) and a conveyor (of the content of the entries), but rarely an interactor or collaborator. Therefore, the skills that a qualitative diary researcher needs to hone are often deployed at the data-crunching phase: observing, interpreting, analyzing, and writing. Reflexivity through this process is especially important, as the researcher must take days and weeks of data across participants and use it to provide meaningful answers to the research questions they posed. Shank (2002) describes three different roles of a qualitative researcher that may help inform the approach a diary research takes. The lantern uses a light to illuminate certain parts of a story—wherever the researcher helps shine a light, a small reality is revealed. Lanterns can only illuminate certain parts of a phenomena, and that is all that is expected. The window provides a peek into an experience, so the clearer the window, the clearer the view; thus, the role for a researcher is to keep themselves as much out of the interpretation as possible. The third analogy is a mirror. In this case, the researcher attempts to reflect the material in the diaries, with little interpretation, but as a tool for allowing people to see what is there.

Rapport is extremely important in any role of a diary researcher because the diarists need to feel comfortable enough to report their experiences to the outside observer. A diary project may require additional staff or research assistants who serve in a variety of roles as liaisons. Some may help recruit and retain diarists, or encourage diarists to stick with making entries. If there is technology involved, there may be a need for technical assistants for upkeep and troubleshooting of electronic equipment. Because diary studies tend to produce a massive amount of data, research assistants can be enormously helpful, and it is important to maintain a good rapport with the whole research team to keep the project well organized. If the project has ethnographic qualities, the researcher may need to recruit community liaisons. For example, in my own research on everyday prejudice, liaisons to the communities completing diaries worked with their own in-group members so that diarists felt more comfortable and as if they had an ally in the project. Sometimes, when analyzing data, researchers may pull in stakeholders either to help code the data for themes or to help review themes. Even though the interaction between the researcher and the diarists is often only indirect, rapport is still important to nurture. The more diarists understand and trust in the goals of the project, the more informative their entries will be. It can also help if diarists meet in a group to encourage each other as they explore the phenomena of interest.

Solicited Diary Entry Format

The obvious benefit of the solicited diary study is that the researcher has more control over who writes the diaries and the format of the diaries. Solicited diaries can be as simple as a pack of plain paper for freeform writing, but there is a vast array of other design choices, such as the degree of structure, the medium of communication, the timing of entries, use of supporting data collection, and intended audience. The choice of format is influenced by considerations of the skills and abilities of the sample of participants, the content of the phenomena of interest, and the epistemological framework of the project. A slower process and longer ongoing contact with participants in diary research often affords opportunities to make adjustments to questions, if need be.

Variations in the Degree of Structure in Diary Soliticted Entries

Solicited diaries can be relatively unstructured or highly structured. A completely unstructured diary entry form is rare, as most studies provide *at least* some minimal instructions on what, when, and how the person is to record their entry. Semi-structured forms (sometimes referred to as "unstructured" in the literature) ask for open-ended (unstructured) answers to carefully selected prompts such as short sensory or emotional commands (e.g., "Please describe how you felt today") or to a sentence stem (e.g., "Looking back at my day . . ."). Some repeatedly pose open-ended questions about a specific scenario of interest (e.g., "Was there any time today when you felt treated unfairly?") or cue the participant to account for certain times of day (e.g., "Describe any times you had difficulty concentrating during the work day," or "Describe any times you had difficulty concentrating while at home this evening").

The *Thousand Journals Project* (www.1000journals.com) is an example of a highly unstructured solicited diary study, containing simple instructions to add to the journal, but then to relinquish that diary to any other person, after taking a picture of one's entry and posting it on a webpage. With the intention that "Those who find the journals add something to them. A story, drawing, photograph, anything really. Then they pass the journal along, to a friend or stranger, and the adventure continues" (http://www.1000journals.com), these journals contain poems, essays, sketches, and photography. This study has been going on over two decades and includes diarists from over 40 countries.

As an example of a more typical diary study design, Välimäki, Vehviläinen-Julkunen, and Pietilä (2007) asked more than 80 adults who were caregivers for family members with Alzheimer's disease to keep semi-structured diaries for two weeks, with these instructions:

> The basic question was: "What is your life like now that a member of your family has Alzheimer's disease?" The written instructions were somewhat more specific about the possible themes of writing, which covered a wide range of topics about daily life, the impact of Alzheimer's disease on this, emotions and events experienced in the different stages of the disease, ways of solving problems, and moments of contentment. Caregivers were given an A5-sized notebook containing 40 pages and a prepaid envelope. (p. 72)

At the participants' own will, the diaries varied from one to 19 pages, with a mean length of five written pages. The slimmest diaries included what the researchers called "meager" entries, such as, "There have been no changes for good or bad during this period, everything has stayed the same (Wife 71 years)" (p. 72). The more elaborate diaries included entries that the researchers referred to as "reflective":

> I just can't help thinking about how I'm going to cope when all my strength runs out and the illness gets worse. . . . Who is going to help us then? I haven't needed outside help as yet, but that time will soon be at hand (Husband 80 years). (p. 73)

This poignant entry was not made in response to an emotional prompt since the diary forms themselves consisted of blank lines. Therefore, in the unstructured format, some participants who feel so compelled may share vivid feelings, while others may not. This can be both a benefit, in that participants who did share did so more spontaneously; however, others might not think to share certain aspects of their experience.

Structured diaries are often viewed as more efficient (Rosner, Namazi, & Wykle, 1992), and they are a far more common format in contemporary diary research. Structured diaries standardize the way participants report on the event, with dedicated sections of the entry within which the experience is dissected into focused information (e.g., about the event, any contextual details, etc.) that the researcher predetermined to be important. The structured diary form has the look of a more sterile intake survey form rather than the nostalgic look of one's private "Dear Diary."

Structured diaries can be both qualitative and quantitative. While there are many examples of structured diaries that are solely qualitative, often the choice to use a highly structured diary entry form opens the researcher to incorporating some quantitative items, therefore making the qualitative diary study into more of a mixed-method design.

An example of a structured diary form that is solely qualitative is found in a study by Ballantyne, Hansford, and Packer (1995) on mentoring beginning teachers:

> Blank pre-dated journal entry forms containing five general questions for reflection were sent to participants by mail on the set dates in order to prompt completion. Participants were asked to use these forms to record their thoughts, feelings and reflections and to return the completed forms using a reply-paid envelope. In each journal entry beginning teachers were asked to report on the needs, concerns and professional development they had experienced during the preceding 3 or 4 weeks, the professional assistance they had received from various sources and the nature and value of the "buddy" mentoring relationship. Mentors were asked to describe and reflect on their concerns and feelings about working with a beginning teacher, the types of assistance they had been able to offer and its perceived effectiveness. (p. 1)

This qualitative structured diary form on mentoring can be contrasted with a mixed method qualitative and quantitative structured diary form my colleagues and I used to assess mentoring of teachers (Hyers, Cochran, Syphan, & Brown, 2012; see Figure 3.1).

Diary Entry Form

1. Please indicate what week of the 15-week semester you are making this diary entry (check one):

☐ Week 1	☐ Week 6	☐ Week 11
☐ Week 2	☐ Week 7	☐ Week 12
☐ Week 3	☐ Week 8	☐ Week 13
☐ Week 4	☐ Week 9	☐ Week 14
☐ Week 5	☐ Week 10	☐ Week 15

2. Did you have any mentoring experiences this week (check one)?
☐ No (please go on to the last question number 6 at the bottom of the sheet)
☐ Yes (please continue to the next question number 3)

3. What type of mentoring did you receive this week (check all that apply):
☐ Meetings with Other Junior Level Colleagues
☐ Meeting with Mentor/Close Advisor/Assigned New Faculty Buddy
☐ Informal/Brief Conversation with (check all that apply):

☐ Junior Colleagues	☐ Administrator
☐ Senior Colleagues	☐ Mentor
☐ Chair	☐ Other (briefly describe):_____

☐ Workshops, Retreats, Orientation Programs (briefly describe):_____
☐ Social Get-Togethers (briefly describe):_____
☐ Consulted Printed Handbooks/Manuals/Cheat Sheets (briefly describe):_____
☐ Other (briefly describe):_____

4. On what topic did you receive mentoring (check all that apply):
☐ Teaching Issues
☐ Tenure and/or Promotion Matters
☐ Universities Policies
☐ Service/Committee Matters
☐ Research Matters
☐ Grants/Awards
☐ Student/Student Advisement Issues
☐ Campus Climate/Politics
☐ Other (briefly describe):_____

5. Overall, how satisfied are you with the mentoring you received this week (circle one):

1	2	3	4	5
Very Dissatisfied	Somewhat Dissatisfied	Neither Satisfied Nor Dissatisfied	Somewhat Satisfied	Very Satisfied

6. On reverse, please share further thoughts/reflections about your mentoring experiences this week.

Figure 3.1 Example of diary form, from Hyers, Cochran, Syphan, & Brown, 2012.

The quantitative items included check boxes concerning types, topics, and satisfactions of mentoring. The qualitative items included open-ended short answers and a blank back page for them to add any more comments about their mentoring experience each week. A combination of checklists or logs along with open-ended spaces of free writing can accommodate varying types of participants, those who are comfortable writing long narratives and those who are not. Such mixed-method structured diaries also allow the researcher to quickly summarize a number of contextual variables as well as to more easily compare qualitative experiences, but as a function of categorizable variables.

There are positives and negatives, whichever structure one chooses. As Radcliffe (2013) described in a study on work–life balance decision-making:

> [H]aving trialled various diary structures, semi-structured diaries, consisting of four open-ended questions for each day, were decided upon. During the pilot studies unstructured diaries consisting of a blank page for each day led to daily reports that were not entirely relevant and lacking sufficient detail with regards to the decision-making processes involved in conflict resolution. Participants explained that without the prompts of the semi-structured diary, they "would just have written what happened and not any feelings or why" and that they "did think about it more" when completing the semi-structured diary. Overall the semi-structured diaries tended to produce more detail regarding the decision-making process. However, there was still concern regarding restriction of participant expression resulting in information loss since the aim of this study was to capture participants' experiences from their point of view therefore a compromise was reached by including an extra space for further comments each day. (p. 21)

As long as the demands of the diary do not dissuade participants from staying with the study, a combined strategy of structured and unstructured, quantitative and qualitative, may provide the best data. Instructions themselves can be necessarily quite elaborate, because the participants are left on their own to work with whatever form they are provided. As an example, in a study my colleagues and I conducted of daily experiences with prejudicial incidents, we provided a full page of instructions on the cover of their diary packet (Hyers, 2012). Helpful information should include:

- Summary of the larger purpose of the study:
  - Research questions
  - Why participate

- Reminder of participant rights (refer to informed consent)
- A reminder of the procedure:
  - When to begin and when to stop keeping the diary
  - An estimate of how long an entry will take
  - What is the procedure of making an entry
  - What an entry should be about, if applicable
  - Where and how diary entries should be stored
  - Where and how diary entries are to be submitted
- What to do (can be in the form of "Common Q & A"):
  - If additional forms are needed
  - If support/resources are needed (refer to informed consent)
  - To submit final diary
  - To contact the researcher

Just like a more commonplace survey, the structure and wording of a diary form itself is essential to getting the best data. As Foddy (1994) notes, when asking for descriptive accounts of phenomena, the same prompt can elicit wildly different answers, as in response to the question "Where did you read that?" to which one could respond "in an advertisement" or "in the *New York Times*" or "at home in front of the fire." So in order to obtain the information one wants, the prompts need to be explicit. Ultimately, he suggests:

> The researcher can decide to indicate to the respondents whether they should take a moral, instrumental, domestic or political point of view, whether they should give personal or cultural answers; what sort of explanation should be given— if an explanation is called for; what standards of evaluation should be used—if evaluations are called for. In sum, the researcher can elect to specify a response framework for respondents. (p. 89)

If the nature of the response does not matter, (e.g., any interpretation they may make of a prompt "where" will suffice), then such detail is less necessary. Nonetheless, one still may find variability in the quality of their data. Välimäki, Vehviläinen-Julkunen, and Pietilä (2007) noted four types of variations in the nature of diary data they obtained: meager, simply reporting on the phenomena, descriptive of the phenomena, and reflective. Often a pilot test of a diary entry will quickly reveal if diarists need more specific instructions in how to respond. Stopka and colleagues (2004) asked participants to keep a diary as part of their instruction, were given feedback, and then used it as a model for what types of content the researcher was looking for in the entries.

Medium of Solicited Diary Entries

Diary studies also vary as a function of the medium of communication of entries. Written diaries have been the most pervasive; however, technology has expanded the options considerably to include entries that are not just handwritten or typed, but also emailed, blogged, tweeted, instant messaged, Facebook posted, audio recorded, visually generated either by hand or with a computer or hand-held technology, and video recorded. It is not unusual to find diary studies that involve no writing at all in an entry. Which method one chooses, from the more old-fashioned to the technologically advanced, depends on the budget and aims of the study.

- *Handwritten entries* may be the preferred choice for many reasons. Obviously, they can be useful in areas where electricity, the Internet, batteries, and equipment are scarce or awkward or with people who are unaccustomed to technology. In off-the-grid communities, the wilderness, or in religious settings, handwritten diaries are more convenient and have the added advantage of being more easily toted around. The handwritten form of self-expression is more intimate, may prime nostalgic diary writing of childhood, and can be a real treat for some participants. Some people feel that handwriting can open up their thoughts into more of a "stream of consciousness," so beneficial as to be dubbed "scriptotherapy" by Riordan (1996). In primary school educational settings, it can provide an opportunity for students to practice penmanship. Diaries handwritten offsite will need to be mailed, faxed, or manually delivered back to the researcher. Typically, the researcher will type the entries and anonymize the narrative, removing all identifying information, before working with the data.[1] In the rare cases where participants would need to be contacted to clarify any illegible words, it helps if the transcribing of diaries happens swiftly, while participant contact information is still up to date. If diaries contain sketches or scribbles, permission would also need to be sought to reprint such images in any publications. Participants should be given the option of having their diaries returned to them once they are transcribed, if they so choose.

- *Typed entries* are the most common format today where computer technology is available. The advantages include legibility, ease of writing (for most people), and ease of transfer back to the researcher. Typing of diaries may occur on one's home computer, cell phone, or other electronic devices such as an iPad. The diaries can be electronically transferred (e.g., via email, an encrypted website) to the researcher, while the participant can still retain an electronic copy for themselves. They can also be printed off and faxed or mailed. Typed files should then be anonymized by the researcher. Electronically produced entries can also automatically include a date and time stamp, word count, and even data on active writing time. Unlike handwritten diaries that may be more "off the cuff," typed diaries may be "wordsmithed": spell-checked, edited, and self-censored by participants, producing data that have been fashioned by the participant in the service of some incalculable effort toward impression management. There is no question that this has become the most "natural" form of contemporary written communications, so charges that handwriting produces more "genuine" self-expression may be open to debate.

- *Audio recorded entries* diaries might remind one of the scenes in old movies, where a reporter, detective, or author is seen huddled over a small microphone, quietly dictating the events of the day in a dimly lit office. The audio diary is an exciting format because the speaker can turn "the mic" off, think, and restart as they want, unlike an in-person interview, though audio diaries are ultimately transcribed, just like interviews (Monrouxe, 2009). The content can be cued just like "interviews" as well, if the diarist is provided a list of questions to answer; however, like a written diary (and unlike an interview), the entry is made by the participant alone, with no one to interrupt their expression. For example, Palen and Salzman (2002) had participants call their diaries in to a message machine:

> In the voice-mail method, participants use mobile or landline phones to make reports to a dedicated voice-mail line instead of recording events on paper. We found this to be an easy and less time-intensive way of reporting activities of research interest. With paper diaries, users must stop their activity and manually record it; this is not so troublesome when users work at a desk and the activities of interest occur there but becomes problematic when participants are mobile. (p. 2)

Old-fashioned audio can retain more emotion and nonverbal aspects of language that would be lost if translated automatically to text. Audio recordings can be saved on tapes or digital storage and mailed or uploaded and emailed to the researcher. The talk-to-text technology that automatically converts audio to script is improving, so that audio entries can then be returned to the researcher already transcribed. Thompson (2015) in *Wired* magazine cautions that dictation software not only *changes the way* we talk (and "write") but also *changes what* we say and write:

> In a sense, voice-writing requires people to change their cognitive style. It's relatively free and easy, more like speech than writing. But because it's hard to edit and tinker, dictating to a phone is most like working on an old manual typewriter, where you have to map out each sentence in your head before clacking away. (p. 1)

If a diary entry is simply audio recorded with no assumption that it is to be transcribed by a computer, the speaker may feel less concern about slowing speech, thus audio files may still contain longer, rambling sentences and more complex speech. If participants feel comfortable with other audio self-expression such as poetry or singing, they could do so. Songwriter Tracy Chapman said that, "Music was never just a hobby for me. I'd pick up a guitar every day to work on whatever I was writing at the time. I would put my ideas in songs the way some people might put them in diaries or journals" (Hilburn, 1988, p. 1). Whatever their method of oral expression, the current state of research reporting will probably lead to the material's being transcribed into written form; however, researchers would be advised to listen to the audio and then ultimately work back and forth from transcripts to audio when working with the data.

- *Visual entries* are a less common variety of diary studies, perhaps in part due to what Twine (2016) has described as an "academic apartheid" that has over-privileged textual over visual data in the social sciences. Photography, artwork, and visual collage can be used when they are more effective for displaying experiences or thoughts visually—with young children, for international or cross-lingual groups, in research on esoteric or hard-to-describe experiences, for studies of media in our lives, and for those who find visual self-expression more genuine. Participants can be asked to express themselves through diaries made of images from printed or electronic media, self-made collages, drawing, photography, or painting (Latham, 2004). Picasso (1965) is quoted as saying, "Painting is just another way of keeping a diary . . . . For those who know how to read I have painted my autobiography" (cited in McArdle & Wright, 2014, p. 22). The visual diarist does not have to be a master artist. The images can be somewhat mundane, typically an accounting of activities, emotions, triggers, people, spaces, or any subject matter that either the participant chooses or the researcher asks them to represent with visual images. For example, in a sociological study of everyday domestic kitchen practices (Wills, Dickinson, Meah, & Short, 2016), the authors' use of visual diary data "meant everyone in a sample of 20 household cases, from children through to adults in their 80s, could show and tell their own stories" (p. 470):

Households were given disposable cameras, a notebook, pens and some coloured pencils so that they could capture information they thought was relevant between our visits [and] examples of how they could use the notebook, including as a diary, to log photographs they had taken, or as a scrapbook. Photographs taken by participants with the disposable cameras were processed and a set of prints used to elicit further talk about practices. (p. 476)

Visual diary entries can be less time-consuming for participants and can often be perceived as more creative and quite fun for participants, the images infused with semiotics and symbolism that verbal expression may lack—*a picture is worth a thousand words.* Researchers may present the actual images in reports, with permission, in some cases cropping or blurring images to protect participant anonymity. Researchers can also code, organize, or discuss the visual data for themes alone or in conjunction with interviews or written captions in diaries.

- *Video diaries* are more dynamic than audio-only, visual-only entries. They have become more common as video equipment has become more accessible. Video diary methodology is considered an important tool in contemporary community-based ethnographic and participatory action research (McClelland & Fine, 2008). In a study of the media and sexualization of girls, Jackson and Vares (2015) relied on "the potential of video cameras to not only enable diverse ways of responding but to ground the project in the everyday lived worlds of the girls . . . . [V]ideo cameras provide scope for participants to use multiple modalities of expression—talk, gesture, movement, performance and so on" (p. 3). Pocock, McIntosh, and Zahra (2011) advise that, once participants have the video camera and a basic set of instructions, "Encourage them to record scenes that are meaningful to them. Minimize the researcher's influence on the scene selection. Ask participants to narrate their video diaries to explain the scenes they are filming." The typical nature of a video diary is revealed in a prompt card that they included in their study of the meaning of "home" (p. 108):

  ### Tips for Filming

  - Record scenes from your personal perspective
  - Talk to the camera to explain why a particular scene is meaningful to you

- Your thoughts and feelings are more important than the technical aspects of filming
- Don't worry if your scenes don't fit nicely together
- Don't try to film everything—sample shots of meaningful scenes will be sufficient
- If you are unsure when to start or stop recording, think to yourself "Does this scene mean home to me?"
- Video strangers at a distance so as not to invade their private space with the camera
- If you are videoing people you know, please make sure they are comfortable with you videoing them first

The last two advisements point to a problem with video diaries, as they are especially problematic for anonymity (Anderson & Muñoz Proto, 2016). In a video diary study exploring the undergraduate student's first-year university experience, Cashmore, Green, and Scott (2010) struggled with the video diary conundrum:

> It was generally agreed that student confidentiality was one prime concern—it was essential that no video footage found its way to any web-site because this medium could quickly spread, and even with false names could lead to future embarrassment for the students. It was commented that the openness of the students was a particular strength of the project. One participant suggested using the audio tracks from the video as the form of shared data, however, it was agreed that this would lose the richness of the communication from the students. (p. 109)

Similar to visual diaries, some researchers just report video diary examples (as one would quotes or extracts in textual data) in the form of participation narration about the video, and some even combine that with video still frames. Analyzing the video data for the themes can reduce the richness to a less identifiable abstraction, although it does accommodate concerns for confidentiality and anonymity. Researchers can describe the video and/or their accompanying narration in order to retain some of the richness. For example, in a study of older women as lifelong learners, Kamler (2006) relates: "Rich images from the video diaries show Vietnamese women meditating in serene, early morning domestic spaces; praying in temples with their communities; exercising with diligence and humour; singing while chopping vegetables, creating rhythms of food preparation and giving to community and family" (p. 159). Similarly, Cherrington and Watson (2010) used video diaries to explore the embodied everyday contexts of a university basketball team. The authors detailed a jovial video diary of a participant in the midst of partying, pointing out,

> Had we interviewed Paul or even asked him to put these experiences down in words, he might have given us a quick, convenient and sporadic account of what unfolded that night, which would have been limited by his memory, literacy and temperament: Paul turns the camera on. He has just returned after initiation and is very drunk. He is wearing a straw hat, a flower necklace, a white vest and a flowery wrist band. His eyes are red, his words are slurred and his actions are slow and disoriented. After firing obscenities at the researcher (in a jovial way), he talks (or tries to talk) about initiation and he had "defeated" the majority of the first years. He finishes (whilst laughing) with some more lurid comments about the researcher and says he is off to drink more with his flat mates. (p. 275)

In some ways, "reality" television has supplied the video diary method *en masse*, of course, this is for entertainment and not for research purposes. The drawback of perpetual videoing is that the reflective time for repose that the diary entry provides, the stepping back from performing and just quietly documenting what has occurred, is lost. As one moves into video "live action" journaling, one moves away from the diary and toward naturalistic observation. The participant making the entry is perhaps performing differently due to observation, and the researcher-observer can choose what aspects of the performance on which they will focus their attention. Reflection in some respects is compromised.

- *Online diaries* go by other names, such as weblogs, blog posts, and digital diaries; however, they are essentially diary entries made electronically and posted on public websites or semi-public password-accessed websites on the Internet. Online diaries are an especially practical format for soliciting entries on behaviors and experiences, as they take place on the web such as on Internet communities, online behaviors, social media, cyber education, Internet games, or any interface with the technology of the Web (Griffiths, Lewis, De Gortari, & Kuss, 2014). The mechanical act of making an online diary entry is essentially the same as the mechanical act of any other Internet activity, which makes switching from those other activities to write a diary entry very convenient, and even more so if the online diary entry can be embedded within the website or online activity itself (Clark & Gruba, 2010). Other advantages of soliciting online diaries include a potentially unlimited geographical range for drawing participants, the ability to recruit a large and diverse sample, and little expense for the researcher (Kaun, 2010). The online diary in some respects may be similar to the video diary, in that the individual diarist is not simply reflecting and documenting, but actively performing. Kaun (2010) points out that solicited online diaries require informed consent and often some statement about the level of privacy of the material produced. Offering a thorough examination as the genre that was solidly emerging at the turn of the 21st century, Serfaty (2004) rejected views of "oxymoronic" online diaries that "smack of exhibitionism." Nonetheless, as Cardell (2014) notes, there has evolved a new genre of self-expression associated with statements made on the Web that the general public has gotten quite comfortable with:

> In the twenty-first century, the diary as blog responds to the unique public/private juxtaposition of online spaces and to a cultural moment that values and commodifies the first-person personal in a multitude of ways. . . . In tandem with rapidly evolving technological modes, life narrative scholars have been interested not only in new digital forms of self-representation but in the experience of self produced when life itself shifts into online and virtual spaces. Whether through e-mail, blogs,

web browsing (and the personalized data caching that results), social media, or virtual online communities, for rapidly increasingly numbers of individuals the Internet is an aspect of everyday life that offers opportunities for self-expression, or for self-assimilation. (p. 98)

The *Thousand Journals Project* is one example of a study soliciting the posting of public online diary entries; however, it starts by the intimate recording of an entry in a very traditional book that is passed to participants. Only after the intimate interaction with making their entry on the pages of a bound journal is the writer invited to then take a photo of it and upload it to the public database. It should be noted that even for "typewritten" online diaries, the flexibility of electronic communication may enable diarists to upload pictures with their text, even if unsolicited (Kaun, 2014).

Privately posted online diaries offer an easier mode for participants who can access the Internet to submit entries (Boynton & Richman, 2014). For example, "diary rooms" can be set up, usually through a host Web page, for the larger project or study. Participants can access the room to post their entries as often and as lengthily as they wish. The posts are then accessible and downloadable by the researchers only. A study by Cohen and colleagues (2008) used online diaries as part of their data to assess the ways that healthcare interventions ultimately get implemented in the field. They offered an online "diary room" where members of the intervention team could go online to make private diary entries every two weeks on the intervention process, a convenient and helpful way to for them to reflect on the ongoing implementation.

Personal Mobile Digital Technology (PMDT) has enabled the digital daily diary and is changing social science methodology. According to Roberts (2014), this leads to data that are dynamic and living and collaborative:

[T]he creation of "daily diaries" via PMDT . . . can alter the cultural and "political" relationships between those involved, such as the participant, researcher(s), audience, publishers, funders, and so on as new avenues for involvement and dissemination arise. They can contribute to challenging the notion of research as merely "linear" in time (past-to-present); increasingly, it will be recognized that its practice is operative in other modes—e.g., as circular, even "multi-linear" in composition. (p. 18)

Convenience, mobility, accessibility, and communication are all facilitated through PMDT and digital diaries, not just for participants, but for researchers and readers, as well.

Timing of Solicited Diary Entries

The timing of entries depends on the goals of the study—some research questions require more rapid and frequent entries, and others require longer-range reflections. Diary entries can be thought of from a sampling perspective: similar to sampling individual participants to be in a study, diary entries represent a sampling of the hours, days, weeks, and months of an individual's ongoing experiences. As a general rule, studies with a greater emphasis on life narrative and meaning-making are designed with longer time spans between entries. In contrast, studies with a greater interest in the specificities of immediate experiences are designed with more on-the-spot entries. Timing also depends upon what triggers an entry, be it intervals of time passed or after an event occurs. There are some basic types of timing:

- *Daily*: Because of the well-known custom of writing a journal entry as a day's end reflection, solicited diary entries are often designed with the assumption that they will be registered at the day's end. If a daily reflection on some aspect of the day's events is all that is required, this works fine. In some cases, a daily diary is used to start the day; however, this is often a more hectic time for participants. A dream diary might be written in the middle of the night or first thing in the morning.
- *Weekly*: A week is an easy demarcation for many experiences, and it takes the pressure off the diarist to some degree. The weekly diary is useful especially for documenting work-cycle–related events, time-use reflections, exercise (because people often alternate exercise activities daily in order to repeat the routine each week), learning (because syllabi often have weekly objectives), and social experiences (because a full week

puts an individual into a range of varied work and leisure settings). Although, when a week "ends" is somewhat arbitrary, often the week's "end" occurs just before the next week's cycle starts (e.g., the work week).

- *Monthly/seasonally:* Calendar months can be good for entries on activities that have monthly demarcations, such as a growing pregnancy, menstrual periods, grade-marking periods, or financial accounting. Monthly reflections are also useful for life-narrative and reflective processing. If monthly diaries are submitted on short-duration activities, it is not uncommon for participants to keep smaller interval notes that can inform their entries at the month's end. If a research project occurs during holidays or other seasonal events, the monthly diary model applies similarly to a seasonal diary.

- *Interval/timed:* Interval or timed diaries have also been referred to as "beeper" studies because the earliest designs made use of beeper technology to signal the time to make an entry. Qualitative research is less likely than quantitative to use such rigid, by-the-clock entry solicitations, but it can be useful. For example, a mixed-method design interval diary-like design that Csikszentmihalyi, Larson, and Prescott (1977) referred to as "The Experience Sampling Method" is conceptually related to the diary study method in that experiences are sampled in daily living. To study the subjective states of people in naturalistic settings, investigators signaled to participants as many as ten times a day (at the researcher's discretion) and asked them to make entries. Participants did not determine when an entry was made.

- *Event-contingent:* In event-contingent diary studies, the participant is vigilant for an event to occur, after which, or soon as possible after which, they make an entry about some aspect of the event. For example, in a study of insulin levels, insulin injection, and mood states, a participant may complete measures before and after mealtime—a time that they determine. Waddington (2005) had participants make entries after an incident of gossip had occurred, giving a detailed operational definition of what that trigger event should look like.

Essentially the researcher is sampling their experiences only when an event occurs. If there is no meal in the afternoon, there is no entry. For these types of studies, the researcher can only estimate how long the diary study itself needs to be to actually capture the events of interest. With meals, one can assume daily; with other behaviors, such as drinking alcoholic beverages, one may need a few weeks. Events upon which the entries are contingent are supposed to occur spontaneously, although sometimes participants feel so obligated to have the event occur that they seek relevant contexts or otherwise artificially elicit the events (even if advised that eliciting the event is not an obligation of participation).

An additional consideration when it comes to the timing of entries is how long the study should go on. If a certain number of events are to be sampled, the researchers have to make careful decisions about the length of time needed to get to that number, without too much participant attrition. For example, in my own research on everyday prejudice in university settings, it takes about a week for a participant to encounter an experience of prejudice note-worthy enough to document in a diary entry, so a two-week-long diary-keeping period usually results in at least one incident being documented per person. Of course, such information is not always available from past research, but if there is time, a pilot could be run. If a certain number of entries is desired, and the entries are labor-intensive (e.g., hourly entries or long entries), a shorter active diary-keeping period would reduce dropout due to fatigue. Generally, the more entries or the more information in each entry, the less often participants can be asked to make them. If there is attrition, it is helpful to know the types of participants who dropped out and their reasons for leaving. It may help to offer participants a chance to opt out of certain busy days or weeks and still stay in the study.

Variations in the Solicited Diarist's Actual or Presumed Audience

One consideration in the use of solicited diaries is the issue of the audience, for which there are some methodological variations.

This may seem obvious—other than the diarist, the researcher who asks for the diaries is the audience. In fact, this can be viewed as somewhat of a problem, making the "purity" of diaries somewhat contrived, as Pini and Walkerdine (2011) have noted. There are uncountable diary researchers who can attest to their own presence in diary entries, when they see that the entries are often written directly to the researcher, sometimes even by name. If there is a potential for policy change as the result of a research project, sometimes diaries will be written to persuade potential or imagined readers of any research report.

There are some types of studies in which, by design, the researcher is not the only intended viewer of the participant's complete set of diary entries, and some studies where the researcher does not even see the diary entries at all. The participant may be asked to write the diary only for the purpose of learning about themselves, observing their behaviors, or processing an experience, all of which ruminations are kept to themselves. The researcher may then only be interested in the diarists' post-diary reflections. There are other studies in which the diary is written by participants who then are asked to look back at their entries and classify their experiences into categories for the researcher to work with. This type of participant-coding study is sometimes used by researchers who feel that this makes for a more valid characterization of the data because the participants are rating their own (e.g., Swim, Hyers, Cohen, Fitzgerald, & Bylsma, 2003). In some studies, the diaries are exchanged between participant pairs who write to each other, a partner, or a group (e.g., as in round-robin journaling mentioned earlier, Morawski & Rottmann, 2016), and then the data come from focus groups or other interviews by the researcher. Contemporary online forums may also be used, in which, along with the researcher, the entire Internet-using public can simultaneously view the posts. Some benefits of making the diaries immediately and publicly available is that one avoids the problem of the researcher as a "middleman." Diary entries are full of rich contextual information, and to have such documents only represented through the distilled observations and reductionist categorization of the researcher's eye can potentially limit what can be understood from them. This allows a diary study to pass the classic test of naturalistic observation what's termed the "dead social scientist test" or the "autopsy principle" (Potter, 2010, p. 667) asking if the same experience happen whether the researcher was there to witness it? If it is truly naturalistic, the diarist who is the immediate witness of their experience can then directly document it in an entry, for whoever chooses to witness the entry, rather than the diarist conveying it through the limited view of a "middleman" research coder.

Supporting Documents for Archival and Solicited Diaries

Although diaries can sometimes be the supporting documents for studies of other media, it is also the case that other documents can be the supporting documents for a diary study. In an archival diary study, supporting documents may include other writings or interviews with the diarist(s) of interest or other historical documents. As Smith (1994) remarked, "no one library or home study, contains all of the papers that are important for a life story. Pools of data exist in all sorts of likely and unlikely places" (p. 9). Common supplements to diary studies of individuals or groups are letters. Interviews may be used as well. The "diary interview" method involves diary keeping along with regular interviews about the entries soon after they are written (Kenten, 2010). In the case of famous individuals who have produced works of art or published, their works may be part of the study as well (e.g., Da Vinci, Darwin). For a solicited diary, similar such materials could certainly be used, although they would typically be actively solicited. There is also the option to solicit new and different data from participants for supporting data collection in mixed-method designs (e.g., pre-tests, post-diary focus groups, or before or after one-on-one interviews). The slower process and longer ongoing contact with participants in diary research often affords opportunities to adjust questions/procedures along the way, if need be. Sometimes mid-study interviews can help with clarification, and a focus group also brings people together. The most common type of supporting data collection is in the form of an interview, either individual or focus group. Zimmerman and Wieder (1977) developed their own version of the "diary-interview" method, involving a pre- and post-interview. Their method was viewed less as a way to supplement the diary, but rather as advocating for the diary as an alternative to regular participant observation methods. In the diary-interview, the diarist is essentially a participant observer who takes field notes on their life (so the researcher doesn't need to), and the interviews simply help the researcher understand the "field notes." Of course, this method of interview combined with diary can be used even if the primary intent of the study is to collect diary data for its own sake. The other supporting documents collected may be part of a pre-test/pre-diary form, in which basic demographic information would be collected (e.g., gender, age, ethnicity, etc.), along with any information about individual differences relevant to the phenomena of interest (e.g., in a study of workplace stressors, information on type of workplace, organizational structure, and employee job position might be collected).

A Look Ahead to Analyzing and Reporting

Diary data can be vast and overwhelming. Entries will need to be organized, indexed, perhaps transcribed, probably anonymized, and notations made about each entry, each diarist's complete diary, and observations recorded about overall patterns in the entire sample of diaries. To distill the content into a meaningful account, the researcher faces the daunting task of qualitative analysis and summarization. It is rarely the case that the researcher simply reprints or publishes all the diary entries without offering some analysis. The diaries are discussed by the researcher in light of the research question and relevant theory. The analysis is a matter of equal importance in both archival and solicited diary research. Certain elements of the entries are explored, striking excerpts are identified, some interpretive framework is offered, and a story is fashioned. It would be wise for the researcher to not get overly ambitious the first time running a diary study and end up with more data than they can humanly process. As the tool in qualitative research is in large part the researchers themselves making observations, they need to design a study that generates a reasonable-sized dataset to be able to do the subsequent analysis justice.

Note

1. There are rare cases, such as historical studies, biographies, and some case studies, where anonymizing would not occur, and the researcher would leave places and names intact, an uncommon practice in the social sciences.

4

ANALYZING AND WRITING A REPORT ON QUALITATIVE DIARY RESEARCH

QUALITATIVE RESEARCH is a mode of inquiry that emphasizes storytelling as a means of knowledge production. In qualitative diary studies, the narrative developed by the researcher is just as integral as the narratives provided by participants. Once the diary entries are collected, qualitative diary researchers must negotiate numerous compositional tensions: between featuring the unique voices of diarists and reflexively revealing their own; between capitalizing on the contextual richness of serial diary entries and conceding to the reductionism demanded by summarizing them in a single report; and between respectfully honoring the private nature of diaries and expressly intending to exhibit their contents in some outside forum. These and other challenges face the diary researcher as data analysis gives way to the development of a cohesive narrative. This is where the work starts for the diary researcher.

The inductive nature of qualitative research anchors the entire project of qualitative report-writing in the Results. Induction requires the research to lead with the Results. Thus, the analytic process of "coding" or analyzing qualitative data for themes is essentially the first act of writing. The data must be witnessed and labeled so that units of meaning or themes can be identified. Naming these themes is an iterative process not entirely separate from the composition of the report itself. In order to produce a cohesive report, data analysis and report writing become reciprocal activities. With this in mind, this chapter discusses data analysis and composition of the report as complementary parts of a larger writing process. The bulk of the chapter will focus on analyzing diary data and scholarly report-writing, after a brief discussion of outlets for diary study reports.

Outlets for Sharing Diary Research Reports

There are three primary outlets for writing up a diary study that correspond with the researcher's goals. They include non-academic outlets, applied consulting, and scholarly outlets. In some cases, a diary researcher may write up a project for two or perhaps all three of these outlets, depending upon the scope of the project, for these do not have to be mutually exclusive paths (Applegate, 2016).

Writing Qualitative Diary Research for Non-Academic Outlets

For centuries now, private diaries have been accessed by the general public through the popular press. Diary research intended for commercial outlets are traditionally released in book form; or more recently, displayed online on websites and blogs, and occasionally prepared for temporary or permanent museum exhibitions. Non-academic outlets are more common when diaries are written by figures of historical or general cultural significance. The diary researcher edits and organizes the entries to guide the reader through them. In single-diarist reports, often non-diary supplemental materials are included. Often a short biography will start off the collection, or photographs will be added. If the volume includes multiple diarists rather than one, there is a greater need for an analytical structure to explain how the various voices are linked. Some online diary reports are ongoing, taking the form of "living" documents, expanding with new diary entries that are either self-posted or essentially "juried" by the researcher who curates the display of the entire compendium (e.g., www.1000journals.com). It is more commonly the case that diary studies going to print or displayed as physical exhibits in museums will be conclude at the time of publication or exhibition.

Writing Qualitative Diary Research for Applied Consulting Projects

Applied diary reports for intervention and consulting may be published as scholarly articles in applied journals, prepared for an organization, presented to a legislative body, submitted to a news periodical, or relinquished directly to the stakeholders in the community from which the diarists originated (e.g., as in participatory action research). With a greater emphasis on "evidence-based" institutional policy and programming (Solesbury, 2002; Young, Ashby, Boaz, & Grayson, 2002), decision makers prefer the style of scholarly reporting that generally stays true to contemporary values of scientism, so the content guidelines for publishing in scholarly outlets will likely be preferred by policy makers. Applied reports can often include a needs assessment (prior to an intervention for program and policy development purposes), and informational about program delivery integrity, or effectiveness (for program evaluation purposes). Such reports will include comprehensive recommendations in the final discussion and conclusion section beyond what would be necessary in a research-orientated scholarly piece.

Writing Qualitative Diary Research for Scholarly Outlets

Scholarly qualitative diary reports are most commonly prepared for presentation in academic settings, at conferences, or submitted to peer-reviewed scholarly journals.[1] For those intending to submit a diary study report to a peer-reviewed scholarly journal, the selection of the target journal may be based on the subject matter of the diaries (e.g., diary research on study habits could fit well in a journal of education), or the selection may be based on the method (e.g., phenomenological diary research may fit well in an existential journal). There is a growing number of academic conferences and journals intended expressly for qualitative researchers, though there are none, as yet, aimed specifically at qualitative diary research. Ultimately, the approach to writing the scholarly diary report will depend upon the epistemological bent, not only of the researcher, but also of their audience: editorial staff, scholarly associations, and the larger academic field. There are slightly different reporting expectations mandated by the editorial style of the journal, as well. The major scientific journals in the United

States follow the editorial styles of the American Psychological Association (APA) or Modern Language Association (MLA); however, there are many other academic scholarly editorial styles that vary from these, dictated by the discipline, the scholarly association, and the country of the publisher. The editorial style generally alters the citation and reference format, and sometimes the required sections of the report, though each may follow the basic reporting model of conventional positivistic science.

Making a Qualitative Research Report Fit a Positivistic Scientific Framework

In the positivistic/post-positivistic realm of contemporary academia, most readers (and writers, for that matter) are trained in more conventional scientific and quantitative research methods. The writing of a traditional scientific research report is by design rigid, faithfully following in the order of (1) introduction to the theoretical framework and statement of hypotheses, (2) method for hypothesis testing, (3) results of hypothesis testing, and (4) discussion of results as they pertain to theory. Scholars, journal editors, and association members who have little training in alternative methodologies may be less accustomed to the qualitative mode of inquiry that emphasizes flexibility, reflexivity, and narrativity in reports (Bryman, 2015). Moreover, given the variety of qualitative methods, reviewers may lack simultaneous expertise with both the subject matter *and* a very specific qualitative method (e.g., narrative analysis, participatory action research, etc.). In such cases, qualitative diary researchers often need to simultaneously describe and defend their methods. Qualitative diary researchers may find they need to explain the epistemological values of qualitative research. "Reflexivity" (first-person reflection on the research process) can contribute to this through the transparency of methods, but even this practice may need to be explained. In general, it is very important that the methods and procedures be written with clarity. Here is a short list of the types of qualitative methodological devices that often conflict with traditional social science writing and thus, may need more explanation and justification.

- *Lengthier manuscript:* A qualitative study may be longer than is usually expected in a quantitative study overall, but also shorter in some parts. The Method section is typically longer, because it often takes more manuscript pages to explain the design and coding of a qualitative study. If the methods used are novel or tailored to a specific question, explaining them leads to a lengthy methods section. Furthermore, the methods may be iterative, evolving while data are being collected either expectedly or unexpectedly, which can further add to the length of the methods description. The Results section, with lengthy extracts (quotations) often contributes the largest share of the manuscript's overall length. Obviously the Results section of a qualitative study will be less likely benefit from the concise manner in which quantitative studies summarize findings. Although a qualitative results section may include some numbers and occasionally including frequencies, there is typically less reliance on such statistical values, displays, and figures that can take up space. Nonetheless, narrative results, especially in participants own words will often be quite lengthy.

- *Shorter Introduction section:* Sometimes, the Introduction to a qualitative study will devote less space to reviewing past literature or to framing the project around past theory than would that of a quantitative study. This is because qualitative research emphasizes "bottom-up" inductive inquiry, placing less emphasis on making predictions from past research or past theory. Likewise, an explicit Hypotheses section may be replaced with a less precise set of overarching research questions.

- *Reflexivity:* A qualitative study may include first-person accounts of the process of doing the study. This practice, referred to as "reflexivity," or personal reflection, is antithetical to scientific modes of inquiry. Whether epistemological reflexivity, methodological reflexivity, or personal reflexivity, such self-aware commentary often includes the first-person pronoun "I" and leads the reader to learn something about the researcher and their process. Reflexivity may be peppered throughout the manuscript or occur only in the Introduction or the Discussion. Reflexivity can be an optional part of one section (e.g., Introduction or Discussion) or of each and every individual section (from the Introduction to the Discussion), enabling the researcher to be transparent about their reflections on the process of qualitative analysis and writing.

- *Unconventional organization of sections:* A qualitative study may diverge from the typical organization of a scientific report. A qualitative researcher may combine sections or use them in a way that a scientific report would not. The most common type of combination is Results/Discussion, facilitating analysis of quotes and examples. In some cases, it may be useful to combine Methods and Results, if the method has evolved during analysis. There may be additional sections, including Reflexivity or Social Applications. There may also be a heavier literature and theoretical review in the Discussion rather than in the Introduction—after data are in, some inductive qualitative researchers tie the results back to other extant theories on the subject after the fact.

- *Contextualizing:* While a scientific report may develop around the goal of generalizing to a larger population, a qualitative report may be focused exclusively on developing a well-rounded description of the context of their participants' experiences. Qualitative researchers will be less concerned about the random selection from or representativeness of a population. Instead of forcing a false universalism on the experiences of participants, a qualitative study will be more concerned about contextualizing their experiences. This is also why a qualitative study will often have a smaller sample and describe these fewer participants in richer detail, sometimes in the Participants section.

- *Informal language:* Grammar, language, and literacy levels for qualitative research reports are often set at a more universally accessible level. The use of specialized jargon and technical terminology is often limited. The use of the first-person pronoun, which often feels awkward to traditionally trained researchers, is part of the anti-elitism that some researchers aim to project in the qualitative style.

- *Overlap of writing and analysis:* Qualitative researchers need to be more flexible because writing and analysis are more cyclical. Researchers may begin with one set of research questions that may lead them to an additional set of questions, necessitating reframing of the Introduction section. At times, even the method may change slightly mid-study and sometimes even mid–report-writing, as additional data may be collected or new themes coded. This is quite contradictory to quantitative positivistic report writing, where the methods and hypotheses are locked in before any analysis takes place. (Of course, this does not mean a qualitative diary researcher goes into a study without a plan. Certainly, grant-funded and programmatic academic research projects will require a prepared and planned set of research methods ahead of time for the review and approval of overseeing award agencies and Institutional Review Boards [IRBs]. Before even recruiting participants, researchers will have an anticipated coding strategy—the coding method to be used, the research questions guiding the coding, the number of coders who will read and analyze the data, and how to handle confidentiality and anonymity. Furthermore, any significant revisions to the method, such as recruiting a different set of participants or changing diary entry forms, would need to be approved by the agency overseeing the project, and this would be noted in the final report, as well.) Nonetheless, the potential for changes to the relevant background research and to the coding strategy make it most logical to begin by writing up the research report around the methods and the results.

I recommend that researchers first compose a rough outline of the project report, and then after the data are collected, compose the Methods section, move on to analyze the data, then write the Results, revisit the Methods outline to adjust for any changes, followed by writing the Introduction and finally the Discussion. After explaining each of these steps, reflexivity will be discussed last; however, it can occur at all stages.

Preparing a Pre-Study Project Report Outline

Before running the study, the researcher should begin with an outline to frame the whole project and anticipate the final written report. The amount of writing for this basic outline is not far removed from what would already be necessary for any grant or human subjects proposal that would need to be submitted before the study begins anyhow. This outline represents the general vision that the researcher has for the research project, including what the final written product might look like. Some of that vision may change, depending upon the nature, richness, quality, and content of the collected diary entries. Completing the following suggested outline is a helpful first step in starting the project and preparing for the ultimate final report.

Introduction

A. Brief introduction: Provide a short statement of the topic of interest or issue of concern to the readers and participants.
B. Opening reflexivity: This is more acceptable in qualitative journals, and involves a first-person commentary on what the researchers bring to the study.
   1. Personal reflexivity: Why is the topic of interest to the researchers doing the study as a function of their personal experiences, values, and assumptions about this topic?
   2. Epistemological reflexivity: What are the researchers' beliefs about the acquisition of knowledge and their methodological or disciplinary standpoint that informs this research project?
C. Literature review: Review the past research on the topic as it is necessary and relevant for setting up the research questions to be addressed in the present study. This illustrates the typical way the topic has been studied in the past and what is uniquely offered in the present study.
D. Research questions: These are the overarching research questions to be posed in the study. This is similar to a Hypotheses section in a quantitative report (and it is not

the specific questions that might appear on the diary form itself, which are actually described in detail in a Method section). There may be one or several overarching questions. This can be a numbered list, but paragraph format is more typical.

E. Brief overview of the design of the present study: This is the present study in a nutshell. The method and participants should be described briefly.

Methods

A. Overall design and rationale: Provide a description of the particular method to be used (by name if applicable) and the rationale for using it. Address why qualitative research in general and diary research in particular are good for the topic. In a positivistic quantitative study, the Methods section often begins with a design statement, which is an overall methodology description. In a qualitative study, it is helpful to begin the Methods section with an equivalent or parallel statement of the overall design and rationale, which explains why qualitative research, in general, is good for the topic. Then specifically state why the diary method is best in this situation. This section can be a paragraph or two, and it may even include some reflexivity.

It is worth noting that the rationale for any qualitative study is roughly the same, although the rationale for a diary study is more specific. For the qualitative rationale, the major reason is that it gives voice to the participants and gives them more control over their self-expression. Furthermore, qualitative research gives flexibility and freedom to researchers to explore the topic with fewer constraints. Qualitative research is useful for topics that we know less about, so it is excellent for pilot and exploratory studies. It is also useful for uncovering processes that cannot easily be revealed in a rigid, quantitative, forced-choice measure. The rationale for qualitative diary research is multifaceted; it is useful for a range of reasons. The researcher can discuss how the topic and behavior of interest are best measured with diary data.

B. Participants: Describe the sample of participants by including (1) the characteristics of the participants that are used as the selection criteria aimed for in the potential sample of participants, (2) how many participants were sought, and 3) the plan for outreach and recruitment.

C. Materials: Describe the basic diary data entry format of the study, what they will be recording and how, and what the scheduling/signaling of entries will be.

D. Procedure: Describe how informed consent will be obtained, the instructions that will be given, and the plan for distribution, instruction, and collection of entries (and how long the study will go on). Also describe what form the data will be in, if/how they will be transcribed, if/how they will be anonymized, how they will be systematically analyzed or coded, and how they will be stored.

Expected Implications

A. Anticipated outcomes: Describe what potential findings, strengths, and weaknesses or challenges are expected in conducting this study.

B. Anticipated reflexivity: Perhaps add some anticipated reflexivity—what the researchers, participants, stakeholders, and readers might expect to take away from the study. This helps contribute to any reflexivity because the researcher can look back at these pre-study expectations after the study is completed.

This outline is best written in future tense. There may be variations in the outline as a function of one's institution, funding agencies, or thesis requirements as relevant. However, once composed, this can help keep the researcher and research staff grounded. Diary data can be richly overwhelming, so having this outline not only helps with report writing but also serves as the how-to manual as the researchers begin to sift through their data and get to work on making sense of it all.

Preparation of Diaries for Coding

Before one can begin the process of analyzing and coding the diary data, the entries must first be organized. If the entries are handwritten or audio-recorded, they will need to be transcribed. Transcribing from written entries can be very time-consuming. There may also be visual data that, if there is no participant-generated caption, will have to be visually described by the researcher. Names and identifiable images of participants and the people and places they refer to should be changed and ano-nymized. Each entry should be labeled and indexed in a system-atic way. If any dates are missing or text is illegible, a method for approximating dates in the context of the larger diary (e.g., num-bering them in order) and deciphering illegible words should be established.

Each participant's diary should be reviewed. Depending on the scope of the study, the researcher might read over each diary in its entirety for each participant, to get a sense of the scope and qual-ity of the data set they have gathered. After this cursory review of the diaries, reconfirmation should be made with regard to the intended coding strategy. The researcher can return to the origi-nal methods outline to refresh their memory of their game plan established before they had diaries in hand. Are the entries written as expected? Is the sample size adequate? Is the total number or size of entries what was expected? Is something about the quality or nature of the entries different from what was expected? Some of the anticipated methodological plans will inevitably be altered in some way. Does the coding strategy still make sense? Do more data need to be collected?

Analysis and Coding

As with any qualitative study, where *process* is as important as the final *product*, there is great importance placed upon transparency in describing one's method of analysis or coding. Coding of rich qualitative data is often an inevitably and regrettably reduction-ist act. The researcher provides some structure, organization, and analysis of the complex data they have amassed, and the reader needs to understand this process. As much as possible, each step should be described in detail.

Coding involves the process of identifying segmented units of meaning from the diary entries. As Miles and Huberman (1994) explain, codes are "tags or labels for assigning units of meaning" that are "attached to 'chunks' of varying size—words, phrases, sentences, or whole paragraphs" that often "take the form of a straightforward category label" (1994, p. 56). There are many choices for the researcher at this stage with regard to whether coding will be focused word by word, line by line, paragraph by paragraph, page by page, section by section, or even diary by diary. Coding in smaller chunks usually produces more categories. What is often described in the literature is a somewhat vague process of "isolating meaning bearing units" or "identifying units of meaning" (e.g., Ahmadi et al., 2014).

In cases where some participants have written many diary entries and others only a few (and still others have dropped out of the study entirely), decisions have to be made about resulting variability in voice. As Scollon, Prieto, and Diener (2009) point out, not every participant can follow the full time-consuming research protocol in a solicited diary study, leaving researchers to contemplate just "who volunteers for such intrusive studies and who completes them?" (p. 14). Of course, the answer is, "Not everyone!" If participants who wrote more are over-represented in the study overall, does this risk (what quantitative methodologists refer to as) over-representation and/or selection bias, or is that over-representation a natural accounting of the phenomena on some abstract global scale? The answer depends in part on one's epistemological assumptions. In some cases, the researcher has to decide how to balance voices so that one or two very expressive participants are not carrying the weight of the coding scheme and thus (perhaps unfairly) over-represented in the narrative written up by the researcher. One solution is for participants themselves to decide which entries the researchers should code, selecting their most vivid, typical, or representative entry, for example. This will depend upon the research question and the researchers' methodology. For example, in her study of women serving life sentences in prison, Lempert (2016) explained, "As is common in feminist research, the participants exerted considerable informational control . . . they determined what to include and exclude from their two-week diaries" (p. 31). The longitudinal nature of diary data can also offer some solutions to variations in the number and length of diaries, as well as introduce new decisions to be made. In particular, the way in which time is woven into the analysis of a diary study will depend on the researcher's methodological orientation and research questions. Again in Lempert's (2016) study of women serving life sentences, she collected just two weeks of contemplations in the diaries solicited from incarcerated women serving life sentences; thus, dramatic or even detectible changes in their experience of prison life over that time would be unlikely to surface in that short period. In fact, as one of her participants, Kari, said, temporality may be irrelevant:

> My mind isn't in here. Everything I do is focused around my friends on the outside and preparing myself for the demands of life on the outside. I never have looked at my being in prison as permanent. I just get through my days as simply "going through the motions," something I must do, surviving, and before you know it, it's 5, 10, 15, 20 years later." (p. 185)

Had Lempert's diary collection spanned several years in the lives of her participants, diary order and developmental changes in their experiences may have been more of a factor. Thus, in studies where short samples of much larger experiences are amassed through diaries, collapsing them and analyzing them without temporal considerations is a reasonable coding strategy. In these cases, coding is conducted with data collapsed across time (taking no account of the point in time during the diary study when any particular entry was made). Other studies for which collapsing across time makes sense are those where the diary method was employed to capture a fleeting experience that might have been forgotten or overlooked. These types of diary studies are typically done to capture snapshots of very short-lived experiences that are not explicitly developmental in trajectory (e.g., a diary study of conversation topics at the dinner table, or times when one gets angry on the road, or chocolate cravings).

For diary studies in which attention is paid to when an entry was made, the primary reason for doing the diary study is to explore change in that experience over time, or the impact of a prior experience on a later one. Studies about developmental phenomena of growth, maturation, change, learning, healing, disease progression, or interventions will need to explore diary themes within the context of time and over time. For example, McIver, O'Halloran, and

McGartland (2009) explored the effects of a yoga program on binge eating through the diary entries of women, explaining the care they took to attend to "where they were located in time" and how patterns were revealed over the course of the training. They noted, "As the program developed over time, journal entries suggested distinct phases of progression among the women . . . . Similar experiences seemed to be occurring at similar times" across the diaries (p. 1237). Diary researchers are often interested in change over time, so in those cases, their coding may occur with the first half of diary entries and then again separately with the second half. Another simple way to manage a large and varied distribution of entries across participants and over time is to assemble a collection of all *first* diary entries from all participants and another collection of all *final* diary entries from all participants.

Coding may also be organized by the type of diarist or type of experience described. There may be naturally emerging group differences that warrant a segregation of participants or entries into subgroups for coding. Diaries from a particular subgroup may then be pulled to be analyzed separately, based upon demographic or background information gathered. For example, in my research on anti-gay prejudice (Hyers, 2010), the participants who were "out" faced more prejudice than those who were not. Whether the greater experiences of anti-gay prejudice for those who were in the public eye "over-represents" the phenomenon is a representational matter. It depends on the kind of question asked. This may or may not be an issue for any particular study, but if it is a concern, researchers may select only one entry from each participant for coding. Similarly, in research with my colleagues on everyday sexism (Swim, Hyers, Cohen, & Fergusen, 2001), a concern that affected the quantity and perhaps the nature of entries was whether the lesser frequency of men's versus women's experiences of sexism might also indicate a qualitative difference in the phenomena and a need for them to be coded separately. Whether the researcher will select one versus many diary entries for each participant, whether they will assay full entries versus a sentence or two within an entry, and whether the experiences of certain groups will be examined separately is entirely dependent upon the design of a particular study and the research questions at hand.

The style of coding is determined by the underlying epistemological framework of the study. As Gläser and Laudel (2013) note,

"The enormous variation between the approaches, their partial overlap, and the breadth of legitimate research goals in qualitative research make it impossible to construct a framework in which all methods can be located" (p. 1). One might take it for granted that a *universal* first step in diary analysis is for the researchers to carefully read, listen to, and/or view the diary entries they have collected. Yet there are even coding variations in which the researchers never see the raw entries at all. One example is when diaries are used only for consciousness raising. In such studies, other data, perhaps from post-diary interviews become the subject of analysis rather than the diaries themselves. Or, as another example, participants may be asked to reflectively code their own entries at the close of the study. Self-coding has been employed to get around positivist's concerns of validity and at the same time qualitativists' concerns for voice when a researcher dares to classify another person's words and experiences. The charges of naïve realism and reductionism make the act of coding open to criticism. For those staying true to the qualitative research value system, St. Pierre and Jackson (2014) warn that if a coding plan is too reductionist, it will be at odds with the "post" (a.k.a. post-modern) and social constructionist sensibilities that inform so much of qualitative research:

> There is something nonsensical in this practice of coding if one thinks about it, because in the logic of coding, words can be both data—brute, waiting to be interpreted—and code—meaningful. Even if one accommodates that incommensurability—which coders do—such a project is thinkable only in logical positivism that presumes that language can, indeed, be brute and value-free. To restate, it is logical positivism that claims a word can be brute data. Other social science approaches such as interpretive, critical, and "post" approaches assume that language is always already entirely contaminated by meaning, exploding with meaning deferred. (p. 716)

The choices and mechanics of coding and analysis are diverse and will be unique to each study. In some studies, the diary data are all that is coded, whereas in others, triangulation of diaries with interviews and supporting documents may require coding from multiple sources. In some cases, sources will be kept separate for coding, but many times it makes sense to code across all these sources. For example, in a healthcare study, Kielmann and colleagues (2010) coded simultaneously across three data sources: diaries, telephone interviews, and focus group discussions. This may be difficult to manage, given what is often an enormous data set already generated in diaries themselves. Nonetheless, there are some basic steps and a few common coding methods in the human sciences. Four types of analysis or coding are most typical with diary data, each using slightly different language and processes: content analysis (Berelson, 1952), biographical analysis (Runyan, 1982), grounded theory coding (Glaser & Strauss, 1968), and thematic analysis (Braun & Clarke, 2006). All four involve coding descriptively for patterns and themes after an extensive review of the diary entries and any supporting materials.

Content analysis is the most generic method of categorizing content. It has been employed across a broad range of disciplines and in both qualitative and mixed-method designs. The diary entries can be read through, and any patterns observed can be sorted into categories. Hseih and Shannon (2005) describe three different types of content analyses. In *conventional content analysis coding*, the coding is bottom-up and starts with observation for patterns, with codes, code labels, and code definitions derived from the data. In *directive content analysis coding*, the coding is top-down and starts with a theory, with codes derived from past theory before or during data analysis. In *summative content analysis coding*, the coding keywords are derived from and informed by existing literature before data analysis. The steps of a content analysis outlined elsewhere (Chelimsky 1989; Hsieh & Shannon, 2005; Mayring, 2010) can be applied to the coding of most diary studies:

- *Step 1:* Identifying what portion of the total set of diaries will be explored. One needs to decide how one will use the "data"—the entire set of diaries one has collected, a certain year or month or week of diaries, only one entry from each person (e.g., only the first), or only a subsection of each diary. These are sometimes referred to as the "sampling units," the material within which further attention and classification will take place. These sampling units in their entirety are not themselves being classified or coded, as they are too large. For example, in a diary study of participants receiving mindfulness-based chronic pain-management training, a researcher may select one diary entry from the beginning of the study and one from the end.

- *Step 2:* Identifying the boundaries around what will be classified. One then identifies the exact portions or components of the sampling units that will be subject to classification. These are sometimes referred to as "recording units." A recording unit is a specific part that will be categorized. Taking the hypothetical chronic pain study again as an example, the researcher may select as the recording units any short emotional phrases in the selected entries (e.g., "I am feeling like giving up," or "I feel like everything I do is futile") that would then be coded for type of emotion (e.g., "hopelessness" and "helplessness"). Larger recording units might be whole stories or short narratives. For example, a researcher studying family conflict might select as the recording units the entire paragraphs wherein diarists described arguments, which would then would be coded for the trigger of the conflict (e.g., childcare, politics, financial issues, etc.).
- *Step 3:* Identifying the surrounding context. When coding, researchers look to the surrounding context for meaning. This is sometimes called the "context unit," and the width of the spread to surrounding context is generally held consistent throughout the coding task. Having this surrounding context is very important for understanding. One needs to make a decision about how much context will be considered surrounding each particular recording unit to be coded. The context unit itself can be quite small; for example, in a visual diary, the images in the diary entries may be the recording units, and the accompanying caption for each image could be the context unit. The context unit can be quite large as well, even taking into account mixed-method data. Generally, the context unit is aiding in the understanding of the recording unit to be coded. Returning to the example of a hypothetical chronic pain study, the recording unit (unbolded emotional statement below) that will be coded is surrounded by the context unit (bold

sentences surrounding the emotional statement below) in this fictional entry:

> The kids did not go in to school today they both have dentist appointments. I heard their alarms go off, and they both headed downstairs to get their own break-fast—they are getting so grown up. **Today I awoke and my arthritis was very bad in my left knee despite elevating it with a pillow last night.** I am feeling like giving up because feel like everything I do is futile. **Nothing I try works not even ice or heat take away the pain.** I might try to stop by the pharmacy while the kids are at their appointment to pick up a refill on my prescription pain meds.

The context unit sentences help characterize the emotion.

- *Step 4:* Naming the category labels. This is where the real analysis lies in a content analysis. The categories need to be conceptualized based on one's research questions. Categories are either developed deductively from past theory or inductively from the diaries (bottom-up) or a combination of both. In some cases, lower level codes can be added to *a priori* higher level codes (e.g., Waddington, 2005). For example, in the hypothetical pain management study, the emotions could be classified based on Plutchik's (1980) model of eight types of emotions (e.g., representing anger, sadness, joy, disgust, and trust, etc.), or based on characterizations of emotions generated by participants. Perhaps this might even include emotions that are more closely connected to pain and perhaps highly related but nonetheless distinguishable in the recording units (e.g., hopelessness distinguished from helplessness). Categories should be exhaustive, meaning they should account for all recording units (typically there should be no unclassifiable "other" categories in an inductive coding system, but there may be in a deductive/theory-driven one). In general, categories should be mutually exclusive—so that each recording unit falls into only one category—though this is not always the case. For example, in a study of imagery in nocturnal dreams, Perry (1973) gave participants 21 pages of lined paper on which to record their dreams, which were later classified into just two categories—distorted or not distorted. It is essential that categories labels be meaningful to the reader.

- *Step 5:* All data from entries are given a classification. Now that the codes are developed, the researcher should outline a basic coding guide or instructions. Whether there are research assistants or only the researcher going back through to code all the recording units, detailed written instructions are useful for keeping consistency in the procedure, and they can be put (with minor editing) directly into the final report in the Methods section. If multiple coders code the data, inter-rater reliability between coders will typically be described in some way (see Burla et al., 2008; Krippendorff & Bock, 2009; and Morse, Barrett, Mayan, Olson, & Spiers, 2002, for more information on reliability in content analysis).

By the end of the content analysis, the data will have been reviewed numerous times—while reading, organizing and indexing, establishing sampling units, identifying recording units, and deciding upon context units, and finally when developing and assigning codes. This is a structured process, and the steps need to be explicitly articulated. As an example, Wickens, Roseborough, Hall, and Wiesenthal (2013) conducted a content analysis of offensive driver behavior in an audio diary study on anger and driving to identify major themes, described in their report in this way:

> All diary entries were coded by two primary coders (a postdoctoral fellow and a graduate student, both of whom were experienced coders). Each diary entry could be classified as falling into one or more categories (or sub-categories). For example, in describing their upsetting driving event, one respondent wrote:

> I was driving on the 401, and someone was tailgating me on the highway and I was already exceeding the speed limit a bit, so I didnt [sic] want to go faster. Then there was a bit of traffic so I had to break [sic], and the car behind me had to break [sic] suddenly and I could see her yelling at me through my mirror. So she switched lanes, and I noticed she was tailgating the other car as well [sic].

This diary entry was classified as speeding/racing (Ai), tailgating (B), and perceived hostile driver display (Hi). If the two primary coders were unable to reach agreement on at least one possible classification of a diary entry, a third independent coder (an experienced graduate student) categorised the diary entry. The final classification included categories selected by at least two of the three coders. Upon completion of all coding, the three coders met to discuss and come to an agreement on the classification of diary entries where at least one category was not selected by two of the three coders. (p. 9)

Biographical or case study analysis requires a holistic treatment of entries in order to tell a contextualized life story or history. Using biographical analysis, the researcher reads and reviews the diaries for a cohesive story. As Smith (1994) has noted, the thinking and analysis in a biographical or case study are obscure, iterative, and revelatory:

> One of the most difficult decisions facing the biographer as he or she practices the craft of biography resides in the slant, perspective, or theme that is needed to guide the development of the life to be written. . . . Sometimes the theme comes early based on an insight from preliminary knowledge and an overview of the subject's life. . . . But sometimes also, reconstruals vie with the original decision as new data enter, new facets of the life begin to form, new views on the significance of the story arise, and new audiences appear and become salient. . . . And then, at least in some instances, the writing takes over and transforms things—such as a theme—once again. (p. 10)

To provide a foundation for a biography or case study, a set of diaries can be explored with attention to (embedded) chronology. The themes appearing in individual diary entries are not left as piecemeal daily events; instead, the segregated stories are taken up and the life is reconstructed. A biographical analysis involves forming a narrative, usually around a thesis and sometimes organized by stages of life or phases of a career. Beller (2015) cautions that hindsight "conceals rather than reveals" the life:

> Most biographers conspire to deliver "a story," a seamless continuum of incidents and quotes as neatly packaged as the subject pictured on the book's jacket cover. Cured of

discrepancies, order reigns, disappointment and want word-processed into a tidy deployment of situation and sequence. Against this, the true experience of being here is not determined by an invisible architecture undergirding all. Life is muddled and messy, talk discursive and rambling, not a stenographic transcription of "mindful" soundbites. There are emotional misfirings, relational miscarriages, and closures coming apart. The biographer's plot is more often an entombment of a life than a gateway to it. (p. 100)

There are as many different foci of biographical methods as there are research questions. The biographical researcher will read the diaries looking for information for their particular thesis. A generic life history biography would involve a general static comprehensive accounting of a life lived (Miller, 2003). Narrative analysis focuses on the elements of a story in the biographical material. An intellectual biography focuses on the evolution of thought and philosophy revealed in the diaries of the subject of interest (Wallace, 1992). A group of biographical methods called psychobiography, psychodynamic biography, or biographical structuring (Fischer-Rosenthal, 2000) focuses on the diarists' personality and identity development revealed in their entries. Biographical action research focuses on how the diarists' entries reveal a persons responses to certain social problems and situations (Zinn, 2005). In studying and relaying the story of a case, the researcher needs to be aware of the limitations of their own analysis. Some degree of reflexivity is part of this process because the biographer brings their own historical era and cultural background to bear in interpreting the biography of another (Każmierska, 2004, 2012). At the same time, some argue that the researcher must actively insert their analysis. In biographical analysis, Renders, de Haan, and Harmsma (2016) argue against "simply presenting it in the form of an explanation from a distant, omniscient narrator" encouraging the biographical researcher to form an argument as *plot*:

How, then, does the biographer "make an argument"? By transposing your "argument" into a "plot," and your "thesis question" into a "plot question" . . . in which conflicting desire—both internal and external, conscious and unconscious—are the engines of change . . . the patterns of desires as they are shaped by upbringing, social context and personality, as they are pursued, thwarted, negotiated, ful-filled or abandoned. (p. 16)

Thematic analysis (Braun & Clarke, 2006 & 2013) is a more recent term for "systematic coding" that some researchers have been erroneously mislabeling as "grounded theory" (described in the next section). Themes can be *emic* (favoring context, language, narrative style) or *etic* (favoring *a priori* categorizing, reducing). With regard to emic themes, Braun and Clarke reject the "naïve realist" notions that themes simply "emerge" from the data or that researchers merely "give voice" to participants as a sort of excuse for not thinking through and explaining their process clearly. The stages or phases of Braun and Clarke's (2006) thematic analysis can be applied to diary research coding:

- *Phase 1:* Get familiarized with the data. For diary research, the familiarizing stage may occur in an ongoing fashion, as entries roll in, or not until the entire set is collected. Diaries will need to be compiled into an organized set of documents: handwritten or audio diaries may be transcribed; visual diaries may be watched and then edited into a single stream or a series of snapshots; in mixed-method designs, quantitative categorical data will be entered. This is also a time when background information and any supporting documents or interviews would be explored in some fashion. If the sample size allows for it, the idiosyncratic life stories of each participant can be explored, and it may be helpful to familiarize oneself with a complete data set, one participant at a time: review the background information to contextualize the diary, then review the diary entries, most likely in chronological order. If the sample size is larger, it may not be idiosyncratic life stories that one can explore. Instead, diaries may be combed through for general patterns, repeated experiences, or specific phenomena that are of interest. If multiple coders are involved and it is feasible, they should also review the documents, or a subset they will work with.
- *Phase 2:* Generating initial codes. This phase is not unlike the beginning stages of coding in any other qualitative

study. It involves perusing data and beginning to look for events of interest, units of meaning, patterns, or unusual events. Because diaries are often about sequential and unfolding events, attention may also be paid to chronology, sequence, story, and characters. Notes may be taken on a separate sheet or within diary documents themselves, unless multiple coders are using the same documents.

- *Phase 3:* Searching for themes. Notes and initial themes are reviewed to develop an organized set of themes. This is where the analysis comes in. What are the patterns seen within a story, within a diary, or across participants? The researcher goes from themes to diaries, from entry to entry, from participant to participant. Although much of the work of this is private mental work, if multiple coders are involved, they may meet to discuss themes they generated through conversation.
- *Phase 4:* Reviewing themes. Once themes are tentatively identified, at this point in the coding, the researcher focuses on the integrity of the themes. Are certain themes interrelated, or are they different manifestations of a single common experience? The researcher explores whether there is internal homogeneity in a category. Does this theme fit one participant's experience but not others'? Do the extracts (quotes) where an initially theme was spotted all have something in common? The researcher also explores the external heterogeneity of the themes. Does an extract labeled with one theme fit into other themes? It probably should not. Do different themes really differ?
- *Phase 5:* Defining and naming themes. This is part of the storytelling of qualitative data analysis. The researcher needs to decide on a name for each theme and define each theme. This is similar to operational definitions in quantitative research. The researcher will name, define, and then identify examples of the themes. It is important to go back to the data and come up with extracts or quotes for each theme.
- *Phase 6:* Producing the report. The final part of the thematic coding process is described in more detail later in

Chapter 4, and it involves writing up the story of the study. The set of fully worked-out themes are then described in detail in the Results section, including any final analysis as part of the write-up of a report. As Braun and Clarke (2006) declared, "The task of the write-up of a Thematic Analysis, whether it is for publication or for a research assignment or dissertation, is to tell the complicated story of your data in a way which convinces the reader of the merit and validity of your analysis" (p. 24).

Thematic analysis is somewhat similar to content analysis and at the same time somewhat similar to grounded theory. Thematic analysis is more firmly anchored in qualitative methods than is content analysis, and somewhat tied to theory like grounded theory. The researcher will need to decide which method speaks most clearly to how they are approaching their coding and follow that system.

Grounded theory (Glaser & Strauss, 1968) is the most elaborate of these three coding systems. It involves the progressive identification and integration of categories of meaning from data. Qualitative researchers' use of grounded theory as a coding method has been a part of qualitative methods for some time. Grounded theory has its foundations in sociology. The end product of grounded theory coding is not just a list of categories, but an explanatory framework with which to understand the phenomenon under investigation. It allows new theories to emerge from data, to liberate the researcher from being bound to positivistic hypothetico-deductivism and is often more explanatory. What counts as a theme is a decision, or a series of decisions in itself. A theme may capture something important in the data in relation to the research question. Or it may be a patterned response, a unit of meaning, or a consequence. Sometimes an important theme is one that is intense or even unusual. Because grounded theory is supposed to be an accounting of all observed phenomena, if one has a category called "Other," they need to get back to work! There are four levels of coding for a grounded theory analysis that can be applied in a diary research project:

- *Level 1:* Open coding: In grounded theory, the initial exploration of the data for themes is the first step, not unlike Phase 2 in thematic analysis. The reading of Phase 1 in thematic analysis and the reviewing of Phase 2 are essentially combined in Level 1. Large quantities of raw qualitative data are focused on and labeled. In diary research, there is much to explore. Whether the researcher goes diary by diary or across participants is an individual choice, although the holistic nature of grounded theory style coding would favor staying with one participant's story at a time.

- *Level 2:* Focused coding and category development. This phase is similar to Phase 3 in thematic analysis. The researcher reexamines Level 1 codes and further focuses and refines themes. Redundant themes may be combined, and patterns within diary entries and across participants may be highlighted. If there are multiple coders, they may meet to review just before Level 3.

- *Level 3:* Axial or thematic coding. Previous coding is studied to develop highly refined themes. At this phase, the themes are reviewed and finalized, and extracts or examples are amassed. Grounded theory coders follow a number of guidelines to enrich the coding process, such as constant comparative analysis, a process of moving back and forth from category to category to refine categories. They also engage in negative case analysis, which involves exploring instances that don't fit. Theoretical sensitivity is the process of moving back and forth from the data to the categories. This can be especially difficult given the richness of diary data. This is the final phase of code generation in thematic analysis, but in grounded theory, this may be the phase where the need for new participant samples and/or more diaries will be identified. Grounded theory coding's open-ended data collection allows for this.

- *Level 4:* Theories can emerge from "saturated" categories and themes. Theoretical sampling is the process of collecting more data, often from new samples of participants, in light of categories that emerged, to further explore them. More of an ideal than a reality, theoretical saturation involves the commitment to continue collecting more data and code until no new codes emerge. In this regard, diary studies lend themselves well to continuing to collect data if the end date is not firm. Participants can continue to complete entries, and new participants or domains can be added.

Some other variations in coding may be tied to research questions. Coding may focus on between-group differences, comparing entries of two different participant groups (e.g., older and younger diarists). One may code, not for what is said, but for how it is said and in what context, as in phenomenological or discourse analysis. Related to this is narrative analysis coding, in which how one tells a story and the story itself are of interest, rather than the event itself. Coding can also be longitudinal, with a focus on the chronology of certain events. Or it may focus on process rather than isolated events per se, looking at how one works through certain events in everyday life behaviors and/or their intrapsychic processing, as told through the diary entry.

In the process of coding, it is helpful to develop a handbook or codebook for internal organization, as well as potentially to include in the final report. The coder's handbook or codebook typically consists of three key elements. First, the label or name for each theme should be listed. Second, a definition (sometimes called "operational definition") of the code should be listed. Third, examples or excerpts should be identified from the diaries. It may also be important in some studies to list the number of people who reported the experience. This will ultimately go into the Results section of the report. For example, Table 4.1 is an excerpt of a codebook my research lab used in coding a study of Christians' experiences with prejudice (Hyers & Hyers, 2008). Though it is not always the practice in coding, for our manuscript, it was helpful to depict it as a chart in the final manuscript. Sometimes inter-rater reliability will be reported as well. This may depend on the nature of the project and the journal to which the manuscript is submitted. Some qualitative researchers have at least two researchers code all of the data. Some employ a research assistant or a coding team of three (to deal with tie-breaking in disagreements) to code all of the passages into the categories in the codebook. Some have a second coder just code the first 10% of the passages with them to "affirm" that the researcher's views are

Table 4.1

Codebook: Excerpt from Hyers & Hyers, 2008

CODE	EXCERPTED QUOTES	*n*
Derogation: Ridiculing remarks or judgements perpetrated at Christians		**64**
at Christian beliefs	My professor seems to try to make Christians question their beliefs. Tonight he mentioned several beliefs I hold and started to say contradictory things about them.	24
at Christian people	I was at a restaurant with my father and we heard a couple behind us talking about how "hypocritical" Christians could be . . . referring to Christians as "they" and "those people."	19
at Christian practices	I was called a goody-goody because of going to church and for not doing things others do such as drinking and sex. I was made fun of because of the decisions I make.	14
at Christian churches	A person in the campus ministry made directly derogatory comments about another campus ministry.	7
Cultural Insensitivity: Lack of sensitivity or accommodation of Christian beliefs or practice		**37**
General insensitivity	I was scheduled to work regular and overtime hours, which would have required me to work seven days in a row, which would have violated my religious beliefs.	24
Vulgarity	Me and a few of my friends were playing pool and each of them know I'm a Christian. One guy kept on saying God *ammit if he missed a shot.	7

(*continued*)

CODE	EXCERPTED QUOTES	*n*
Sexualized	I was offended by the way a male professor was looking at me, though he didn't think I saw him.	4
Assumed not to be Christian	A friend was reading me a questionnaire about how well you know your friend and I was answering. One question he asked me was "Do you believe in God." He answered, "I hope not."	2
Teasing: Mocking, joking, or sarcasm from others		**17**
(and so on . . .)		

Table 4.1
Continued

Reprinted with permission from John Wiley and Sons.

shared by another who uses the same codebook. As Pedhazur and Schmelkin (2013) explain:

> Generally speaking, interobserver agreement consists of assessing the extent to which two (or more) observers agree in their codings, ratings, categorizations, and the like. Although many interobserver agreement indices have been proposed, they are basically aimed at estimating the percentage of agreement among the observers. (p. 145)

In many qualitative journals, these inter-rater validations are deemed unnecessary, and in fact, some may view it as a futile exercise in appeasing naïve realists. *Member checking* is sometimes used to confirm the validity of any coding. This involves presenting or sharing, in some form, the codebook with participants to ask if they feel their experiences have been adequately reflected.

After the data are coded, it is not a good idea to immediately archive and/or return diaries until the final report writing is done. It is very common to need to revisit the diary for reference while writing the report, to recode some portions, and even to code new portions of diaries, once the bigger picture of the results begins to emerge. If the diary data are to be accessed well into the future for longitudinal studies, permission to store and access the data for any period longer than the standard five years would need to be sought from participants as part of the informed consent procedure. This is especially important when one considers the increasing popularity of opening archival diary data to other researchers.

Composing the Methods Section

After the coding is complete, this is the time to review the original outline and begin to compose the final report, starting with the Methods as outlined previously. At this point, the researcher is describing how they ultimately worked through the data set. (Of course, any substantial change to the methods that requires reporting back to any overseeing body such as one's IRB approval, granting agency, or academic committee should have already been cleared before acting upon it.) The final Methods section should include the same content as in the outline, this time rewritten in past tense, with a good deal more detail on the coding. The exercise of changing tense from future to past helps keep reflexive thinking at the fore.

First, restate the study's rationale. Are there any changes or additions to the overall methodological rationale? Although the rationale is not likely to change, one's own understanding of the undertaking may be clearer after having run the study.

Next, the Participants section will be further elaborated on. Describe the final recruitment method and selection criteria. What was the total number of participants? Were any additional participants sought? The Participants section will have much greater detail than in the proposal. There is likely to be a range of background demographic material that was gathered so that the participants can be more richly described. If the sample has just a few participants, this section might devote a paragraph to describing each one. The larger the number of participants, regrettably, the less individualized information can be provided about each one.

Next, describe the Materials information on the diaries. What was the total number of diaries and entries generated? How were they transcribed, anonymized, and organized? Ultimately, what parts were selected for coding?

Next, flesh out the Procedure section. Describe the informed consent protocol, participant instructions, and data management procedures? How was coding conducted? The description of the coding should include how and who did the analysis in detail and whatever system was followed. The inter-rater reliabilities, if any were calculated or the conclusions of the member checks, if any were done, should be described if such validation of the coding is conducted Member checks can also be shared in the Discussion section under a Strengths/Limitations section).

Composing the Results or the Findings

The Results section of the report is the most exciting part to write. This may also be the lengthiest section. It is best to first restate the overarching research questions that were listed in the initial outline and then begin to structure the Results around those questions and the resulting codes or themes. A strong Results section will also include extracts or quotes that exemplify the codes generated in the coding, and an indication of the person quoted if there are multiple participants.

The Results may be organized a number of ways. If the sample of diarists is small, the Results may be organized participant by participant. If the sample is larger but divisible by a demographic group or shared experience, the Results may be organized by group. In some cases, the Results may be organized and described as a function of the timing of the entries (e.g., early in the study or late in the study; morning versus evening). If the sample is too large to contextualize in either of these ways, the Results might be organized around the themes in the codebook. This is actually the most common way a qualitative diary study is presented.

It is important to note that, in qualitative research, the extracted quotes are the "data." So, in writing the Results, some considerations include the length and selection of quotes reprinted, and how to designate the participants who are speaking. Some researchers report basic demographic information along with a pseudonym to protect anonymity (e.g., "Lucy, 30-year-old law student"). It is important to balance the voices of the participants. If a study has ten participants who will be identified in the results under a pseudonym, pay attention to whether examples are being drawn as equally from all participants as possible.

Sometimes in writing out the results and choosing extracts or quotes, the researcher will realize an alternative perspective or a more suitable way to organize the themes in the codebook. In a qualitative study, this is the point where the researcher needs to keep a flexible and open mind and be patient. In crafting the Results, sometimes new insights are revealed, and the researcher may find the need to go back to the diaries to rethink the codebook and possibly recode. This post-hoc analysis would not be an acceptable practice in a positivistic design, but in some respects, it represents the final phase of inquiry in the qualitative research process.

Composing the Introduction

The Introduction introduces the topic of interest, the question or series of questions that the researcher is raising about the topic, and the reason why diaries are a compelling way to address these matters. As with the Methods write-up, the original outline should be revisited when writing the final Introduction. So that the introductory material can frame the results as concisely and practically as possible, that initial outline does not need to change dramatically. The initial brief introduction and reflexivity should not change at all, to speak of. The literature review will probably be fleshed out a little more, and the research questions may be refined or changed.

In general, introductions in qualitative research tend to be shorter and more concise. Part of the reason for this necessity, in that qualitative research tends to explore topics for which there is less research available to review. However, another reason is methodological, as qualitative research moves away from the conventional post-positivistic scientific framing of research inquiry as theory-derived hypothetico-deductivist. Qualitative research is more inductive, which contraindicates an elaborate, theoretically heavy introduction. In general, in a qualitative design, the best language of inquiry used would be to explore, describe, or reveal rather than to determine, predict, or test.

Background Literature Review

Qualitative introductions provide a literature review; however, they are less exhaustive than in Positivistic quantitative research introductions which require the entire study to be justified in the Introduction, via hypothesis-testing of a particular theoretical framework. Qualitative researchers are often seeking information on topics, questions, and voices of participants, none of which have been explored in the particular way they are approaching it in their qualitative study. Qualitative diary researchers are often seeking diarists' perspectives to turn existing theory on a topic in a new direction and focus, into uncharted terrain. One problem that can arise with the literature review is that the researcher ends up not reviewing the past research literature thoroughly enough, and overlooks a framework that could have actually informed the research design or the language of the coding. It is important, in addition to thoroughly reviewing the literature (even if it is not all cited in the initial outline), to be sure to review related work that might not seem immediately relevant. Oftentimes qualitative work is very grounded in one particular context and experience, and researchers can fail to move outside these parameters to see what is related (something more typical in quantitativist work). Moreover, the qualitative researcher needs to be sure to review both quantitative and qualitative literature, and both diary and/ or non-diary designs, so as to include studies using a range of methods.

Research Questions

This is the section in which the researcher poses the overarching questions to be asked. The Introduction to a qualitative diary study is less likely to include explicit hypotheses; however, some deductive coding and mixed-method designs of positivistic bent may include predictions and even hypothesis testing. Regardless, the research questions that are posed in this section must provide structure for the forthcoming Results section, so posing them in the same order in which the Results section flows best is key. One common mistake with the posing of research questions is not articulating them in a clear and organized manner to lend structure to the whole report. Also, the research questions may have changed slightly in wording since the researcher used them in approaching the subject, and may have evolved to be more precise. It is best to present the research questions that are ultimately addressed through the study-as-run. If in the act of carrying out the diary study, the researcher ends up answering a slightly different question than was initially posed, or if a key term or concept has been given a more precise name after interacting with participants, it is acceptable to use that new knowledge and incorporate it in the introductory writing. If the researcher wants to explain the evolution of their research questions as they designed, carried out, or analyzed data from their study, they should use the reflexivity section to do so.

Many researchers will face some struggles between writing in the mode of traditional scientific writing and in the mode of qualitative research. Some manuscripts need to be rewritten in the scientific style because of the demands of the audience, the editors, the reviewers, or the journal. This is often faced by those Kidder and Fine (1987) refer to as "big Q" researchers—those qualitative researchers who do not conceptualize their projects within a positivistic framework. Inversely, those who do follow the positivistic framework will find themselves in an equal and opposite struggle of resistance to giving up that scientific writing style in writing to a big Q audience.

Composing the Discussion

The three main goals of the Discussion section in a standard academic article, be it quantitative or qualitative, are to (1) summarize the major research findings, (2) tie them to past literature and theory, and (3) make suggestions for future research, social policy, and practical applications, as relevant. The qualitative discussion is also often a place where qualitative researchers choose to share some final reflexivity to discuss how the study influenced them and their perspective on the subject.

To begin the Discussion, summarize the major research findings. It is best to summarize the answers to the key research questions that were stated in the Introduction. In doing so, this is not the place to insert diary excerpts or quotes; this should be in the researcher's own voice. The terms that were devised in the coding analysis should continue to be used in the Discussion, since the analysis has brought those concepts to light. Any interesting contradictions, coding challenges, or interrelationships across the phenomena observed can be discussed here as well.

Next, tie the findings back to past literature. Any past research of a descriptive or theoretical nature that the researcher feels is relevant should be discussed at this time. Some qualitative researchers may use the Discussion section to bring in more theory, even more than was mentioned in the Introduction. This may be a larger or smaller part of the Discussion, depending on how much past work there is on the subject. In contrast, other qualitative researchers may keep their final discussion on more of a descriptive level, paying less attention to how their observations connect to past theoretical or scholarly approaches to the subject.

The Discussion should then turn towards suggestions for further research or applied implications of the work. It is in this section that the researcher will discuss limitations and strengths of their design and possible future research steps. Future research considerations include changes to participant recruitment, diary study design, and/or coding and analysis. For some qualitative studies, it may include a final Reflexivity section. Ideally, the researcher makes a connection between reflexive statements made in the Introduction. If the Introduction included personally reflexive statements about the researcher's personal values and assumptions about the topic, then they may discuss if and how their participants' perspectives affected the researcher's own. If the Introduction included epistemological reflexive statements about the researcher's assumptions about their methodological or disciplinary approach to the subject, they can discuss whether and how that has changed from conducting the study. As Gilgun (2010) has noted:

> The core concept of my working definition of reflexivity is the idea of awareness—that researchers are reflexive when they are aware of the multiple influences they have on research processes and on how research processes affect them. (p. 2)

Qualitative modes of inquiry view researcher subjectivity as a natural and unavoidable part of any research, from design, to data collection, to analysis, to the final write-up and sharing of the report. Reflexive statements are best written in first-person, and explore not only one's perspective at the beginning of conducting the study, but also how one affected and was affected by the process.

Composing the Title and Abstract

Compose a detailed title or else the study can be hard to locate. Researchers may not include the words "qualitative" or "diary" in their title or abstract, and this makes it difficult for researchers interested studies containing both features to locate them. Saldaña (2011) also points out the importance of listing one's major themes in the abstract. "Front-loading" the method and main themes/conclusions as early as in the title, the abstract, and if feasible, the Introduction, increases the accessibility of the article as a whole. Suspense in the form of withholding methods and findings does not contribute to the ease with which other readers and researchers can locate and digest the manuscript.

Collective Copyediting and Proofreading

Qualitative researchers typically value accessibility of writing. The target audience can be a bit wider than in more technical scientific, quantitative research. Therefore, it is good to have a range of readers proofread the project once written. It can be good to receive feedback from both academic and non-academic readers, experts on the topic and novices, qualitative as well as quantitative readers, researchers and applied professionals, and if feasible, participants or individuals similar to the participants themselves. This can improve the writing and the conceptualizing, as well as contribute to the validity of the report, a topic that will be discussed in the chapter ahead. Feedback from a range of readers can be viewed as part of the iterative writing process and can even result in changes to some of the coding or the conceptualization of themes. Often deadline pressures can stunt this process, but if possible, a collective and collaborative editing phase can help strengthen the analysis and the final report in ways that are not possible in highly technical positivistic research. Take advantage of this great benefit that comes with the accessibility of qualitative design.

Summary

The qualitative researcher does their hardest work in doing analysis and then summarizing their whole project to share with others. Their goal is no different than in positivistic science—to contribute to our collective knowledge base in a systematic way. The best means of doing this are with reflexive, intentional, and transparent methodology and reporting. This can contribute to the integrity of the project and make the efforts put into the project by all involved, including the researchers, the diarists, and the readers, all worth their while.

Note

1. Here, "journal" is not synonymous with "diary," but rather refers to an academic publication in which scholars and scientists publish systematic studies or reports that have been reviewed by their respective peers.

PUTTING IT ALL TOGETHER

PLANNING, EVALUATION, AND ETHICS OF QUALITATIVE DIARY RESEARCH

DIARY RESEARCH is an unusual qualitative method that can produce extraordinary results. Qualitative diary researchers count on the method itself to offer perspectives on interesting and complex research questions. The measure of success will be different for every diary study. For one project, success might be defined as the discovery of a cache of archival diaries that contain unknown perspectives on a historic event. For another, success might mean gaining new insights into some transitory aspect of the daily experience. Some researchers may deem their project a success in terms of whether the solicited diarists found diary-keeping to be a meaningful personal experience for them. Some will measure their success by whether their final report prompted a positive social change. All diary researchers hoping to develop a successful qualitative diary study will need (1) to have a solid plan for project management, (2) to be aware of potential methodological strengths and weaknesses, and (3) to pay attention to the special ethical considerations in doing qualitative diary research.

Diary Project Planning and Management

As different as one diary study might be from the next, there are some common parts to the whole process of planning and management. Most of these steps are no different than what is done for any other type of research study in the field of human sciences and humanities. It is best to review the whole picture before one embarks on a diary research project. In a nutshell, for both archival and solicited diary studies, there is a pre–data collection phase, a data collection phase, and a post–data collection phase.

Pre–Data Collection Phase

- *Conceptualizing*: Before researchers commit to using a qualitative diary design for their study, they should spend some time conceptualizing and brainstorming about the project. This can be a very active, interactive, and intentional process. For those new to qualitative research design, it might be useful to read about the epistemological underpinnings of qualitative inquiry and how it differs from quantitative approaches (e.g., Lincoln & Guba, 1985; Yilmaz, 2013). Qualitative researchers do not identify their research questions and research design via the more circumscribed path laid out in positivist deductive theory-testing. Qualitative researchers are more likely to explore phenomena at the margins and in unchartered territories. So, as they decide on a research design, qualitative researchers should spend some time exploring, engaging in a discussion of ideas, and not just with the "experts." They will peruse scholarly theoretical pieces, but they will explore popular writing on the subject as well. It is important to read some of the basics about the method, the data it produces, how one works with it, and the philosophy behind the method. If one is using a mixed-method design, one needs to be familiar with the conflicts and compatibilities of the two methodological orientations (qualitative and quantitative).

  This is also a good time for thoughtful personal, methodological, and epistemological reflexivity. Personal reflexivity focuses on what questions one wants to ask and why, what experiences one brings to the table, and what assumptions one already has about the subject matter. Methodological reflexivity focuses on what methods one thinks are appropriate and why it seems a diary might give better-quality information than, say, an interview or a survey; or why a qualitative diary entry seems it will reveal the phenomena better than a quantitative diary entry. There is probably a great answer to both these questions, and advocates for qualitative diary research would surely support a decision to use their method, but it is important to have the answer to these questions thought through, just the same. When the researcher is immersed in data management and coding, it is good to go back and remember why one has chosen to put oneself in this position in the first place! Also, consider whether it is better to solicit new, targeted diaries if possible; or are there archival diaries that will address the research question? Take the time to solicit others' opinions about the design, and draw up some possible diary forms and coding sheets. Imagine what the projected data might end up looking like, and why. Epistemological reflexivity focuses on grander questions of what actually can be known and what one's philosophy of science may be. This may not make it into the report, but it helps to position one's method in the larger picture of human science inquiry.

In addition, think about what resources are needed and available: funding sources, time, research staff, accessible diaries or interested diarists, and outlets for reporting results. If the diaries are archival, where would they be found? How would they be accessed? What form would they be in? If participants will need to be recruited, consider whether there is a good source for outreach to them. What networks could be tapped? What kinds of incentives could be offered for their time? Would travel be necessary? Take a note of the calendar and consider what would be the best timing for starting what can be a substantial commitment of continuous time for researchers and participants alike. What are some possible outlets for any final report, such as a book publisher, a community organization, a government agency, an academic conference, or a peer-reviewed scholarly research journal? It may be useful to discuss ideas with potential stakeholders and readers of any final report.

- *Writing the basic study outline or proposal*: Once one is convinced that a qualitative diary study is feasible and is the best method for their research questions, it is time to commit to a particular plan. At this point, it is essential to compose an outline of the Introduction and a detailed Methods section. This will probably be needed for gaining any necessary approvals before the study starts, as well as for keeping the project on track once it is underway. A well-laid-out design can also help work out (most of) the potential kinks in the research plan before it is underway. Even though qualitative researchers are flexible with changes in design, care should be made in documenting the plan and any changes that happen along the way.
- *Seeking institutional approvals*: The next step is to obtain any approvals necessary for the study. This could begin as much as a year in advance of the study, if not more in some cases. The more institutions and agencies involved, the longer this process will take. Approvals may be needed from overseeing agencies such as human subjects institutional ethical review boards, educational supervisors, project funders, and/or any community or organizational stakeholders. Usually, the basic study outline (described in Chapter 4) will serve as a good start for writing any such proposals.

Data Collection Phase

Sourcing and accessing existing diaries (for archival diary studies). Archival diaries come from libraries, private collections, university research holdings, and online. There is no one story for how an archival researcher sourced their diary data. Electronic storage is increasingly opening up access to more diary data globally, but there is still likely to be substantial footwork involved in obtaining most diary data.

- *Locating diaries:* Certainly, there are some researchers who got involved in diary research because of the fortuitous acquisition of a set of archival diaries at the outset. However, more often, serendipity will not bring a collection of rich diary material to the researcher, so they will instead need to go out and locate the material. It may be buried deep in an archive and only to be found by manual searching onsite, or it may be conveniently indexed and Internet-searchable. Idiosyncrasies of one's particular research questions will dictate the particular strategy for locating material, but strategies may include Internet searches, crowdsourcing, email and postal advertisements to local, regional, and national libraries and archives, and personal outreach to members of historical societies, museums, individual experts, and universities.

- *Seeking additional consent from collection holders:* In addition to institutional consents, there may be informed consents, permissions, and copyright clearances to obtain. In some cases, permissions will need to be granted for access to diaries through estates and lawyers representing the collection (e.g., when in private holdings) before the study is approved by an overseeing agency.

- *Accessing diaries:* Because the archival diary researcher is handling documents that they do not have authority over, they can expect to negotiate with others about when and how access to the diaries. It is important to establish good relationships with any archival staff, who are often pleased to see that someone is interested in their documents. Depending on the location of the diaries, the archival researcher may need to relocate to the archive for an extended period of time to do their research. If the diaries can be removed offsite, this is ideal. There are many international efforts underway to convert written documents in collections around the world into electronic form (Pandey & Misra, 2014), which can allow easier access to documents in remote locations. Often, however, they will only be in physical copies, perhaps microfiche, and rarely can the researcher take these offsite. If digital diaries are not available, they may often be photocopied, photographed, or scanned, which would be very helpful for long-range, offsite writing of an analysis. At a minimum, handwritten transcription and detailed research notes will be essential for those who cannot access the location of diaries on a regular basis. Archival researchers may also wish to use non-diary materials that may be in a different location. Onsite, there is basic etiquette and respect for preservation and protection of the documents. The Society for American Archivists (http://www2.archivists.org/usingarchives/typicalusageguidelines) lists a number of rules researchers will need to respect (Typical Usage Guidelines in Archival Repositories, n.d.):

Registry and personal identification: Many archives ask researchers to fill out an application, registry card, online form, or acquire a researcher card before they begin using materials. The forms typically include name, address, institutional affiliation, materials to be used, and a description of the research project. Photo IDs may also be requested. Such registration practices familiarize the archival staff with the researchers to better serve their research needs and interests, and may also be used to aid a criminal investigation in the event that theft is discovered. Some archives also require a note of recommendation or special permissions before admitting researchers.

Removal of coats and bags: Another method used to discourage theft is requiring that researchers remove bulky outer clothing and store purses, bags, binders, and laptop cases outside of the research area. Many archives have lockers or other monitored areas that researchers can use to store personal possessions. If the only storage option is a nonsecure environment, such as a public coat rack, be sure to remove valuable items like keys and wallets from bags and pockets.

No food, drink, or gum: This guideline is designed to help preserve the collections. Spills can irreparably damage documents or require costly repairs by a conservator. The presence of food may also attract insects or rodents that infest archival materials.

Use of pencil only: This is a preservation practice in case accidental marks are made on archival materials; pencil can be erased while pen marks cannot.

Request forms: Forms are used in a variety of situations, from "call slips" that specify the boxes or books a researcher would like to see, to forms requesting reproductions (such as photocopies). Some forms have very practical uses, like verifying that the correct materials are retrieved, calculating fees, or keeping track of usage for statistical and preservation purposes. By recording exactly which materials were used and by whom, forms can also serve as a theft deterrent. Finally, forms can be useful in notifying the researcher of any legal requirements to take into consideration for how materials are used. Example: Photocopies of unpublished materials provided for a researcher may require additional permissions before they are published. The researcher's signature on the request form indicates that the signer has read and understood these stipulations, and that the archival repository has done its duty informing researchers that those conditions exist.

Gloves: In most cases clean hands free of lotions or perfumes are sufficient for handling materials. Gloves may be necessary for handling objects or photographs in order to protect the materials from the oils and other residues left by hands. The archives should provide gloves if they are required.

Laptops, cell phones, cameras, recorders, and personal scanners: Many archives allow the use of cameras, laptops, and other personal digital devices, but restrictions may exist. Materials may require permissions before they are reproduced, and the lights used by cameras and scanners can cause text and images on documents to fade if they are overexposed. Hence, guidelines in these areas are for security and preservation purposes, as well as for ensuring that all researchers can work in a relatively quiet, distraction-free environment. Archival staff may also ask to inspect any devices researchers bring with them before entering or leaving the research area.

Careful handling and maintaining order: To ensure that materials are maintained for future use, all archives ask researchers to handle materials carefully. While older materials are generally thought to be more fragile, even new materials need to be handled with care so they remain available to the next generation of researchers. Archives may provide specialized tools like book pillows to help preserve materials during use. It is also important that materials remain in the order in which the researcher received them so they can be located later and observed in their proper contexts. Misfiling or changes in order can lead the archival staff to assume that items are missing and inconvenience future researchers. Repositories generally provide place markers to help a researcher keep materials in order and to mark items requested for photocopying. An archive may have additional guidelines like removing one folder from a box at a time, leaving reshelving to archival staff, etc.

It is worth nothing that all of these guidelines are as important for managing one's own documents as for those of a public library or a borrowed private holding. Researchers might establish a similar set of ground rules for any of their own research staff working with the documents as well.

- *Data organization:* The data will then be compiled and organized in preparation for coding and analysis. All diaries will need to be labeled with the source, date, and any other identifying information. If additional supporting documents are accessed, they will need to be part of the indexing system. Researcher notes may be important, and perhaps the only data used for coding and analysis, depending on the restrictiveness of the archival source.

Generating and organizing new diaries (for solicited diary studies). For those who are soliciting their own new research diaries, this is the active data-collection phase.

- *Outreach and recruitment:* If diaries are going to be solicited, the researcher will need to do outreach to find the sample that fits the selection criteria for participants. Additional approvals will be required if going through an organization to solicit diarists (e.g., when going through an institution). Unless the sample is already identified, researchers will need to reach out to potential participants with information on the study so that they can decide if they are interested. This may be through paper fliers, email, social media, mail, phone, or in-person recruitment contacts. Participants need to be given time to decide if they are interested and respond, so initial recruitment letters should describe the topic succinctly, the researchers and their contact information, the timeframe for responding and participation, along with any potential benefits (such as self-knowledge, social change, or monetary incentives), all in a very short paragraph along with where and how to sign up or get more information.

- *Seeking participant informed consent:* Once participants indicate interest (responding via email, phone, etc.), the full informed consent form should be distributed for their perusal. If they are not meeting with the researcher in person, as in the case of an online diary study, they can complete the informed consent form at this point. If, however, they will be meeting with the researchers, the final informed consent and form signatures can be taken care of in person in the instructional phase.

- *Instruction for completing diaries:* Commonly an initial, in-person meeting will occur, either with individual participants or with a group, to go over the diary study instructions. At this time, informed consent forms can be reviewed again and signed. Instructions should include how to complete the forms, what signals making an entry (e.g., after a certain time or event), how diary entries are submitted to the research staff, and how long the diary-keeping phase is to last. It is important to include advice about how to safely store their materials while the study is ongoing and the materials reside in their own home space (whether the entries be handwritten, electronic, video, etc.), given that (unlike most social science research studies) the research materials are not immediately in the protective custody of the researcher. For participants' own safety, if the entries they produce have the potential to cause strife if others have access to them, they may wish to anonymize their diaries as they generate them and keep them in a secure location with lock and key or password-protection. This is the choice and responsibility of each participant, but the importance of considering the security of their diaries should be clearly emphasized. They will also be given information on who to go to with questions, any other resources that are available to them, and how any incentives will be distributed (if applicable).

- *Pre-diary phase*: There are some pre-study measures that will probably be collected for any qualitative diary study, including demographic information and information on the traits of the participants that caused them to meet the selection criteria. Contextualizing phenomena is a hallmark of qualitative design, so a thorough description of the sample is essential. This information is also helpful if attrition—not uncommon in a labor-intensive diary study—is going to be tracked, so researchers can know what kind of participants stopped complying with the participation protocol.

- *Active diary data-collection phase*: At this point, the diary entries are being generated. The researcher will probably check in with participants to see if they have any questions and to ensure participation. Studies in which diaries are submitted regularly and in which there is consistent and regular contact with the researcher encourage greater participation and retention of participants. Some studies use strategic incentivizing such that rewards are given for each diary or each day/week, etc., of participation.

- *Data organization:* The data will need to be compiled and organized in preparation for coding and analysis. The plan for data organization will be spelled out as much as possible in the basic project outline, but there are likely to be nuanced aspects of data management that cannot be anticipated ahead of time. Generally, the diaries need to be anonymized and indexed, date and time stamped, matched to participant demographic information and any pre- or post-diary documents, transcribed as applicable, and safely stored.

- *Wrap-up and debriefing:* Once the diary-keeping phase is over, there may be a final collection of materials, sometimes in person, either with individual participants or with a group of participants. There may be post-study measures to be collected and debriefing forms and procedures. There may be additional background information about any changes to participants' situation or demographics. Are there any questions that were not asked, and were realized afterwards—such as demographics, unexplored content areas, or other questions (as long as approved by any institutional research oversight agency)? Researchers may also seek feedback about the process. Looking back over the process, were there complications or comments they would like to make about their participation? If a post-study individual interview or focus group needs to be run, it can be helpful to do that when final incentives are disbursed, and debriefing and resource forms may be distributed.

Post–Data Collection Phase

- *Analysis and Report Writing:* The next step is the analysis and writing up of the report, alone or with a research team. At this point, archival researchers will most likely be done with orienting themselves in the collection, or the solicited diary participants will most likely be done generating entries. If research assistants are included in the process of coding, they will need to be trained and brought up to speed on the methods and content of the diaries. Analysis and writing are quite elaborate, given the complexity of any diary data set. The amount of time to work through the data might be equal to or exceed the time spent up until this point. Dissemination/application/ theoretical contribution plan: Reconsider the publication outlet considered prior to beginning of the study. Is the initial publication plan still a suitable goal, given the way the project is unfolding? Do other publication outlets need to be considered? What will happen with the final project and results; how will the results be used (inform theorists, activism, public policy?) For applied projects and action research, it may be important to consult with members of the community, stakeholders, and the diarists themselves when making decisions about sharing results.
- *Data archiving:* At the conclusion of the study, after analysis and report writing, the diaries may be returned to participants, retained in a research archive (e.g. in a university), or destroyed depending on the research plan and any institutional requirements. Again, members of the community, stakeholders, and the diarists themselves may

be included in such decisions. Any changes to pre-approved protocols for dispersing, archiving, or destroying of diaries and diary coding files would need to be approved by participants and the IRB overseeing the project.

Methodological Strengths and Weaknesses of Diary Research

General Strengths of the Diary Method as a Qualitative Research Method

Qualitative diary research is a unique tool with strengths that set it apart from other ways of exploring phenomena. Whether in its historic or contemporary form, the diary prioritizes the centrality of daily experience and the transitory minutiae of how we think, feel, and act. The diary is an antidote to psychological and sociological conceptions of human personality and behavior as predetermined constants locked-in by one's personal traits or secured by one's status in the social structure. The perspective offered through the diary serves to destabilize these constants (e.g., self-esteem, pain, satisfaction in the workplace) and reveals their transitory nature. In addition, the diary entry exposes the intersectionality of an individual by group, by context, and by time. This has been echoed by many. For instance, Allport (1942) emphasized that "Personal document items in a life are put together as and when the subject sees them to belong together" (p. 145). For Terman (1934) "a true personality cannot be pieced together from any number of test scores. . . . The total is organisimic, not an additive total" (p. 609). Similarly, Wiseman, Conteh, and Matovu (2005) advised, "In many instances, simple 'snap shots' of behaviour can be misleading. Diaries can also help to place events in a broader social, economic and political context" (p. 395). A collection of diary entries can reveal how unreliable and complex cause-and-effect predictions are in the life of an individual. Moreover, diary data can help bridge the gap between, on one hand, the proceedings of everyday experience, behavior, and choices, and on the other hand, global measures of mental health and adjustment. As Cantor and colleagues (1991) explained of the "interactionist mandate":

> A critical issue when studying personality and daily life experience is to find units of analysis that simultaneously reflect

the personality of the individual and the features of the life context in which daily life experience takes shape. (p. 425)

Without the ability to count repetitive behaviors in daily entries, such as tallying routine chores, individual foods eaten, and steps taken in a day, there are many phenomena, such as domestic labor, quality of diet, and activity level, for which we could never get the big picture. These little details of the context, timing, and frequency of behaviors can reveal so much about our lives and lifestyles that we would not otherwise keep track of.

Diary data also feature what some non-Western cultures and philosophies have emphasized—the preeminence of the immediate moment that Western psychologies have slowly moved away from in favor of psychological constants (Dewey, 1986; Kabat-Zinn, 2003). At a most basic level, entries in a diary are descriptions of phenomena locked in the present moment. They reveal phenomena as they occupy our most immediate conscious attention. A century ago, there were some voices in the Western human sciences attempting to address this, such as mid-century president of the American Psychological Association, John Dewey, who argued for a need to focus on "this individual thing existing here and now with all the unrepeatable particularities that accompany and mark such existences" (Dewey, 1986, p. 181). Diaries help reveal this desirable, Eastern concept of human existence promoted as the "present moment" by Kabat-Zinn (2012), the "nonillusory present" by Borkovec (2002), and the "now moment" by Stern (2004).

Finally, diary research is a versatile, fairly nonintrusive way to obtain very valuable data. From a programmatic research perspective, it can contribute to theory-building alone or in combination with other more typical retrospective methods when researchers are looking to use mixed methods in strategies of triangulation. From an applied perspective, it can be used to evaluate and design successful community programming and policy development.

General Weaknesses of the Diary Method as a Qualitative Diary Research Method

The method has some weaknesses. In contrast to the qualitative interview or observational methods, the participants for most types of diary studies must be fairly literate, although video, audio, and visual methods accommodate different literacies. Diarists must be fairly self-regulating or have someone who can assist them with following a diary-keeping protocol.

In addition, the ironic twist with this method is that the secretive nature of "diary keeping" so familiar to the general public is really not what happens in a diary study. For most designs, the diary keeping is not personal, private, and secret, but rather is written for a researcher. This makes the secretive name "diary" somewhat contrived in a diary study because the diarist knows there is a future audience. This is even the case with many archival diaries as well, when the diarist half-expects their writing to be read in the future. Again, using the interview as a comparison, diary research is quite different—an interview is obviously an interaction. The information shared is not construed as audience-free.

Diaries can also produce their own side effects. These side effects are not necessarily bad, but they can affect the phenomena the researcher is interested in studying. Diary keeping about daily events has some of the therapeutic benefits purported of "mindfulness," slowing down and disentangling affective, cognitive, and behavior responses as diarists reflexively engage in reconstructions of the day's experiences (e.g., Wheeler & Reis, 1991). The introspective self-monitoring can also artificially accentuate emotions, encourage rumination, alter self-awareness, affect thoughts and feelings, and interfere with daily life tasks. Furthermore, diary surveillance (by the researcher who will ultimately read the diarists' entries) creates a sense of accountability in day-to-day life that can create experimenter demand (such that participants begin performing and then writing entries about things they think the researchers would like to see) or self-presentation concerns (such that participants write entries about themselves in a way that puts them in a better light).

There is also a cultural lens in measuring phenomena by individuals writing about their lives. The diary method emphasizes individualistic values of self-focus, introspection, and self-as-subject. Diary keeping may be inconsistent with cultures that are non-documenting and cultures that follow oral traditions. In addition, in some cultures, diaries and private self-reflective rumination are inconsistent with certain social roles—such as in the United States, where the keeping of a diary has been viewed at times as somewhat of a feminine and juvenile activity.

Specific Design Issues and Strengths in Qualitative Diary Research

Individual diary studies have their own strengths and weaknesses. Some issues are the result of an oversight in the design, some are only a problem due to resource limitations, and still others are a problem because of the nature of diary research (Mackrill, 2008). Table 5.1 highlights some of the most common weaknesses and strengths across the three phases of diary research. Researchers can look ahead to this list and work to amend or address these design issues, when possible, before they begin. For reviewers, this list can provide a rubric for evaluating and strengthening diary research under scrutiny.

To minimize some of the issues in the pre–data collection phase, researchers should be sure to "do their homework." Most researchers are not well trained in qualitative methods and assume they can just dive right in. Although qualitative research is definitely more accessible in many ways, it has a cohesive epistemological foundation and one that is quite different from that of traditional positivistic science. Related to this is the struggle that some researchers may have in their review of past literature. The tendency for qualitative researchers to craft lightweight introductions to their investigations does not mean that they are naïve about related research on their topic. Knowing the extant research on the topic is not a detriment in designing a more exploratory study, as long as the researcher does not mold their own research design strictly around existing models. An open mind is important in qualitative research; however, one should not turn to a qualitative diary study to get raw daily experiences of a phenomenon without knowledge of other approaches that might be more efficient or appropriate. It could be frustrating when a particular data collection method, research question, or relevant theoretical orientation is discovered but not until after an elaborate diary study is already designed, conducted, and in the process of being analyzed.

It is also important to think about where any reports on the study are destined to go. Waiting until the manuscript is written to decide where to submit it is a particularly bad move in qualitative research, because qualitative work tends to be more methodologically and topically interdisciplinary. Although there are more and

Table 5.1

Weaknesses and Strengths in Archival and Solicited Diary Studies

Design Weaknesses in the Pre-Data Collection Phase	Design Strengths in the Pre-Data Collection Phase
Researcher has limited understanding of their own epistemological assumptions and does not adequately position themselves reflexively in the qualitative inquiry/ quantitative inquiry debate	Researcher has a solid understanding of their own epistemological assumptions and reflexively considers their project, their research questions, and their method in light of their position
Researcher does not adequately review past research on the topic, or in contrast, allows past research to constrain their approach to the topic	Researcher has thorough understanding of past research and theory on topic but does not allow it to restrict their openness to new perspectives
Researcher does not carefully consider the eventual reporting outlets for the project	Researcher considers possible reporting outlets so the project is relevant to their audience
Researcher does not adequately seek perspectives from stakeholders, networks for diaries/diarists, or funding and project support	Researcher seeks multiple perspectives, taps stakeholders and networks for source materials or participants, and secures adequate support
Design Weaknesses in the Data Collection Phase	**Design Strengths in the Data Collection Phase**
Researcher has trouble accessing diaries or soliciting diarists, hence the sample of diaries is not as rich as intended	Researcher succeeds in obtaining a rich set of diary materials or a good source of solicited diarists
The archival or solicited diarists are not very diverse with regard to characteristics that would enhance conclusions from the project, or not homogeneous enough on relevant characteristics	The archival or solicited diarists are as diverse as possible with regard to characteristics that would enhance conclusions from the project and homogeneous enough on relevant characteristics

Table 5.1
Continued

Diaries contain irrelevant information, not related to the topic of interest, or the diary forms do not function as expected, or participants are not following protocol	Archival diary entries have substantial relevant content, the entries get at the core of the issues of interest, and solicited diary participants have diligently recorded entries according to protocol
Entries not carefully organized; authors, dates, or accompanying materials are poorly indexed	Entries are carefully organized; authors, dates, or accompanying materials are properly indexed
Transcription and anonymizing of entries results in excessive amounts of words that are not identifiable and references that are either too revealing or taken too much out of context	Thorough transcription of entries with majority of incomprehensible words resolved and name and place references sufficiently anonymized in a manner so as not to detract from their relevance
Design Weaknesses in the Post-Data Collection Phase	**Design Strengths in the Post-Data Collection Phase**
Researcher misinterpretation due to lack of information, unknown or misunderstood cultural references	Researcher recognizes and attempts to address potential for interpretation issues due to lack of awareness of full intent of diarist
Fatigue or resource limitations lead researcher to cease coding before the richness of the diary data is adequately explored	Researcher thoroughly codes and analyzes all data across diarists and over time, doing justice to the rich data set produced in diary research
Researcher reflexivity is insufficient with regard to design, process, and/or participant feedback	Researcher reflexivity is sufficient with regard to design, process, and/or participant feedback

more qualitative and interdisciplinary journals, there may be other journals that are good content fits, and knowing that is the goal ahead of time may mean including additional measures or exploring additional aspects of an experience so that it answers questions of interest to that audience.

An additional consideration in the pre–data collection phase is with regard to networking and resource seeking. Diary research is not a quick pop-in/pop-out method. It takes substantial time commitments from the participants and the researcher. Failing to explore the issue with stakeholders may mean leaving gaps in possible design, source materials, and content that would have otherwise been so helpful to understanding the issue. More resources could enable more data collection from each participant or from different participants, more time with each person (longitudinal), triangulation of data from other voices or sources on the issue or topic, and the grounded-theory ideal of saturation (a thorough and exhaustive exploration of the issue from all possible perspectives; Strauss & Corbin, 1997). Diary research is not necessarily expensive, but it does take substantial resources of time, so the more support a researcher has for a diary study, the stronger it will be.

There are several challenges in the phase of actual data collection. A good diary project requires rich diary data. Archival researchers, for instance, may not know how rich their source materials will be until they are immersed in a collection. The hope is that the entries will speak to the issue of interest and provide entries that are directly related to the issue, but also diverse in content or voice. The same is true for solicited diary studies. It is so important to have as many dedicated diarists as one intended in the proposal, that the diarists are interested in participating and have the relevant experiences to write about, and that they are diverse in background in a way that might contribute to the depth and breadth of conclusions made.

For both archival and solicited diary studies, the large amount of data that may come rolling in needs to be carefully and painstakingly organized and indexed—the more diaries and the longer-running the study is, the more data there are to keep in order. Decisions will need to be made about whether to keep partial data from some participants who inconsistently make their entries, creating a variation on the intended protocol.

Once the data are in, researchers need to take care to transcribe and anonymize the data. One issue that is presented is how to anonymize without losing the information. This is a judgment call for each researcher and each project. In some cases, the diarists are not anonymous, so the main issue in transcribing is to accurately decipher materials. In the case of anonymous diaries, changing names of participants is easy enough; however, decisions about how to change occupations, geographical locations, institutional references, and names of public figures are more difficult to make. The researcher wants to retain the context and spirit of comments; however, some of that will be lost in the necessary anonymizing of the documents.

The approach to data interpretation depends on the epistemological framework of a diary study. There will be researchers who follow a realist perspective, taking the diary entries as statements of fact or truth. There will also be researchers who will follow a phenomenological or social constructionist perspective and will be more concerned about the symbolism and discourse in and of itself. However, regardless of their approach, generally researchers will want to understand something of the intention of the diarist. All researchers can do is try their best to understand the meaning of the entries as the diarist intended them. The researcher's understanding prevails, because, unlike in a more interactive design such as an interview, a diary researcher cannot easily ask a quick follow-up or ask for clarification.

Because diary studies are labor-intensive and can span over an extended time period, participants' efforts may wax and wane. Problems with diarists not getting really invested in the project, under-rapport, lack of trust, and discomfort with openness can inhibit participation. As a result, they may "fake" data, record it at a time not indicated as part of the protocol, or engage in a "response set," entering a "pat" answer to day after day of diary prompts. They may not want to share some of the very information the researcher is looking for—as de Beauvoir's (1967) diarist mused, "What an odd thing a diary is: the things you omit are more important than those you put in" (p. 130). Some of this can be prevented by maintaining a good rapport with participants. For example, the more trust, openness, and interaction that solicited diarists have with the researcher running the study, the better they will be able to discuss and handle any difficulties they are having with the protocol.

There are also a few interpretation issues that can happen beyond the awareness of the participant and the researcher. For example, participants may unconsciously fall prey to experimenter demand and write about *and even engage in life experiences* that they think the researcher wishes to hear about. Related to this, in studies using diary recording to evaluate interventions, sometimes the diary itself has palliative qualities and can improve participants' well-being, irrespective of any effects of the intervention under study.

All of these issues present challenges when the researcher begins to read through the diaries for coding and analysis. Not until coding may the researchers notice that some questions should have been worded differently or asked in a different order. Even after coding, researchers may realize that the coding framework could have incorporated different themes or been approached with a particular preexisting framework or a different epistemological orientation entirely. Researchers who are sifting through extensive diary entries will struggle, not only with confusing or "suspicious" data, but also with the sheer volume. They will often face tough decisions due to time constraints over how much data to give full analysis and attention to. Sometimes diary entries about which researchers are confused or skeptical will simply be eliminated, but they must expect to make unanticipated decisions on the spot about how to manage the whole set of diaries. Some of these decisions come at the point of writing up the final study, and some beforehand.

Once most of the report is being composed, the researcher should return to engage in the personal and methodological reflexivity that they began with and contemplate how the study turned out. Did they learn what they expected? Did the procedure go along well? Did they gather good diary entries and analyze them as anticipated? Qualitative research should be carefully evaluated just as any research should, but not in an identical way. As Johnson (2015) said:

> Positivists have deployed criteria to evaluate their research that centre on particular conceptions of validity and reliability to ensure "scientific" rigour . . . . Whilst such criteria may be eminently appropriate for the evaluation of

hypothetico-deductive research—this patently in not the case for qualitative research. (p. 320)

So how do we evaluate the validity of a qualitative diary study? The more reflexive a qualitative researcher is, the more they will understand their phenomena and their own role in bringing the phenomena to light through the diary entries. It is ultimately the researchers themselves—their ideas, their compilation of the data, and their insights into themes that lie within it—that contribute to knowledge generation. Critical anthropologist Edith Turner (1993) provides one of the most thorough descriptions of the reflexive process from start to finish:

> The first need then, as ever, is to sink oneself in the society. . . . Then note the circumstances when one slips in and out of familiarity; use all possible means to situate and contextualize others as they experience feelings . . . ; reflect back on all one feels and sees . . . write one's own story by means of a narrative, along with other people's accounts of the events and how those accounts affect one, one's own memories and knowledge, their memories and knowledge . . . be faithful to the order in which things occurred to one, so that the whole will have organic coherence and so that insights will be true ones. Thus the art of writing will render the instrument transparent so that all concerned will have a sense of recognition, both those who originally experienced those events and the readers. (p. 47)

Common Evaluative Terminology Applied to Qualitative Diary Research

In evaluating diary research, many of the same criteria used for evaluation of other qualitative projects apply (Cho & Trent, 2014; Guba & Lincoln, 1994; Seale, 1999; Johnson, 1997; Johnson, 2015; Sandelowski, 1986). Some dimensions used in evaluating qualitative research have been borrowed from the quantitative sciences, such as the concept of *validity,* which has many variants now in both the qualitative genre and in the quantitative sciences from which the term is borrowed. Other dimensions of quality are unique to qualitative research, such as the concept of member checking. Following is a range of criteria by which a qualitative diary study can be evaluated with regard to its overall quality:

- *Credibility:* Credibility focuses on the authenticity, descriptive validity, fidelity, and dependability of the diarist's telling and the researcher's retelling of phenomena of interest. Authenticity is both enhanced and called into question by the very nature of the form itself. There are many who feel that it is the mere act of private writing, rather than the outcome of writing, that contributes to self-understanding. As Oliver Sacks (2016) explains:

  > I started keeping journals when I was fourteen and at last count had nearly a thousand. . . . The act of writing is itself enough; it serves to clarify my thoughts and feelings. . . . But for the most part, I rarely look at the journals I have kept for the greater part of a lifetime. The act of writing is an integral part of my mental life; ideas emerge, are shaped, in the act of writing. My journals are not written for others, nor do I usually look at them myself, but they are a special, indispensable form of talking to myself. (p. 380)

  More precisely, Toni Morrison (2015) describes that it is the *safe space* provided by the medium that contributes its self-revelatory potential:

  > The writing is—I'm free from pain. It's the place where I live; it's where I have control; it's where nobody tells me what to do; it's where my imagination is fecund and I am really at my best. Nothing matters more in the world or in my body or anywhere when I'm writing. It is dangerous because I'm thinking up dangerous, difficult things, but it is also extremely safe for me to be in that place. (p. 1)

  Others have pointed out the potential for self-deception to occur in narrating the self. For example, Lalonde (2016) suggests that diary writing encourages a deceptive self-absorption:

If we consider the example of Tolstoy keeping two diaries, one for himself—locked up in a drawer—and one for his nosy wife to peruse, then it is clear that fiction exists in so-called factional intimate literature, such as diaries, journals, memoirs, and autobiographies. Even if intimate literature may appear closer to the truth, it does contain strands of fiction, just as life does. . . . After all, narrative does not simply capture aspects of the self for description; it builds the self as it relates stories about the self. (p. 4)

Likewise, Watson (2016) suggests that there are three ways in which "the diary . . . seeks to persuade readers of its authenticity while simultaneously calling its own veracity into doubt" (p. 108). First, it is a private document, giving the impression of more honesty, yet an audience is probably in the diarist's consciousness. Second, a diary's mere existence—the document with its diligent documentation of specific moments—gives credence to the experiences, yet individual entries may be fantasy or fabrication (e.g., the infamous forged "Hitler Diaries"). Third, the immediacy of the documentation implies that any problems of memory distortions that come from a retelling of long-distant moments are corrected; however, this is only a matter of degree, as immediate perception and short-term memory also have their limitations.

There are other issues of credibility related to the researchers as well, for they must reduce and retell on behalf of their diarists. Does the researcher take care in describing the diarist's expressions in the diarist's own words? To what extent is the researcher describing the feelings and emotions of the participant's experiences in a faithful manner? Are the researcher's descriptions of or themes developed to classify the phenomena described in the diaries recognized by those who share the same experience? Credibility is enhanced when researchers provide quotes or extracts from diary entries to illustrate their themes, and when researchers use semantic labels for their themes that are as close as possible to participants' own conceptualizations and/or words. Others can also judge the quality of the researcher's work through *auditing* (someone external to the project reviews the diary data, the research process, and/or research report conclusions) and *intercoder reliability* (whereby more people than just the researcher analyze and code the content of the diary entries to corroborate conclusions). One can also support credibility with a query of participants and other stakeholders who validate the themes, the process called member checking. This is questionable, though, in cases where researchers' conceptions of phenomena become too abstracted from diarists' experiences for participants to be able to confirm their conclusions. As Cope (2014) warns:

> Such an approach is, however, problematic because the participants and the researcher will, to a greater or lesser degree, have different agendas and perspectives. A completed research study will, to some extent, conflate the accounts of all participants in order to obtain saturation of categories and should provide a shift from substantive situations to a more generalized and theoretical discussion of their underpinning concepts. Sandelowski (1993), for example, comments that, within her own work, she found that participants may have possessed a greater interest in their own substantive situation than in any abstract synthesis of their own accounts with those of others. Morse (1998) argues that, as theory is developed from a synthesis of the perspectives of a number of participants, it is inappropriate to expect that individual participants will have the ability to validate the findings of the research study as a whole. For the foregoing reasons, it may be inappropriate to return the findings from a study to participants for comment, in order to obtain participant validation. (p. 90)

The researcher will need to determine in each project whether their final analysis of a set of diaries is so far removed that member checks may not be possible. There are other dimensions for which highly abstracted reports can be evaluated, such as *interpretive validity*, which refers to the accuracy of the qualitative researcher's analytical interpretations and coding of the participants' expression; and *theoretical validity*, or whether the account contributes to and fits with the theory developed from it. Both of these are evaluated through an internal comparison between the diary entries presented in the report and the researcher's theorizing from the diaries.

- *Transparency:* A good research process is systematic and transparent. Of course, transparency as a criterion for quality implies an audience *to be transparent to* (including the researchers, diarists, and readers). Therefore, transparency is especially important at the write-up. More precise terminology in qualitative research over the last several decades has helped qualitative researchers better describe their methods and has helped improve transparency. In order to be transparent about one's research process, however, significant notes as one goes along will help immensely, as there may be a series of contingent decisions, the reasoning for which may swiftly be forgotten. A qualitative diary study has good transparency if the whole procedure, from participant outreach, to data organization, to all the steps in coding, is described in detail, each and every step of the way. This is related to the concept of *confirmability,* which refers to the degree to which—if someone walked through all steps of the current study, including the pre–data collection conceptualizing, the organization of the study's data, the coding of the set of diaries, and the eventual report writing—they would be able to confirm that the process the researcher described is accurate. Of course, it is difficult to imagine many diary researchers as being able to find someone to evaluate their entire research process, especially given the large amount of diary entries that can be generated. Therefore, the researcher can walk their audience through this to some degree, by carefully describing how conclusions and interpretations were established, and exemplifying that the findings were derived directly from the data.
- *Utility and application: Application* or *utility* refers to how much social relevance the study has and how it makes new contributions to a topic. Although a diary study can contribute so much to description—and merely digesting

and processing private diary entries and putting them in public view is a transformation of sorts—it is necessary to make the case for the utility of the exercise. A strong archival diary study that explores archival diaries, no matter how obscure, will make a case for their theoretical, historical, or social import. Similarly, a strong solicited diary study must show social relevance. This is not to say that a very small event or obscure phenomena would have no value on other dimensions; however, the effort and resources involved make measurements of the usefulness of the findings worth consideration. If a study falls short in regard to its utility and application, it is most often a case of underdeveloped thinking and framing on the part of the researcher, for there may always be an audience interested in the perspectives offered by even the remotest and most marginalized of diarists.

Special Ethical Considerations in Qualitative Diary Research

As a final topic for discussion, the uniqueness of diary research raises equally unique ethical considerations. After a short review of the basic ethical considerations for human subjects research in general and qualitative research in particular, some of the unique concerns raised in diary research will be addressed. There are ethical review boards and policies that speak to the specific guidelines a research study is bound by that are disciplinary, institutional, national, and international. This review is not exhaustive, but rather serves as a short primer for evaluating the ethics of qualitative diary research.

There are international standards for ethics that have been developed out of a concern for biomedical and psychological research subjects. There are some basic similarities in the ethical guidelines in that they aim to protect the agency, the well-being, and the rights of research participants. The Declaration of Helsinki (GAWMA, 2014) was inspired by concerns similar to those addressed in the policy adopted in the United States' Belmont Report (National Commission for the Protection of Human Subjects of Biomedical and Behavioral Research, 1978), which emphasizes three fundamental principles of respect for persons, beneficence, and justice. Individual societies and professional organizations have their own as well, such as the American Psychological Association, which provides more details on what participants should be informed of in the consent procedure (www.APA.org):

- The purpose, duration, and procedures of the research
- Their rights to decline to participate and to withdraw from the research once it has started
- The factors that may influence their willingness to participate
- Any risks, discomfort, or adverse effects
- Any prospective research benefits
- Any researcher-provided incentives for participation
- The limits of confidentiality in data transcribing, coding, sharing, archiving, disposing
- Whom participants can contact with questions

There are also some additional special considerations with regard to qualitative data. In fact, the Belmont Committee has been taken to task for failing to adequately address the unique ethical considerations that need to be addressed in a range of human subjects research protocols such as in qualitative sociological and humanities research (e.g., Thomson et al., 2006). The ethics standards were by and large developed with assumptions of biomedical, psychotherapeutic, and behavioral-experimental research designs, with little attention given to research methods of a more naturalistic and qualitative orientation. Some of what makes qualitative research so appealing is the lesser need for deception (as used in many experimental designs) and the less-invasive methods; however, there are some special parts of the qualitative design that introduce special, more nuanced ethical concerns that researchers need to be aware of and sensitive to.

For one thing, the methods are often more personal. Although many qualitative researchers take pride in their rejection of a cold-hearted Scantron form and the poking and prodding from a distant researcher, the personal nature of qualitative methods makes them in some ways more intrusive. Diary methods, in particular, are more intrusive still, given that the data collection takes place in the everyday world of the participant and is given a very familiar and private name—"diary"—often stationed in its familiar location on the bedside table. In their article reflecting on the ethics of diary research, appropriately titled "'I'm Really Embarrassed That You're Going to Read This . . .': Reflections on Using Diaries in Qualitative Research," Day and Thatcher (2009) point out that the diary writer is thinking of their audience when they write and process daily life events—so much so, that the researcher is essentially and perhaps arrogantly inserted their outsiders gaze into the very private and personal ruminations of a participant. So, a day in the life of participant X is actually now a day in the life of X with researcher Y in tow. This may even affect what experiences participants seek out, not to mention what they may write about.

Furthermore, there may also be expectations on the part of the diarists that social change will result from their participation. Researchers doing applied research should be clear about what the diary study can and cannot do in the effort toward social change, so that participants do not put themselves at undue risk toward their own personal goals of affecting an institutional outcome.

Participants may even erroneously assume that a study is applied and that researchers have goals for social change when that is not the express purpose of the project. Such assumptions can impact their willingness to participate and influence what they share in their diaries. An additional risk is related to unintended audiences. Specifically, participants need to be careful not to have their diary unsecured if information in the entries could put their relationships, reputation, or livelihood at risk. For example, in a drug-use study, Singer and colleagues (2000) reported, "One participant was arrested while in possession of his diary, which contained potentially incriminating information. This led us to change our procedures to retain each day's diary entry and to request participants to delete specific locational references" (p. 1052). Related to this are concerns over appropriating others' personal stories and the importance of "responsible speaking" (Alcoff, 1991). When researchers take stories of private lives and share those accounts in a public forum, they have many responsibilities. In the case of archival data, the diarists themselves may not have had a say in whether they are in a study, though their trust or collections holder may. For such private and personal diaries, the writers probably did not assume they were writing to an audience of a modern-day academic researcher. How does one negotiate that? How does one respect the privacy of writing when one may reveal the writers and all their once-private conceits? The answers to these questions are idiosyncratic to each study, each subject, and each diarist.

There are very different concerns for the solicited diary study, foremost of which is to protect anonymity and confidentiality, which can be difficult given the "thick description" that comes with diary writing. In both archival and solicited diary research, there are many concerns about confidentiality. Care should be taken, as most archival diary collections are kept in a locked, supervised space. For solicited diaries, the data are in the protection of participants while in their control (at home or online), so advising participants about where to keep them can be helpful. Data will need to be anonymized with care to fully protect the identity of participants. This can be especially important if the community is tight-knit, and the research staff may even include its members, which is not uncommon in qualitative research.

Furthermore, there are two issues with regard to what is viewed as a hallmark of qualitative research—honoring the "layperson's" wisdom and entering into the study of a phenomenon with a child's eye view open and unassuming. When it comes to diary research, a naïve solicited diary recruit is given a good deal of agency over sharing as part of the research. They may not exactly imagine how their text could be presented in a research forum. They may not realize how they will feel about having shared intimate details with a researcher. Essentially, they may not know what they are getting themselves into in producing regular documents on their life, how it might change them, what they might realize, and how this will become data and the focus of academic discourse or community activism. On the flip side, if qualitative researchers are working true to the principles of this mode of inquiry, they will be equally naïve about the phenomena because they are exploring new territory. They may get access to a population and exposure to an issue, bringing the participant with them, both somewhat unaware of what they are getting themselves into. The best solution to this is to acknowledge these shortcomings at the outset and practice careful observance of ethical guidelines.

When the diary topic is one of socio-emotional significance, there are numerous delicate issues that may be raised. For one, regularly documenting emotional topics can make them more potent, as the diarist becomes more aware of the regularity of the phenomena. What does this mean for their relationships with the people in their lives, and what does this mean for their relationship with the researcher they entrusted with their potentially effusive diary entries? While there is no one answer and no one way to navigate such challenges, there are some important things the researcher can and should do in such cases. Begin any potentially emotionally charged diary study with rapport building, then engage in regular check-ins. In addition, provide resources for participants, so that if issues come up, they have proper outlets to turn to *besides the researcher.* There can be some amount of bonding with the researcher, the research team, and other participants, so it is important at the close of the study to attend to potential feelings of loss and abandonment. Ending the project with focus groups and supportive community networking can help. A post-diary questionnaire in which the researcher asks participants to share any new self-knowledge or new social knowledge can help with the process. Finally, since the participants may walk away from the study handing over as much as a month's or a year's worth of personal narrative, it is important to maintain open channels of communication for some time after the conclusion of the study, in the event that they wish to reach out with questions, clarifications, or reflections about the project.

In conclusion, there are enormous benefits to conducting a qualitative diary study. It can produce very detailed, exhaustive, unusual data and a wealth of material for the researcher and their audience. The mere mention of an "audience" in the context of the diary is an obvious oxymoron, a testament to the oddness of diary research and a caution for researchers who wish to do justice to the method, as well as to the diarist. Echoing a longstanding cultural maxim, American humorist David Sedaris cautions, "If you read someone else's diary, you get what you deserve." Diary researchers are breaking away from this cultural etiquette, *though with permission*, and they are headed straight to where others have known better than to tread. The result of this unconventional foray into the personal musings of the diarist can be to unlock a wealth of information that might otherwise remain untapped.

REFERENCES

Abdelouahab, F. (2005). *Journeys and Journals: Five Centuries of Travel Writing* (J. Sims, Trans.). Dayton, OH: Kubik Publishing.

Affleck, G., Tennen, H., Urrows, S., Higgins, P., Abeles, M., Hall, C., & Newton, C. (1998). Fibromyalgia and women's pursuit of personal goals: A daily process analysis. *Health Psychology, 17*(1), 40–47. http://dx.doi.org/10.1037/0278-6133.17.1.40

Agnew, V. (1999). Dissecting the cannibal: Comparing the function of the autopsy principle in the diaries and narratives of Cook's second voyage. In R. Langford & R. West (Eds.), *Marginal Voices, Marginal Forms: Diaries in European Literature and History* (pp. 50–61). Amsterdam, Netherlands: Rodopi.

Ahmadi, N. S., Månsson, J., Lindblad, U., & Hildingh, C. (2014). Breathlessness in everyday life from a patient perspective: A qualitative study using diaries. *Palliative & Supportive Care, 12*(03), 189–194.

Alcoff, L. (1991). The problem of speaking for others. *Cultural Critique,* (20), 5–32.

Allport, G. W. (1942). The use of personal documents in psychological science. *Social Science Research Council Bulletin, 49,* xix + 210.

American Social History Project. (2017). Retrieved on January 1, 2017 from https://ashp.cuny.edu/

Anderson, J. (1971). Space-time budgets and activity studies in urban geography and planning. *Environment & Planning A, 3*(4), 353–368. doi:10.1068/a030353

Anderson, S. M., & Muñoz Proto, C. (2016). Ethical requirements and responsibilities in video methodologies: Considering confidentiality and representation in social justice research. *Social & Personality Psychology Compass, 10*(7), 377–389. doi:10.1111/spc3.12259

Angenot, V. (2014). Semiotics and hermeneutics. In M. K. Hartwig (Ed.), *A Companion to Ancient Egyptian Art* (pp. 98–119). New York: Wiley.

Aono, Y., & Kazui, K. (2008). Phenological data series of cherry tree flowering in Kyoto, Japan, and its application to reconstruction of springtime temperatures since the 9th century. *International Journal of Climatology, 28*(7), 905–914.

Applegate, D. (2016). From academic historian to popular biographer: Musings on the practical poetics of biography. In H. Renders, B. de Haan, & J. Harmsma (Eds.), *The Biographical Turn: Lives in History* (pp. 186–194). New York: Routledge.

Baddeley, J. L., Daniel, G. R., & Pennebaker, J. W. (2011). How Henry Hellyer's use of language foretold his suicide. *Crisis, 32*, 288–292. http://dx.doi.org/10.1027/0227-5910/a000092

Bailey, K. M. (1991). Diary studies of classroom language learning: The doubting game and the believing game. In E. Sadtono (Ed.), *Language Acquisition and the Second/Foreign Language Classroom. Anthology Series 28* (pp. 64–65). Singapore: SEAMEO Regional Language Center.

Bailey, K. M., & Ochsner, R. (1983). A methodological review of the diary studies: Windmill tilting or social science. *Second Language Acquisition Studies, 31*, 188–198.

Ball, S. J. (1981). *Beachside Comprehensive: A Case-Study of Secondary Schooling.* New York: Cambridge University Press.

Ballantyne, R., Hansford, B., & Packer, J. (1995). Mentoring beginning teachers: A qualitative analysis of process and outcomes. *Educational Review, 47*(3), 297–307. http://dx.doi.org/10.1080/0013191950470306

Barthes, R. (1987). *Criticism and Truth.* Minneapolis, MN: University of Minnesota Press.

Beal, D. J., & Weiss, H. M. (2003). Methods of ecological momentary assessment in organizational research. *Organizational Research Methods, 6*(4), 440–464.

Beckers, R., van der Voordt, T., & Dewulf, G. (2016). Why do they study there? Diary research into students' learning space choices in higher education. *Higher Education Research & Development, 35*(1), 142–157. http://dx.doi.org/10.1080/07294360.2015.1123230

Beller, M. (2015). How not to write a biography . . . perhaps: A preface. *Psychological Perspectives, 58*(1), 95–102.

Ben-Ari, A., & Lavee, Y. (2007). The effect of security-related stress on dyadic closeness among Jews and Arabs in Israel: A daily diary study. *Family Process, 46*(3), 381–393. doi:10.1111/j.1545-5300.2007.00218.x

Berelson, B. (1952). *Content Analysis in Communications Research.* Glencoe, IL: Free Press.

Beresford, P., & Wallcroft, J. (1997). Psychiatric system survivors and emancipatory research: issues, overlaps survivors and emancipatory research: issues, overlaps and differences. In Doing Disability Research (eds C. Barnes & G. Mercer), pp. 67–87. Leeds: Disability Press.

Berg, M., & Düvel, C. (2012). Qualitative media diaries: An instrument for doing research from a mobile media ethnographic perspective. *Interactions: Studies in Communication & Culture, 3*(1), 71–89. https://doi.org/10.1386/iscc.3.1.71_1

Berger Peter, L., & Luckmann, T. (1966). *The Social Construction of Reality: A Treatise in the Sociology of Knowledge.* Garden City, NY: First Anchor.

Berk, S. F. (1988). Women's unpaid labor: Home and community. In A. H. Stromberg & S. Harkess (Eds.), *Women Working: Theories and Facts in Perspective* (pp. 287–302). Houston, TX: Mayfield Pub Co.

Bernard, B. (1952). *Content Analysis in Communication Research.* New York: Hafner.

Black, A., & Crann, M. (2002). In the public eye: A mass observation of the public library. *Journal of Librarianship & Information Science, 34*(3), 145–157.

Blewett, M. H. (1984). *Caught Between Two Worlds: The Diary of a Lowell Mill Girl, Susan Brown of Epsom, New Hampshire.* Lowell, Massachusetts: Lowell Museum.

Blumenthal, A. L. (2001). A Wundt primer. In R. Rieber & D. Robinson (Eds.), *Wilhelm Wundt in History: The Making of a Scientific Psychology* (pp. 121–144). New York: Springer.

Blumer, H. (1954). What is wrong with social theory? *American Sociological Review, 19*(1), 3–10.

Blumer, H. (1969). *Symbolic Interactionism: Perspective and Method.* Englewood Cliffs, NJ: Prentice Hall.

Boerner, P. (1969). *Tagebuch.* Stuttgart, Germany: Metzlersche Verlagsbuchhandlung.

Bolger, N., & Schilling, E. A. (1991). Personality and the problems of everyday life: The role of neuroticism in exposure and reactivity to daily stressors. *Journal of Personality, 59*(3), 355–386.

Bolger, N., DeLongis, A., Kessler, R. C., & Schilling, E. A. (1989). Effects of daily stress on negative mood. *Journal of Personality & Social Psychology, 57*(5), 808–818. http://dx.doi.org/10.1037/0022-3514.57.5.808

Borkovec, T. D. (2002). Life in the future versus life in the present. *Clinical Psychology: Science & Practice*, *9*(1), 76–80. doi:10.1093/clipsy.9.1.76

Boynton, M. H., & Richman, L. S. (2014). An online daily diary study of alcohol use using Amazon's Mechanical Turk. *Drug & Alcohol Review*, *33*(4), 456–461. doi:10.1111/dar.12163

Braun, V., & Clarke, V. (2006). Using thematic analysis in psychology. *Qualitative Research in Psychology*, *3*(2), 77–101.

Braun, V., & Clarke, V. (2013). *Successful Qualitative Research: A Practical Guide for Beginners*. Thousand Oaks, CA: Sage.

Brereton, B. (1998). Gendered testimonies: Autobiographies, diaries and letters by women as sources for Caribbean history. *Feminist Review*, *59*(1), 143–163. doi:10.1080/014177898339505

British Ecological Society (BES). (2014, December 11). Re-discovered diaries shed new light on one of the world's most studied woods. *Science Daily*. Retrieved December 10, 2016 from www.sciencedaily.com/releases/2014/12/141211081110.htm

Brown, L. A., & Strega, S. (2005). *Research as Resistance: Critical, Indigenous, and Anti-oppressive Approaches*. Toronto: Canadian Scholar's Press/Women Press.

Browne, B. C. (2013). Recording the personal: The benefits in maintaining research diaries for documenting the emotional and practical challenges of fieldwork in unfamiliar settings. *International Journal of Qualitative Methods*, *12*(1), 420–435. doi:10.1177/160940691301200121

Bruner, J. (1985). Narrative and paradigmatic modes of thought. *Learning and Teaching the Ways of Knowing*, *84*, 97–115.

Bruner, E. (1993). Introduction: The ethnographic self and the personal self. In P. Benson (Ed.), *Anthropology and Literature* (pp. 1–26). Chicago, IL: University of Illinois Press.

Bruner, J. (1990). *Autobiography as self. In His Acts of meaning* (pp. 33–66). Cambridge, MA: Harvard University Press.

Bruner, J. (1991). The narrative construction of reality. *Critical Inquiry*, *18*(1), 1–21. doi:10.1086/448619

Bryman, A. (2015). *Social Research Methods*. New York: Oxford University Press.

Buckingham, D. (2009). "Creative" visual methods in media research: Possibilities, problems and proposals. *Media, Culture & Society*, *31*(4), 633–652. doi:10.1177/0163443709335280

Bühler, C. (1935). The curve of life as studied in biographies. *Journal of Applied Psychology*, *19*(4), 405.

Bunkers, S. L. (1987). "Faithful friend": Nineteenth-century Midwestern American women's unpublished diaries. *Women's Studies International Forum*, *10*, 7–17.

Bunkers, S. L. (1990). Diaries: Public and private records of women's lives. *Legacy, 7*(2), 17–26.

Burgess, E. W. (1927). Statistics and case studies as methods of sociological research. *Sociology & Social Research, 12*(2), 103–120.

Burla, L., Knierim, B., Barth, J., Liewald, K., Duetz, M., & Abel, T. (2008). From text to codings: Intercoder reliability assessment in qualitative content analysis. *Nursing Research, 57*(2), 113–117. doi:10.1097/01.NNR.0000313482.33917.7d

Butrick, R. (2016). *Diary of Cherokee trek across Egypt*: 1838, December – 1839, January. *Illinois History*. Retrieved August 16, 2017 from http://www.illinoishistory.com/butrick.html

Caine, B. (2010). *Biography and History*. Basingstoke, UK: Palgrave Macmillan.

Calkins, M. W. (1893). Statistics of dreams. *The American Journal of Psychology, 5*(3), 311–343. doi:10.2307/1410996

Cancian, F. M. (1993). Conflicts between activist research and academic success: Participatory research and alternative strategies. *The American Sociologist, 24*(1), 92–106. doi:10.1007/BF02691947

Cantor, N., Norem, J., Langston, C., Zirkel, S., Fleeson, W., & Cook-Flannagan, C. (1991). Life tasks and daily life experience. *Journal of Personality, 59*(3), 425–451.

Cardell, K. (2014). *Dear World: Contemporary Uses of the Diary*. Madison, WI: University of Wisconsin Press.

Carmichael, J. V. (1998). *Daring to Find Our Names: The Search for Lesbigay Library History*. Westport, CT: Greenwood Publishing Group.

Carter, K. (1997). The cultural work of diaries in mid-century Victorian Britain. *Victorian Review, 23*(2), 251–267.

Cashmore, A., Green, P., & Scott, J. (2010). An ethnographic approach to studying the student experience: The student perspective through free form video diaries, a practice report. *The International Journal of the First Year in Higher Education, 1*(1), 106–111.

Caspi, A., Bolger, N., & Eckenrode, J. (1987). Linking person and context in the daily stress process. *Journal of Personality & Social Psychology, 52*(1), 184–195. http://dx.doi.org/10.1037/0022-3514.52.1.184

Chamberlayne, P., Bornat, J., & Wengraf, T. (Eds.). (2000). *The Turn to Biographical Methods in Social Science: Comparative Issues and Examples*. New York: Routledge.

Chassanoff, A. (2013). Historians and the use of primary source materials in the digital age. *The American Archivist, 76*(2), 458–480. http://dx.doi.org/10.17723/aarc.76.2.lh76217m2m376n28

Chelimsky, E. (1989). *Content Analysis. A Methodology for Structuring and Analyzing Written Material*. Washington DC: United States General Accounting Office.

Cherrington, J., & Watson, B. (2010). Shooting a diary, not just a hoop: Using video diaries to explore the embodied everyday contexts of a university basketball team. *Qualitative Research in Sport & Exercise*, 2(2), 267–281. http://dx.doi.org/10.1080/19398441.2010.488036

Cho, J., & Trent, A. (2014). Evaluating qualitative research. *Oxford Handbooks Online*. Retrieved March 18, 2016 from http://www.oxford-handbooks.com/view/10.1093/oxfordhb/9780199811755.001.0001/oxfordhb-9780199811755-e-012.

Clark, C., & Gruba, P. (2010). The use of social networking sites for foreign language learning: An autoethnographic study of Livemocha. *Curriculum, Technology & Transformation for an Unknown Future, Proceedings Ascilite Sydney*, 164–173.

Cohen, D. J., Crabtree, B. F., Etz, R. S., Balasubramanian, B. A., Donahue, K. E., Leviton, L. C., . . . Green, L. W. (2008). Fidelity versus flexibility: Translating evidence-based research into practice. *American Journal of Preventive Medicine*, 35(5), 381–S389. http://dx.doi.org/10.1016/j.amepre.2008.08.005

Collins, P. H. (2000). What's going on? Black feminist thought and the politics of postmodernism. In E. A. S. Pierre & W. S. Willow (Eds.), *Working the Ruins: Feminist Poststructural Theory and Methods in Education* (pp. 41–73). New York: Routledge.

Connelly, F. M., & Clandinin, D. J. (1990). Stories of experience and narrative inquiry. *Educational Researcher*, 19(5), 2–14. doi:10.3102/0013189X019005002

Constas, M. A. (1992). Qualitative analysis as a public event: The documentation of category development procedures. *American Educational Research Journal*, 29(2), 253–266. doi:10.3102/00028312029002253

Converse, J. M. (1984). Attitude measurement in psychology and sociology: The early years. In C. F. Turner & E. Martin (Eds.), *Surveying Subjective Phenomena* (pp. 3–39). New York: Russell Sage Foundation.

Conway, N., & Briner, R. B. (2002). A daily diary study of affective responses to psychological contract breach and exceeded promises. *Journal of Organizational Behavior*, 23(3), 287–302. doi:10.1002/job.139

Cook, S., & Ledger, K. (2004). A service user-led study promoting mental well-being for the general public, using 5 rhythms dance. *International Journal of Mental Health Promotion*, 6(4), 41–51. http://dx.doi.org/10.1080/14623730.2004.9721943

Cooley, C. H. (1902). *Human Nature and the Social Order*. New York: Charles Scribner's Sons.

Cooper, D. R., & Schindler, P. S. (2003). *Business Research Methods* (8th ed.). Toronto, Ontario: McGraw-Hill/Irwin.

Cope, D. G. (2014, January). Methods and meanings: Credibility and trustworthiness of qualitative research. *Oncology Nursing Forum, 41*(1), 89–91.

Cortese, A. J. (1995). The rise, hegemony, and decline of the Chicago School of Sociology, 1892–1945. *The Social Science Journal, 32*(3), 235–254.

Corti, L., & Bishop, L. (2005, January). Strategies in teaching secondary analysis of qualitative data. *Forum Qualitative Sozialforschung/ Forum: Qualitative Social Research, 6*(1). Retrieved on [NEED DATE] from http://www.qualitative-research.net/index.php/fqs/article/view/509

Costall, A. (2004). From Darwin to Watson (and cognitivism) and back again: The principle of animal-environment mutuality. *Behavior & Philosophy, 32,* 179–195.

Costall, A. (2006). 'Introspectionism'and the mythical origins of scientific psychology. *Consciousness and Cognition, 15*(4), 634–654.

Cowell, C. C. (1937). Diary analysis: A suggested technique for the study of children's activities and interests. *Research Quarterly. American Physical Education Association, 8*(2), 158–172. http://dx.doi.org/ 10.1080/23267402.1937.10761823

Coxon, A. P. M., Davies, P. M., & T. J. McManus (1990). Project sigma, longitudinal study of the sexual behaviour of homosexual males under the impact of AIDS, a final report, *Department of Health, Project Sigma Working Papers*, London: Southbank Polytechnic Project Sigma.

Crane, E. F. (1983). The world of Elizabeth Drinker. *The Pennsylvania Magazine of History & Biography, 107*(1), 3–28.

Cressy, D., & Ferrell, L. A. (2005). *Religion & Society in Early Modern England: A Sourcebook* (2nd ed.). New York: Routledge.

Csikszentmihalyi, M., & Larson, R. (2014). Validity and reliability of the experience-sampling method. In *Flow and the Foundations of Positive Psychology* (pp. 35–54). Amsterdam, Netherlands: Springer.

Csikszentmihalyi, M., Larson, R., & Prescott, S. (1977). The ecology of adolescent activity and experience. *Journal of Youth & Adolescence, 6*(3), 281–294.

Cullum-Swan, B., & Manning, P. (1994). Narrative, content, and semiotic analysis. In N. K. Denzin & Y. S. Lincoln (Eds.), *Handbook of Qualitative Research* (pp. 463–477). Thousand Oaks, CA: Sage.

Curtis, S., Gesler, W., Smith, G., & Washburn, S. (2000). Approaches to sampling and case selection in qualitative research: Examples in the geography of health. *Social Science & Medicine, 50*(7), 1001–1014. http://dx.doi.org/10.1016/S0277-9536(99)00350-0

Czerwinski, M., Horvitz, E., & Wilhite, S. (Eds.). (2004). A diary study of task switching and interruptions. In *Proceedings of the SIGCHI Conference on Human Factors in Computing Systems* (pp. 175–182). New York: ACM.

Darwin, C. (1882). *The Descent of Man, and Selection in Relation to Sex*. London: John Murray.

Davies, P. M., Hunt, A. J., Macourt, M., & Weatherburn, P. (1990). *A Longitudinal study of the sexual behaviour of homosexual males under the impact of AIDS: A final report, Department of Health, Project Sigma Working Papers*, London: Southbank Polytechnic Project Sigma.

Day, M., & Thatcher, J. (2009). "I'm really embarrassed that you're going to read this . . . ": Reflections on using diaries in qualitative research. *Qualitative Research in Psychology*, 6(4), 249–259. http://dx.doi.org/10.1080/14780880802070583

de Beauvoir, S (1967). *The Woman Destroyed*, London: William Collins Sons & Co. Ltd.,

de la Rue, M. B. (2003). Preventing ageism in nursing students: An action theory approach. *The Australian Journal of Advanced Nursing*, 20(4), 8–14.

Deuchar, M., & Quay, S. (2001). *Bilingual Acquisition: Theoretical Implications of a Case Study*. New York: Oxford University Press.

Dewey, J. (1938). *The Theory of Inquiry*. New York: Holt, Rinehart & Wiston.

Dewey, J. (1986). *The Later Works of John Dewey, Volume 12, 1925–1953: 1938–Logic: The Theory of Inquiry*. Carbondale, IL: Southern Illinois University Press.

Dilthey, W. (1977). The understanding of other persons and their expressions of life. In *Descriptive Psychology and Historical Understanding* (pp. 121–144). Amsterdam, Netherlands: Springer.

Dollard, J. (1949) *Criteria for the Life History*, New York: Peter Smith Publishers

Douglas, J. W. B., Lawson, A., Cooper, J. E., & Cooper, E. (1968). Family interaction and the activities of young children. *Journal of Child Psychology & Psychiatry*, 9(3-4), 157–171. doi:10.1111/j.1469-7610.1968.tb02220.x

Drinker, E. S., & Crane, E. F. (1991). *The Diary of Elizabeth Drinker* (Vol. 1). Boston, MA: Northeastern University Press.

Duncan, A. D. (1969). Self-application of behavior modification techniques by teen-agers. *Adolescence*, 4(16), 541.

Duncan, E., & Grazzani-Gavazzi, I. (2004). Positive emotional experiences in Scottish and Italian young adults: A diary study. *Journal of Happiness Studies*, 5(4), 359–384. doi:10.1007/s10902-004-0666-8

Edel, L. (1978). Biography: A manifesto. *Biography*, 1, 1–3.

Egerod, I., & Christensen, D. (2009). Analysis of patient diaries in Danish ICUs: A narrative approach. *Intensive & Critical Care Nursing*, 25(5), 268–277. doi:10.1016/j.iccn.2009.06.005

Epstein, B. (2001). What happened to the women's movement? *Monthly Review*, 53(1), 1–13.

Fals-Borda, O., & Rahman, M. A. (Eds.). (1991). *Action and Knowledge: Breaking the Monopoly with Participatory Action Research*. New York: Apex Press.

Fanon, F. (1994). *A Dying Colonialism*. Brooklyn, NY: Grove/Atlantic, Inc.

Fincher, S. (2013). The diarists' audience. In L. Stanley (Ed.), *Documents of Life Revisited: Narrative and Biographical Methodology for a 21st Century Critical Humanism* (pp. 77–92). Farnham, UK: Ashgate Publishing.

Fincher, S. (2016). Whites writing: Letters and documents of life in a QLR project. In L. Stanley (Ed.), *Documents of Life Revisited: Narrative and Biographical Methodology for a 21st Century Critical Humanism* (pp. 59–76). New York: Routledge.

Fine, M. (1992). Passions, politics, and power: Feminist research possibilities. In M. Fine (Ed.), *Disruptive Voices: The Possibilities of Feminist Research* (pp. 205–231). Ann Arbor, MI: University of Michigan Press.

Fine, M., & Gordon, S. M. (1991). Effacing the center and the margins: Life at the intersection of psychology and feminism. *Feminism & Psychology*, 1(1), 19–27.

Fischer-Rosenthal, W. (2000). Biographical work and biographical structuring in present-day societies. In P. Chamberlayne, J. Bornat, & T. Wengraf (Eds.), *The Turn to Biographical Methods in Social Science* (pp. 109–125). New York: Routledge

Fisher, C. D., & To, M. L. (2012). Using experience sampling methodology in organizational behavior. *Journal of Organizational Behavior*, 33(7), 865–877. doi:10.1002/job.1803

Fisher, K., Egerton, M., Gershuny, J. I., & Robinson, J. P. (2007). Gender convergence in the American Heritage Time Use Study (AHTUS). *Social Indicators Research*, 82(1), 1–33. doi:10.1007/s11205-006-9017-y

Foddy, W. (1994). *Constructing Questions for Interviews and Questionnaires: Theory and Practice in Social Research*. Cambridge, UK: Cambridge University Press.

Foster, M. D. (2009). Perceiving pervasive discrimination over time: Implications for coping. *Psychology of Women Quarterly*, 33(2), 172–182. doi:10.1111/j.1471-6402.2009.01487.x

Fothergill, R. A. (1974). *Private Chronicles: A Study of English Diaries*. Toronto, ONT: Oxford University Press.

Foucault, M. (1978). *The History of Sexuality: An Introduction*. New York: Random House.

Frederiks, A. J., Ehrenhard, M. L., & Groen, A. J. (2013). How do nascent entrepreneurs use imagination in the venture creation process? A weekly diary study. *Frontiers of Entrepreneurship Research*, 33(4), 2.

Freer, C. B. (1980). Health diaries: A method of collecting health information. *Journal of the Royal College of General Practitioners, 30*(214), 279–282.

Friedman, W. J. (2004). Time in autobiographical memory. *Social Cognition, 22*(5), 591–605. doi:10.1521/soco.22.5.591.50766

Gannett, C. (1992). *Gender and the Journal: Diaries and Academic Discourse.* Albany, NY: SUNY Press.

Garfield, S. (2006). *We Are at War: The Diaries of Five Ordinary People in Extraordinary Times.* New York: Random House.

Gaver, B., Dunne, T., & Pacenti, E. (1999). Design: Cultural probes. *Interactions, 6*(1), 21–29.

Gee, J. P. (1989). Two styles of narrative construction and their linguistic and educational implications. *Discourse Processes, 12*(3), 287–307. http://dx.doi.org/10.1080/01638538909544732

Geertz, C. (1974). "From the native's point of view": On the nature of anthropological understanding. *Bulletin of the American Academy of Arts & Sciences, 28*(1), 26–45. doi:10.2307/3822971

Geertz, C. (1986). Making experiences, authoring selves. In V. Turner & E. Bruner (Eds.), *The Anthropology of Experience* (pp. 373–380). Chicago, IL: University of Illinois Press.

Geertz, C. (2003). Thick description: Toward an interpretive theory of culture. *Culture: Critical Concepts in Sociology, 1,* 173–196.

General Assembly of the World Medical Association. (2014). World Medical Association Declaration of Helsinki: Ethical principles for medical research involving human subjects. *The Journal of the American College of Dentists, 81*(3), 14.

Gera, D., & Horowitz, W. (1997). Antiochus IV in life and death: Evidence from the Babylonian astronomical diaries. *Journal of the American Oriental Society, 117,* 240–252.

Gergen, K. J. (1985). The social constructionist movement in modern psychology. *American Psychologist, 40*(3), 266.

Gergen, K. J. (2009). *Realities and Relationships: Soundings in Social Construction.* Cambridge, MA: Harvard University Press.

Gergen, K. J. (2015). Culturally inclusive psychology from a constructionist standpoint. *Journal for the Theory of Social Behaviour, 45*(1), 95–107. doi:10.1111/jtsb.12059

Gersbuny, J., & Sullivan, O. (1998). The sociological uses of time-use diary analysis. *European Sociological Review, 14*(1), 69–85. https://doi.org/10.1093/oxfordjournals.esr.a018228

Gilgun, J. (2010). Reflexivity and qualitative research. *Current Issues in Qualitative Research, 1*(2), 1–8.

Gill, J., & Liamputtong, P. (2009). "Walk a mile in my shoes": Researching the lived experience of mothers of children with autism. *Journal of Family Studies, 15*(3), 309–319. http://dx.doi.org/10.5172/jfs.15.3.309

Gilliam, T. (1985). *Brazil* [Motion picture]. United Kingdom: Embassy International Pictures and Universal Pictures.

Gilman, E. (1921). A dog's diary. *Journal of Comparative Psychology, 1*(3), 309–315. doi:10.1037/h0072585

Giorgi, A. (1975). An application of phenomenological method in psychology. In A. Giorgi & R. Von Eckartsberg (Eds.), *Duquesne Studies in Phenomenological Psychology: Vol. 2* (pp. 82–103). Pittsburgh, PA: Duquesne University Press.

Gladden, W. (1908). *The Church and Modern Life.* New York: Houghton Mifflin.

Glaser, B., & Strauss, A. (1968). *The Discovery of Grounded Theory.* London: Weidenfeld and Nicholson.

Glaser, B., & Strauss, A. (1975). *Theoretical Sampling.* Chicago, IL: Aldine.

Gläser, J., & Laudel, G. (2013, March). Life with and without coding: Two methods for early-stage data analysis in qualitative research aiming at causal explanations. *Forum Qualitative Sozialforschung/ Forum: Qualitative Social Research, 14*(2). Retrieved on [NEED DATE] from http://www.qualitative-research.net/index.php/fqs/article/view/1886

Goffman, E. (1959). *The Presentation of Self in Everyday Life.* New York: Doubleday.

Goffman, E. (1963). *Stigma: Notes on a Spoiled Identity.* Bristol, PA: Simon & Schuster.

Goodson, I., & Gill, S. (2011). The narrative turn in social research. *Counterpoints, 386,* 17–33.

Gregory, J. (1990). The adult dietary survey. *Survey Methodology Bulletin, 27,* 1–5.

Griffin, G., & Hayler, M. (2016). *Research Methods for Reading Digital Data in the Digital Humanities.* Edinburgh, UK: Edinburgh University Press.

Griffiths, M. D., Lewis, A. M., Ortiz de Gortari, A. B., & Kuss, D. J. (2014). Online forums and solicited blogs: Innovative methodologies for online gaming data collection. *Studia Psychologica, 11*(1), 5–18. http://dx.doi.org/10.21697/sp.2015.14.2.07

Grønmo, S., & Lingsom, S. (1986). Increasing equality in household work: Patterns of time-use change in Norway. *European Sociological Review, 2*(3), 176–190.

Guba, E. G., & Lincoln, Y. S. (1994). Competing paradigms in qualitative research. In N. K. Denzin & Y. S. Lincoln (Eds.), *Handbook of Qualitative Research* (pp. 163–194). Thousand Oaks, CA: Sage.

Guly, H. R. (1996). *History Taking, Examination, and Record Keeping in Emergency Medicine* (No. 12). New York: Oxford University Press.

Hall, G. S. (1904). *Adolescence (Vols. 1 & 2).* New York: Appleton.

Harding, D. J. (1997). Measuring children's time use: A review of methodologies and findings. *Working Paper No. 91-1. Bendheim-Thoman Center for Research on Child Wellbeing*, Princeton, NJ: Princeton University.

Harding, S. G. (1987). *Feminism and Methodology: Social Science Issues*. Bloomington, IN: Indiana University Press.

Harding, S. G. (2004). *The Feminist Standpoint Theory Reader: Intellectual and Political Controversies*. Washington, DC: Psychology Press.

Hardy, S., & Gray, R. (2012). The secret food diary of a person diagnosed with schizophrenia. *Journal of Psychiatric & Mental Health Nursing*, *19*(7), 603–609.

Hawkins, M., Ralley, R., & Young, J. (2014). A medical panorama: The casebooks project. *Book 2.0*, *4*(1–2), 61–69. https://doi.org/10.1386/btwo.4.1-2.61_1

Hesse, H. (1920/1972). *Wandering: Notes and Sketches* (J. Wright, Trans.). New York: Farrar, Straus, & Giroux.

Hilburn, R. (Dec. 25, 1988). Taste makers: Tracy Chapman. *Los Angeles Times*, <*Entertainment & 1.*>.

Hill, I. (2014). Finding the manly man in archives. In M. O'Neill, B. Roberts, & A. C. Sparkes (Eds.), *Advances in Biographical Methods: Creative Applications* (pp. 138–150). New York: Routledge.

Hilton, M. E. (1989). A comparison of a prospective diary and two summary recall techniques for recording alcohol consumption. *Addiction*, *84*(9), 1085–1092. doi:10.1111/j.1360-0443.1989.tb00792.x

Hirschman, E. C. (1986). Humanistic inquiry in marketing research: Philosophy, method, and criteria. *Journal of Marketing Research*, *23*(3), 237–249. doi:10.2307/3151482

Hochschild, A. R. (1983). *The Managed Heart*. Berkeley, CA: University of California Press.

Hogan, R. (2009). Much ado about nothing: The person–situation debate. *Journal of Research in Personality*, *43*(2), 249. http://dx.doi.org/10.1016/j.jrp.2009.01.022

Holden, E. (1906). *The Country Diary of an Edwardian Lady: A Facsimile Reproduction of a Naturalist's Diary for the Year 1906*. New York: Friedman/Fairfax.

Howard, D. R. (1980). *Writers and Pilgrims: Medieval Pilgrimage Narratives and Their Posterity* (No. 17). Berkeley, CA: University of California Press.

Hsieh, H. F., & Shannon, S. E. (2005). Three approaches to qualitative content analysis. *Qualitative Health Research*, *15*(9), 1277–1288. doi:10.1177/1049732305276687

Hug-Hellmuth, H. V. (1922). *A Young Girl's Diary*. New York: Thomas Seltzer.

Hughes, J. M., & Callery, P. (2004). Parents' experiences of caring for their child following day case surgery: A diary study. *Journal of Child Health Care, 8*(1), 47–58. doi:10.1177/1367493504041853

Humphreys, M. (2005). Getting personal: Reflexivity and autoethnographic vignettes. *Qualitative Inquiry, 11*(6), 840–860. doi:10.1177/1077800404269425

Hunter, J. H. (1992). Inscribing the self in the heart of the family: Diaries and girlhood in late Victorian America, *American Quarterly, 44,* 59–61.

Husserl, E. (1983). *Ideas Pertaining to a Pure Phenomenology and to a Phenomenological Philosophy* (F. Kersten, Trans.). The Hague, Netherlands: Martinus Nijhoff Publishers.

Hyers, L. L. (2007). Challenging everyday prejudice: The personal and social implications of women's assertive responses to interpersonal incidents of anti-black racism, anti-Semitism, heterosexism, and sexism. *Sex Roles, 56,* 1–12.

Hyers, L. L. (2010). Choosing alternatives to silence in face-to-face encounters with everyday heterosexism. *Journal of Homosexuality, 57,* 539–565.

Hyers, L. L., & Hyers, C. (2008). Everyday discrimination experienced by conservative Christians at the secular university. *Analysis of Social Issues & Public Policy, 8,* 113–137.

Hyers, L. L., Brown, E., & Sullivan, J. (2015). Social psychology of stigma. In J. D. Wright (Ed.), *International Encyclopaedia of Social & Behavioral Sciences Vol 23* (2nd ed., pp. 461–466). Oxford, England: Elsevier.

Hyers, L. L., Swim, J. K., & Mallet, R. M. (2006). The personal is political: Using daily diaries to examine everyday prejudice-related experiences. In S. Hesse-Biber & P. Leavy (Eds.), *Emergent Methods in Social Research* (pp. 313–329). New York: Sage.

Hyers, L. L., Syphan, J., Cochran, K., & Brown, T. (2012). Disparities in the professional development interactions of university faculty as a function of their gender and ethnic underrepresentation. *Journal of Faculty Development, 26*(1), 18–28.

Hynes, S. (1998). *The Soldiers' Tale: Bearing Witness to a Modern War.* New York: Penguin.

Irwin, A. (1995). *Citizen Science: A Study of People, Expertise and Sustainable Development.* New York: Routledge.

Jackson, S., & Vares, T. (2015). New visibilities? Using video diaries to explore girls' experiences of sexualized culture. In E. Renold, J. Ringrose, & R. D. Egan (Eds.), *Children, Sexuality and Sexualization* (pp. 307–320). Basingstoke, UK: Palgrave.

James, H. E. O., & Moore, F. T. (1940). Adolescent leisure in a working class district. *Occupational Psychology, 14*(3), 132–145.

James, W. (1884). I—On some omissions of introspective psychology. *Mind*, *33*, 1–26.

James, W. (1902). *The Varieties of Religious Experience. A Study in Human Nature*. New York: Longmans, Green, & Co.

Jerome, W. S. (October, 1878). How to keep a journal, *St. Nicholas Magazine*, *12*(5).

Jewell, J. (1905). The psychology of dreams. *The American Journal of Psychology*, *16*(1), 1–34. doi:10.2307/1412227

Johnson, P. (2015). Evaluating qualitative research: Past, present and future. *Qualitative Research in Organizations & Management: An International Journal*, *10*(4), 320–324. http://dx.doi.org/10.1108/QROM-07-2015-1303

Johnson, R. B. (1997). Examining the validity structure of qualitative research. *Education*, *118*(2), 282–293.

Jones, H. A. (2016). New media producing new labor: Pinterest, yearning, and self-surveillance. *Critical Studies in Media Communication*, *33*(4), 352–365.

Jones, R. K. (2000). The unsolicited diary as a qualitative research tool for advanced research capacity in the field of health and illness. *Qualitative Health Research*, *10*(4), 555–567.

Kabat-Zinn, J. (2003). Mindfulness: The heart of rehabilitation. In E. Leskowitz (Ed.), *Complementary and Alternative Medicine in Rehabilitation* (pp. xi–xv). St. Louis, MO: Churchill Livingstone.

Kabat-Zinn, J. (2012). *Mindfulness for Beginners: Reclaiming the Present Moment—and Your Life*. Boulder, CO: Sounds True.

Kambouropoulou, P. (1926). Individual differences in the sense of humor. *The American Journal of Psychology*, *37*(2), 268–278.

Kamler, B. (2006). Older women as lifelong learners. In C. Leathwood, & B. Francis (Eds.), *Gender and Lifelong Learning: Critical Feminist Engagements* (pp. 153–163). London: Routledge.

Kandler, R. (2013). Roses of Love, Violets of Humility and Lilies of Suffering: A Phenomenological Hermeneutic Study of Floral Experiences in the Diary of St. Faustina Kowalska (1905–1938) (doctoral dissertation). Retrieved from University of Ottawa, http://dx.doi.org/10.20381/ruor-3226

Kanner, A. D., Coyne, J. C., Schaefer, C., & Lazarus, R. S. (1981). Comparison of two modes of stress measurement: Daily hassles and uplifts versus major life events. *Journal of Behavioral Medicine*, *4*(1), 1–39.

Kaun, A. (2010). Open-ended online diaries: Capturing life as it is narrated. *International Journal of Qualitative Methods*, *9*(2), 133–148.

Kaun, A. (2014). 'I really don't like them!'–Exploring citizens' media criticism. *European Journal of Cultural Studies*, *17*(5), 489–506.

Kaźmierska, K. (2012). Ups and downs of teaching the biographical approach. *ZQF–Zeitschrift für Qualitative Forschung, 11*(2), 183–195.

Kaźmierska, K. (2004). Narrative interview as a method of biographical analysis. In J. Fikfak, F. Adam, F., & D. Garz (Eds.), *Qualitative Research: Different Perspectives, Emerging Trends* (pp. 153–172). Ljubljana, Slovenia: Založba ZRC.

Kierkegaard, S. (1938/1960). *The Journals of Kierkegaard, 1834–1854*. (A. Dru, Trans.). London: Oxford University Press.

Kenten, C. (2010). Narrating oneself: Reflections on the use of solicited diaries with diary interviews. *Forum Qualitative Sozialforschung / Forum: Qualitative Social Research, 11*(2). Retrieved on [NEED DATE] from http://www.qualitative-research.net/index.php/fqs/article/view/1314/2989

Keyserling, H. (1923). *Das Reisetagebuch eines Philosophen*. St. Goar, Germany: Reichl Verlag.

Kidder, L. H., & Fine, M. (1987). Qualitative and quantitative methods: When stories converge. *New Directions for Evaluation, 35*, 57–75.

Kielmann, T., Huby, G., Powell, A., Sheikh, A., Price, D., Williams, S., & Pinnock, H. (2010). From support to boundary: A qualitative study of the border between self-care and professional care. *Patient Education & Counseling, 79*(1), 55–61.

Kiffin-Petersen, S., Murphy, S. A., & Soutar, G. (2012). The problem-solving service worker: Appraisal mechanisms and positive affective experiences during customer interactions. *Human Relations, 65*(9), 1179–1206. doi:10.1177/0018726712451762

Kinsella, E. A. (2006, May). Hermeneutics and critical hermeneutics: Exploring possibilities within the art of interpretation. *Forum Qualitative Sozialforschung/Forum: Qualitative Social Research, 7*(3). Retrieved on [NEED DATE] from http://www.qualitative-research.net/index.php/fqs/article/view/145

Klein, P. D., Boman, J. S., & Prince, M. P. (2007). Developmental trends in a writing to learn task. *Studies in Writing, 20*, 201.

Kowalska, F. (2003). *Divine Mercy in My Soul: Diary of Saint Maria Faustina Kowalska, 1934–1938*. Stockbridge, MA: Marian Press.

Kreiswirth, M. (1992). Trusting the tale: The narrativist turn in the human sciences. *New Literary History, 23*(3), 629–657. doi:10.2307/469223

Krippendorff, K. (2008). Testing the reliability of content analysis data: What is involved and why. In K. Krippendorff & M. A. Bock (Eds.), *The Content Analysis Reader* (pp. 350–357). Thousand Oaks, CA: Sage.

Krippendorff, K., & Bock, M. A. (2009). *The Content Analysis Reader*. Sage.

Krueger, E. T. (1925). The technique of securing life history documents. *Journal of Applied Sociology, 9*(4), 290–298.

Kupky, O. (1928). *The Religious Development of Adolescents: Based Upon Their Literary Productions*. Oxford, England: Macmillan.

Langford, R., & West, R. (1999). Introduction: Diaries and margins. In R. Langford & R. West (Eds.), *Marginal Voices, Marginal Forms: Diaries in European Literature and History* (pp. 6–21). Amsterdam, Netherlands: Rodopi.

LaLonde, S. (August, 2016). Mapping the boundaries of melancholy and depression through psychoanalysis and intimate literature, PSYART: A Hyperlink Journal for the Psychological Study of the Arts. Available http://psyartjournal.com/article/show/lalonde-mapping_the_boundaries_of_melancholy_and. August, 2016.

LaPalio, L. R. (1981). Time study of students and house staff on a university medical service. *Academic Medicine, 56*(1), 61–64.

Larson, R. (1989). Beeping children and adolescents: A method for studying time use and daily experience. *Journal of Youth & Adolescence, 18*(6), 511–530. doi:10.1007/BF02139071

Latham, A. (2004). Researching and writing everyday accounts of the city: An introduction to the diary-photo diary-interview method. In C. Knowles & P. Sweetman (Eds.), *Picturing the Social Landscape: Visual Methods and the Sociological Imagination* (pp. 117–131). London: Routledge.

Laurenceau, J. P., Barrett, L. F., & Pietromonaco, P. R. (1998). Intimacy as an interpersonal process: The importance of self-disclosure, partner disclosure, and perceived partner responsiveness in interpersonal exchanges. *Journal of Personality & Social Psychology, 74*(5), 1238.

Lazarus, R. S., & Cohen, J. B. (1977). Coping Questionnaire, the Hassles Scale, the Uplifts Scale. Unpublished paper. Berkeley, CA: University of California at Berkeley.

Lazarus, R. S., & Folkman, S. (1987). Transactional theory and research on emotions and coping. *European Journal of Personality, 1*(3), 141–169.

Lempert, L. B. (2016). *Women doing life: Gender, punishment and the struggle for identity*. NYU Press.

Le Page, M. (2016). A lab in every pocket. *New Scientist, 229*, 22. http://dx.doi.org/10.1016/S0262-4079(16)30514-0

Le, B., Choi, H. N., & Beal, D. J. (2006). Pocket-sized psychology studies: Exploring daily diary software for Palm Pilots. *Behavior Research Methods, 38*(2), 325–332. doi:10.3758/BF03192784

Lee, E., Hu, M. Y., & Toh, R. S. (2000). Are consumer survey results distorted? Systematic impact of behavioral frequency and duration on survey response errors. *Journal of Marketing Research, 37*(1), 125–133. http://dx.doi.org/10.1509/jmkr.37.1.125.18724

Lee, V., & Anstruther-Thomson, C. (1914). *Beauty and Ugliness.* New York: John Lane Company.

Lejeune, P. (1992). Auto-genèse. L'étude génétique des textes autobiographiques. *Genesis (Manuscrits-Recherche-Invention), 1*(1), 73–87.

Lejeune, P. (2009). *On Diary.* Honolulu, HI: University of Hawaii Press.

Lejeune, P., & Lodewick, V. A. (2001). How do diaries end? *Biography, 24*(1), 99–112.

Lewin, K. (1939). Field theory and experiment in social psychology: Concepts and methods. *American Journal of Sociology, 44*(6), 868–896. doi:10.1086/218177

Lincoln, Y. S., & Guba, E. G. (1985). *Naturalistic Inquiry* (Vol. 75). Thousand Oaks, CA: Sage.

Long, B. H., & Henderson, E. H. (1973). Children's use of time: Some personal and social correlates. *The Elementary School Journal, 73*(4), 193–199. doi:10.1086/460754

Lundgren, I., & Wahlberg, V. (1999). The experience of pregnancy: A hermeneutical/phenomenological study. *The Journal of Perinatal Education, 8*(3), 12–20.

Mackrill, T. (2008). Solicited diary studies of psychotherapy in qualitative research—pros and cons. *European Journal of Psychotherapy & Counselling, 10*(1), 5–18. http://dx.doi.org/10.1080/13642530701869243

Madianou, M., & Miller, D. (2011). Mobile phone parenting: Reconfiguring relationships between Filipina migrant mothers and their left-behind children. *New Media & Society, 13*(3), 457–470. doi:10.1177/1461444810393903

Madianou, M., & Miller, D. (2013). *Migration and New Media: Transnational Families and Polymedia.* New York: Routledge.

Madill, A., Jordan, A., & Shirley, C. (2000). Objectivity and reliability in qualitative analysis: Realist, contextualist and radical constructionist epistemologies. *British Journal of Psychology, 91*(1), 1–20. doi:10.1348/000712600161646

Makdisi, G. (1986). The diary in Islamic historiography: Some notes. *History & Theory, 25*(2), 173–185. doi:10.2307/2505304

Manning, P. K. (1987). *Semiotics and Fieldwork* (Vol. 7). Sage Publications.

Markwell, K. W. (2000). Photo-documentation and analyses as research strategies in human geography. *Australian Geographical Studies, 38*(1), 91–98. doi:10.1111/1467-8470.00103

Mattingly, M. J., & Bianchi, S. M. (2003). Gender differences in the quantity and quality of free time: The US experience. *Social Forces, 81*(3), 999–1030.

Mayring, P. (2010). Qualitative inhaltsanalyse. *Handbuch qualitative Forschung in der Psychologie,* 601–613.

Mayring, P. (2014). Qualitative content analysis: Theoretical foundation, basic procedures and software solution. *Social Science Open Access Repository*. Retrieved on January 2016 from http://nbn-resolving.de/urn:nbn:de:0168-ssoar-395173

McArdle, F., & Wright, S. (2014). First literacies: Art, creativity, play, constructive meaning-making. In G. M. Barton (Ed.), *Literacy in the Arts: Retheorising Learning and Teaching* (pp. 21–38). Cham: Springer International Publishing.

McClelland, S., & Fine, M. (2008). Writing on cellophane. In K. Gallagher (Ed.), *Creative, Critical and Collaborative Approaches to Qualitative Research* (pp. 232–261). New York: Routledge.

McIntyre, C. W. (2013, November 23). Dear diary: Using diaries in marketing research. *Strategic Initiatives*. Retrieved January 10, 2017 from http://strategicinitiatives.ca/blog/uncategorized/dear-diary-using- diaries-in-marketing-research/

McIver, S., O'Halloran, P., & McGartland, M. (2009). Yoga as a treatment for binge eating disorder: a preliminary study. *Complementary Therapies in Medicine*, *17*(4), 196–202.

Mead, G. H. (1934). *Mind, Self, and Society*. Chicago, IL: University of Chicago Press.

Meltzer, H. (1937). Anger adjustments in relation to intelligence and achievement. *The Pedagogical Seminary & Journal of Genetic Psychology*, *50*(1), 63–82. http://dx.doi.org/10.1080/08856559.1937.10534269

Messinger, S. L., Sampson, H., & Towne, R. D. (1962). Life as theater: Some notes on the dramaturgic approach to social reality. *Sociometry*, *25*(1), 98–110.

Miles, M. B., & Huberman, A. M. (1994). *Qualitative Data Analysis: An Expanded Sourcebook*. Thousand Oaks, CA: Sage.

Miller, R. L. (2003). Biographical method. In R. L. Miller, & J. D. Brewer (Eds.), *The A–Z of Social Research: A Dictionary of Key Social Science Research Concepts* (pp. 15–17). London: Sage.

Milligan, C., Bingley, A., & Gatrell, A. (2005). Digging deep: Using diary techniques to explore the place of health and well-being amongst older people. *Social Science & Medicine*, *61*(9), 1882–1892. http://dx.doi.org/10.1016/j.socscimed.2005.04.002

Millim, A. M. (2010). Preaching Silence: The Disciplined Self in the Victorian Diary (doctoral dissertation). Retrieved December 15, 2016 from University of Glasgow. http://encore.lib.gla.ac.uk/iii/encore/record/C__Rb2710471

Mills, W. (1896). Psychic development of young animals, and its physical correlation (Nos. 1–5). *Papers from the Department of Psychology*. Montreal, Canada: McGill University.

Monga, L. (1998). Crime and the road: A survey of sixteenth-century travel journals. *Renaissance & Reformation / Renaissance Et Réforme, 22*(2), new series / nouvelle série, 5–17. doi:10.1002/joc.1594

Monrouxe, L. V. (2009). Solicited audio diaries in longitudinal narrative research: A view from inside. *Qualitative Research, 9*(1), 81–103. doi:10.1177/1468794108098032

Montgomery, A. J., Panagopoulou, E., Peeters, M. C., & Schaufeli, W. B. (2009). Exploring types of interference between work and non-work: Using a diary study approach. *Community, Work & Family, 12*(4), 455–471. http://dx.doi.org/10.1080/13668800903192101

Moore, A. W. (2016). From individual child to war youth: The construction of collective experience among evacuated Japanese children during WWII. *Japanese Studies, 36*(3), 339–360. http://dx.doi.org/10.1080/10371397.2016.1253434

Moran, J. (2013). The private diary and public history. *Gresham College.* Retrieved November 10, 2016 from https://www.gresham.ac.uk/lectures-and-events/the-private-diary-and-public-history

Morawski, C. M., & Rottmann, J. (2016). Multimodal narrative inquiry: Six teacher candidates respond. *International Journal of Education & the Arts, 17*(14), 1–31.

Morrison, T. (2015). NPR Fresh Air Interview. Retrieved on [NEED DATE] from http://www.npr.org/2015/04/20/400394947/i-regret-everything-toni-morrison-looks-back-on-her-personal-life

Morse, J. M., Barrett, M., Mayan, M., Olson, K., & Spiers, J. (2002). Verification strategies for establishing reliability and validity in qualitative research. *International Journal of Qualitative Methods, 1*(2), 13–22. doi:10.1177/160940690200100202

Mowrer, E. R. (1927). *Family Disorganization: An Introduction to a Sociological Analysis.* Chicago, IL: University of Chicago Press.

Murthy, D. (2008). Digital ethnography: An examination of the use of new technologies for social research. *Sociology, 42*(5), 837–855.

Murthy, D. (2013). Ethnographic research 2.0: The potentialities of emergent digital technologies for qualitative organizational research. *Journal of Organizational Ethnography, 2*(1), 23–36. http://dx.doi.org/10.1108/JOE-01-2012-0008

Musgrave, J. (1998). Southern Illinois history lost on Cherokee Trail of Tears. *Illinois History.* Retrieved November 15, 2016 from http://www.illinoishistory.com/trailoftears.html

Naples, N. A. (2003). *Feminism and Method: Ethnography, Discourse Analysis, and Activist Research.* New York: Routledge.

National Commission for the Protection of Human Subjects of Biomedical and Behavioral Research, & Ryan, K. J. P. (1978). *The Belmont Report: Ethical Principles and Guidelines for the Protection of Human Subjects of Research—The National Commission for the Protection of Human Subjects of Biomedical and Behavioral Research.* Washington, DC: US Government Printing Office.

Noyes, A. (2004). Video diary: A method for exploring learning dispositions. *Cambridge Journal of Education, 34*(2), 193–209.

O'Keefe, K. (2005). *The Average American: The Extraordinary Search for the Nation's Most Ordinary Citizen.* New York: Public Affairs.

Ong, Walter J. (1982). *Orality and Literacy, Technologizing of the Word.* London: Methuen.

Orr, D. (2002). *"Slow Knowledge," in the Nature of Design: Ecology, Culture, and Human Intention.* New York: Oxford.

Palen, L., & Salzman, M. (2002). Voice-mail diary studies for naturalistic data capture under mobile conditions. In *Proceedings of the 2002 ACM Conference on Computer Supported Cooperative Work* (pp. 87–95). New York: ACM.

Palmer, V. (1928). A new research manual for the study of local groups and communities. *Journal of Educational Sociology, 2*(2), 117–118.

Pandey, P., & Misra, R. (2014). Digitization of library materials in academic libraries: Issues and challenges. *Journal of Industrial & Intelligent Information, 2*(2), 136–141. doi:10.12720/jiii.2.2.136-141

Paperno, I. (2004). What can be done with diaries? *The Russian Review, 63*(4), 561–573. doi:10.1111/j.1467-9434.2004.00332.x

Parfitt, J. H. (1967). Comparison of purchase recall with diary panel records. *Journal of Advertising Research, 7*(3), 16–31.

Patterson, A. (2005). Processes, relationships, settings, products and consumers: The case for qualitative diary research. *Qualitative Market Research: An International Journal, 8*(2), 142–156. http://dx.doi.org/10.1108/13522750510592427

Peabody, D. (1962). Two components in bipolar scales: Direction and extremeness. *Psychological Review, 69*(2), 65.

Pedhazur, E. J., & Schmelkin, L. P. (2013). *Measurement, Design, and Analysis: An Integrated Approach.* Washington, DC: Psychology Press.

Pelish, A. (2016). How to keep a journal. *Paris Review*, online, downloaded on March 1, 2017, from https://www.theparisreview.org/blog/2016/07/15/how-to-keep-a-journal/

Perry, C. (1973). Imagery, fantasy, and hypnotic susceptibility: A multidimensional approach. *Journal of Personality & Social Psychology, 26*(2), 217.

Pettersen, L. (2013). Video blogging ethnographic field notes. *Popular Anthropology Magazine, 4*(1), 35–38.

Picasso, P. (1965). In F. Gilot and C. Lake (Eds.), *Vivre avec Picasso*. Paris: Le Livre de poche.

Pierre, E. A. S., & Jackson, A. Y. (2014). Qualitative data analysis after coding. *Qualitative Inquiry, 20*(6), 715–719. doi:10.1177/1077800414532435

Pini, M., & Walkerdine, V. (2011). Girls on film: Video diaries as "autoethnographies." In P. Reavey (Ed.), *Visual Methods in Psychology: Using and Interpreting Images in Qualitative Research* (pp. 139–152). Washington, DC: Psychology Press.

Pink, S. (2003). Interdisciplinary agendas in visual research: Re-situating visual anthropology. *Visual Studies, 18*(2), 179–192.

Plowman, P. J. (2010). The diary project: Revealing the gendered organisation. *Qualitative Research in Organizations & Management: An International Journal, 5*(1), 28–46.

Plummer, K. (1983). *Documents of Life: An Introduction to the Problems and Literature of a Humanistic Method*. London: Allen and Unwin.

Plummer, K. (2001). *Documents of Life 2: An Invitation to a Critical Humanism*. London: Sage.

Plutchik, R. (1980). A general psychoevolutionary theory of emotion. In R. Plutchik & H. Kellerman (Eds.), *Theories of Emotion* (pp. 3–31). New York: Academic Press.

Pocock, N., McIntosh, A., & Zahra, A. (2011). Video diary methodology and tourist experience research. In T. Rakić & D. Chambers (Eds.), *An Introduction to Visual Research Methods in Tourism* (pp. 108–125). New York: Routledge.

Polkinghorne, D. E. (1988). *Narrative Knowing and the Human Sciences*. Albany, NY: SUNY Press.

Polkinghorne, D. E. (1995). Narrative configuration in qualitative analysis. *International Journal of Qualitative Studies in Education, 8*(1), 5–23. http://dx.doi.org/10.1080/0951839950080103

Popkin, J. (2009). Philippe Lejeune, explorer of the diary. In *On Diary* (pp. 1–15). Honolulu: University of Hawaii Press.

Popper, K. R. (1959). *Logik der Forschung. The Logic of Scientific Discovery*. London: Hutchinson.

Poppleton, S., Briner, R. B., & Kiefer, T. (2008). The roles of context and everyday experience in understanding work–non-work relationships: A qualitative diary study of white- and blue-collar workers. *Journal of Occupational & Organizational Psychology, 81*(3), 481–502. doi:10.1348/096317908X295182

Possing, B. (2001). Biography: Historical. *International Encyclopedia of the Social & Behavioral Sciences, 2*, 1213–1217.

Potter, J. (2010). Contemporary discursive psychology: Issues, prospects, and Corcoran's awkward ontology. *British Journal of Social Psychology, 49*(4), 657–678. doi:10.1348/014466610X486158

Potts, K., & Brown, L. (2005). Becoming an anti-oppressive researcher. In L. A. Brown & S. Strega (Eds.), *Research as Resistance: Critical, Indigenous, and Anti-oppressive Approaches* (pp. 255–286). Toronto, ONT: Canadian Scholar's Press/Women Press.

Radcliffe, L. S. (2013). Qualitative diaries: Uncovering the complexities of work-life decision-making. *Qualitative Research in Organizations & Management: An International Journal, 8*(2), 163–180. http://dx.doi.org/10.1108/QROM-04-2012-1058

Radcliffe, L. S. (2016). Using qualitative diaries to uncover the complexities of daily experiences. In K. Townsend, R. Loudoun, & D. Lewin (Eds.), *Handbook of Qualitative Research Methods on Human Resource Management: Innovative Techniques* (pp. 191–204). Northhampton, MA: Edward Elgar.

Radcliffe, L. S., & Cassell, C. (2014). Resolving couples' work–family conflicts: The complexity of decision making and the introduction of a new framework. *Human Relations, 67*(7), 793–819. doi:10.1177/0018726713506022

Reichmann, C. L. (2001). Reflection as Social Practice: An In-Depth Linguistic Study of Teacher Discourse in a Dialogue Journal (doctoral dissertation). Retrieved from Universidade Federal de Santa Catarina, Florianópolis, Brazil.

Reis, H. T. (2008). Reinvigorating the concept of situation in social psychology. *Personality & Social Psychology Review, 12*(4), 311–329. doi:10.1177/108886830832172

Renders, H., de Haan, B., & Harmsma, J. (Eds.). (2016). *The Biographical Turn: Lives in History*. New York: Routledge.

Rettberg, J. W. (2008). Blogs, literacies and the collapse of private and public. *Leonardo Electronic Almanac, 16*(2–3), 1–10.

Richardson, M. R. (2012). Trauma and Representation in Women's Diaries of the Second World War (doctoral dissertation). Retrieved January 5, 2016 from University of St Andrews, Scotland. http://hdl.handle.net/10023/3347

Ricoeur, P. (1975). Phenomenology and hermeneutics. *Noûs, 9*(1), 85–102. doi:10.2307/2214343

Riordan, R. J. (1996). Scriptotherapy: Therapeutic writing as a counseling adjunct. *Journal of Counseling & Development: JCD, 74*(3), 263.

Roberts, B. (2014). Biographical research: Past, present, future. In M. O'Neill, B. Roberts, & A. C. Sparkes (Eds.), *Advances in Biographical Methods: Creative Applications* (pp. 11–29). New York: Routledge.

Rosefield, H. (2015, November 13). The diary of the most boring man in the world. *The New Republic*. Retrieved January 15, 2016 from https://newrepublic.com/article/123593/the-diary-of-the-most-boring-man-in-the-world

Rosner, T. T., Namazi, K. H., & Wykle, M. L. (1992). Health diaries and interviews consistency in reporting by older adults. *Research on Aging, 14*(2), 248–266. doi:10.1177/0164027592142005

Roy, P. (1960). *Design and Truth in Autobiography.* Cambridge, MA: Harvard University Press.

Runyan, W. M. (1982). *Life Histories and Psychobiography: Explorations in Theory and Method.* New York: Oxford University Press.

Russell, S. A. (2014). *Diary of a Citizen Scientist.* Eugene, OR: Oregon State University Press.

Sá, J. (2002). Diary writing: An interpretative research method of teaching and learning. *Educational Research & Evaluation, 8*(2), 149–168.

Sacks, O. (2016). *On the Move: A Life.* London: Pan Macmillan.

Said, E. (1979). *Orientalism.* New York: Vintage.

Saldaña, J. (2011). *Fundamentals of Qualitative Research.* OUP USA.

Sampanes, A. C., Snyder, M., Rampoldi-Hnilo, L., & White, B. K. (2011). Photo diaries—A peek into a mobile worker's life. In A. Marcus (Ed.), *International Conference of Design, User Experience, and Usability* (pp. 640–647). Berlin: Springer.

Sandelowski, M. (1986). The problem of rigor in qualitative research. *Advances in Nursing Science, 8*(3), 27–37.

Sandelowski, M. (1993). Rigor or rigor mortis: the problem of rigor in qualitative research revisited. *Advances in Nursing Science, 16*(2), 1–8.

Sandelowski, M. (2000). Whatever happened to qualitative description? *Research in Nursing & Health, 23*, 334—340.

Sandelowski, M. (2010). What's in a name? Qualitative description revisited. *Research in Nursing & Health, 33*(1), 77–84. doi:10.1002/nur.20362

Scannella, C. (2009). Virtual memory: The blog as technological prosthetic. *The New School Psychology Bulletin, 6*(2), 3–14.

Scharff, R. C. (2002). *Comte After Positivism.* Cambridge, UK: Cambridge University Press.

Schlaeger, J. (1999). Self-exploration in early modern English diaries. In R. Langford & R. West (Eds.), *Marginal Voices, Marginal Forms: Diaries in European Literature and History* (pp. 22–36). Amsterdam, Netherlands: Rodolfi.

Schlagman, S., Schulz, J., & Kvavilashvili, L. (2006). A content analysis of involuntary autobiographical memories: Examining the positivity effect in old age. *Memory, 14*(2), 161–175.

Schlissel, L. (2011). *Women's Diaries of the Westward Journey.* New York, NY: Schocken Books.

Schmitz, B., & Wiese, B. S. (2006). New perspectives for the evaluation of training sessions in self-regulated learning: Time-series analyses of diary data. *Contemporary Educational Psychology, 31*(1), 64–96.

Schoppa, R. K. (2010). Diaries as a historical source: Goldmines and/or slippery slopes. *The Chinese Historical Review, 17*(1), 31–36. http://dx.doi.org/10.1179/tcr.2010.17.1.31

Schumacher, K. L., Koresawa, S., West, C., Dodd, M., Paul, S. M., Tripathy, D., & Miaskowski, C. (2002). The usefulness of a daily pain management diary for outpatients with cancer-related pain. *Oncology Nursing Forum, 29*(9), 1304–1313.

Scollon, C. N., Prieto, C. K., & Diener, E. (2009). Experience sampling: Promises and pitfalls, strength and weaknesses. In *Assessing Well-Being* (pp. 157–180). Amsterdam, Netherlands: Springer.

Seale, C. (1999). Quality in qualitative research. *Qualitative Inquiry, 5*(4), 465–478.

Seelig, S. C. (2006). *Autobiography and Gender in Early Modern Literature: Reading Women's Lives, 1600–1680.* Cambridge, UK: Cambridge University Press.

Serfaty, V. (2004). *The Mirror and the Veil: An Overview of American Online Diaries and Blogs* (Vol. 11). Amsterdam, Netherlands: Rodopi.

Shank, G. (1995). Semiotics and qualitative research in education: The third crossroad. *The Qualitative Report, 2*(3), 1–11. Retrieved January 15, 2017 from http://nsuworks.nova.edu/tqr/vol2/iss3/1

Shank, G. (2002). *Qualitative Research. A Personal Skills Approach.* New York: Prentice Hall.

Shaw Clifford, R. (1930). *The Jack-Roller: A Delinquent Boy's Own Story.* Chicago, IL: University of Chicago Press.

Sheble, L., & Wildemuth, B. (2009). Research diaries. In B. Wildemuth (Ed.), *Applications of Social Research Methods to Questions in Information and Library Science* (pp. 211–221). Santa Barbara, CA: Libraries Unlimited.

Sheridan, D. (1993). Writing to the archive: Mass-observation as autobiography. *Sociology, 27*(1), 27–40.

Shiffman, S., Stone, A. A., & Hufford, M. R. (2008). Ecological momentary assessment. *Annual Review of Clinical Psychology, 4*, 1–32. doi:10.1146/annurev.clinpsy.3.022806.091415

Silvertown, J. (2009). A new dawn for citizen science. *Trends in Ecology & Evolution, 24*(9), 467–471.

Singer, M., Stopka, T., Siano, C., Springer, K., Barton, G., Khoshnood, K., . . . Heimer, R. (2000). The social geography of AIDS and hepatitis risk: Qualitative approaches for assessing local differences in sterile-syringe access among injection drug users. *American Journal of Public Health, 90*(7), 1049–1056.

Smith, L. (1994). Biographical methods. In N. Denzin & Y. Lincoln (Eds.), *Handbook of Qualitative Research* (pp. 286–305). Thousand Oaks, CA: Sage.

Smith, L. T. (1999). *Decolonizing Methodologies: Research and Indigenous Peoples*. London: Zed Books.

Smyth, A. (2013). Diaries. In A. Hadfield (Ed.), *The Oxford Handbook of English Prose 1500–1640* (pp. 434–451). New York: Oxford University Press.

Solesbury, W. (2002). The ascendancy of evidence. *Planning Theory & Practice*, *3*(1), 90–96. http://dx.doi.org/10.1080/14649350220117834

Sorapure, M. (2003). Screening moments, scrolling lives: Diary writing on the web. *Biography*, *26*(1), 1–23. doi:10.1353/bio.2003.0034

Sorokin, P. A., & Berger, C. Q. (1938). *Time Budgets of Human Behaviour*. Cambridge, MA: Harvard University Press.

Speed, S. (2006). At the crossroads of human rights and anthropology: Toward a critically engaged activist research. *American Anthropologist*, *108*(1), 66–76. doi:10.1525/aa.2006.108.1.66

Spiegelberg, H. (1975). *Doing Phenomenology: Essays on and in Phenomenology*. The Hague, Netherlands: Martinus Nijhoff Publishers.

Squires, P. C. (1937). Fyodor Dostoevsky: A psychopathographical sketch. *Psychoanalytic Review*, *24*, 365–385.

St. Pierre, E. A., & Jackson, A. Y. (2014). Qualitative data analysis after coding. *Qualitative Inquiry*, *20*, 715–719.

Stanley, H. M. (1897). Psychic development of young animals and its physical correlation. *Psychological Review*, *4*(1), 92–93. doi:10.1037/h0068490

Stanley, L. (Ed.). (2013). *Documents of Life Revisited: Narrative and Biographical Methodology for a 21st Century Critical Humanism*. Farnham, UK: Ashgate Publishing.

Steinitz, R. (2011). *Time, Space, and Gender in the Nineteenth-Century British Diary*. New York: Palgrave Macmillan.

Stern, D. N. (2004). *The Present Moment in Psychotherapy and Everyday Life (Norton Series on Interpersonal Neurobiology)*. New York: W.W. Norton & Company.

Still, W., & Finseth, I. (2007). *The Underground Railroad: Authentic Narratives and First-Hand Accounts*. Chelmsford, MA: Courier Corporation.

Stone, A. A., & Shiffman, S. (1994). Ecological momentary assessment (EMA) in behavioral medicine. *Annals of Behavioral Medicine*, *16*, 199–202.

Stopka, T. J., Springer, K. W., Khoshnood, K., Shaw, S., & Singer, M. (2004). Writing about risk: Use of daily diaries in understanding drug-user risk behaviors. *AIDS & Behavior*, *8*(1), 73–85.

Strauss, A., & Corbin, J. M. (1997). *Grounded Theory in Practice*. Thousand Oaks, CA: Sage.

Strauss, L. C., & Cross, W. E. (2005). Transacting black identity: A two week daily-diary study. In G. Downey, J. S. Eccles, & C. M. Chatman (Eds.), *Navigating the Future: Social Identity, Coping and Life Tasks* (pp. 67–95). New York: Russell Sage Foundation.

Summerfield, P. (1998). *Reconstructing women's wartime lives: discourse and subjectivity in oral histories of the Second World War.* Manchester University Press.

Swim, J. K., Cohen, L. L, & Hyers, L. L. (1998). Experiencing everyday prejudice and discrimination. In J. K. Swim & C. Stangor (Eds.), *Prejudice: The Target's Perspective* (pp. 37–60). San Diego, CA: Academic Press.

Swim, J. K., Hyers, L. L., Cohen, L. L., & Fergusen, M. J. (2001). Everyday sexism: Evidence for its incidence nature and psychological impact from three daily diary studies. *Journal of Social Issues, 57,* 31–54.

Swim, J. K., Hyers, L. L., Cohen, L. L., Fitzgerald, D., & Bylsma, W. (2003). African American college students' experiences with everyday racism: Characteristics of and responses to incidents. *Journal of Black Psychology, 29,* 38–67.

Szabó, M., & Lovibond, P. F. (2006). Worry episodes and perceived problem solving: A diary-based approach. *Anxiety, Stress, & Coping, 19*(2), 175–187. http://dx.doi.org/10.1080/10615800600643562

Szalai, A. (1966). Trends in comparative time-budget research. *American Behavioral Scientist, 9*(9), 3–8.

Szalai, A. (1972). *The Use of Time: Daily Activities of Urban and Suburban Populations in Twelve Countries.* Mouton, The Hague, Netherlands.

Tanner, C., Maher, J., & Fraser, S. (2013). Digital narcissism: Social networking, blogging and the tethered self. In *Vanity: 21st Century Selves* (pp. 150–177). London: Palgrave Macmillan UK.

Terman, L. M. (1934). The measurement of personality. *Science, 80*(2087), 605–608.

Terzioğlu, D. (2002). Man in the image of God in the image of the times: Sufi self-narratives and the diary of Niyāzī-i Mışrī (1618–94). *Studia Islamica, 94,* 139–165. doi:10.2307/1596215

Thies, C. G. (2002). A pragmatic guide to qualitative historical analysis in the study of international relations. *International Studies Perspectives, 3*(4), 351–372. https://doi.org/10.1111/1528-3577.t01-1-00099

Thompson, C. (2015, September 19). Speak and spell: How dictation software makes us rethink writing. In *Wired.* Retrieved August 15, 2016 from https://www.wired.com/2015/09/thompson-2/

Thomson, J., Elgin, C., Hyman, D., Rubin, P., & Knight, J. (2006). Research on human subjects: Academic freedom and the institutional review board. *Academe, 92*(5), 95–100. doi:10.2307/40253500

Todd, M. (1992). Puritan self-fashioning: The diary of Samuel Ward. *The Journal of British Studies*, *31*(3), 236–264. https://doi.org/10.1086/386007

Toms, E. G., & Duff, W. (2002). "I spent 1½ hours sifting through one large box . . . .": Diaries as information behavior of the archives user: Lessons learned. *Journal of the American Society for Information Science & Technology*, *53*(14), 1232–1238. doi:10.1002/asi.10165

Tov, W., Ng, K. L., Lin, H., & Qiu, L. (2013). Detecting well-being via computerized content analysis of brief diary entries. *Psychological Assessment*, *25*(4), 1069–1078. http://dx.doi.org/10.1037/a0033007

Travers, C. (2011). Unveiling a reflective diary methodology for exploring the lived experiences of stress and coping. *Journal of Vocational Behavior*, *79*(1), 204–216

Travers, C. J., Morisano, D., & Locke, E. A. (2015). Self-reflection, growth goals, and academic outcomes: A qualitative study. *British Journal of Educational Psychology*, *85*(2), 224–241. doi:10.1111/bjep.12059

Tuchman, G. (1998). Historical social science: Methodologies, methods and meanings. Strategies of qualitative inquiry. In N. Denzin & Y. Lincoln (Eds.), *Qualitative Research* (pp. 225–260). Thousand Oaks, CA: Sage.

Turner, E. (1993). Experience and poetics in anthropological writing. In P. Benson (Ed.), *Anthropology and Literature* (pp. 27–47). Chicago, IL: University of Illinois Press.

Turzańska, A. (2014). Junior high school learners' ability to reflect in the process of keeping a diary in a foreign language. In D. Gabryś-Barker & A. Wojtaszek (Eds.), *Studying Second Language Acquisition from a Qualitative Perspective* (pp. 71–89). New York: Springer International Publishing.

Twine, F. W. (2016). Visual sociology in a discipline of words: Racial literacy, visual literacy and qualitative research methods. *Sociology*, *50*(5), 967–974. doi:10.1177/0038038516649339

Typical Usage Guidelines in Archival Repositories. (n.d.). *Society of American Archivists*. Retrieved January 15, 2016 from http://www2.archivists.org/usingarchives/typicalusageguidelines

Välimäki, T., Vehviläinen-Julkunen, K., & Pietilä, A. M. (2007). Diaries as research data in a study on family caregivers of people with Alzheimer's disease: Methodological issues. *Journal of Advanced Nursing*, *59*(1), 68–76.

van Dijck, J. (2004). Composing the self: Of diaries and lifelogs. *Fibreculture*, *3*(0). Retrieved January 15, 2016. http://three.fibreculturejournal.org/fcj-012-composing-the-self-of-diaries-and-lifelogs/

van Eeden, F. (1913). A study of dreams. *Proceedings of the Society for Psychical Research*, *26*, 431–461.

Verbrugge, L. M. (1980). Health diaries. *Medical Care, 18*(1), 73–95.

Waddington, K. (2005). Using diaries to explore the characteristics of work-related gossip: Methodological considerations from exploratory multimethod research. *Journal of occupational & Organizational Psychology, 78*(2), 221–236.

Wallace, D. B. (1992). Studying the individual: The case study method. In D. B. Wallace & H. E. Gruber (Eds.), *Creative People at Work: Twelve Cognitive Case Studies* (pp. 25–43). New York: Oxford University Press.

Washburn, D. (2011). *The Pillow Book of Sei Shonagon: The Diary of a Courtesan in Tenth Century Japan.* Clarendon, VT: Tuttle Publishing.

Watson, C. (2016). Between diary and memoir: Documenting a life in wartime Britain. In L. Stanley (Ed.), *Documents of Life Revisited: Narrative and Biographical Methodology for a 21st Century Critical Humanism* (pp. 107–120). New York: Routledge.

Watson, J. B. (1913/1924). Psychology as the behaviorist views it. *Psychological Review, 20*(2), 1–158.

Wechtler, H. (2015). Cross-cultural adjustment of female self-initiated expatriates: A longitudinal diary study. In *Academy of Management Proceedings* (vol. 2015, no. 1, p. 13414). Briarcliff Manor, NY: Academy of Management.

Wells, K. (2011). *Narrative Inquiry.* New York: Oxford University Press.

Wheeler, L., & Miyake, K. (1992). Social comparison in everyday life. *Journal of Personality and Social Psychology, 62*(5), 760.

Wheeler, L., & Reis, H. T. (1991). Self-recording of everyday life events: Origins, types, and uses. *Journal of Personality, 59*, 339–354. doi:10.1111/j.1467-6494.1991.tb00252.x

Wickens, C. M., Roseborough, J. E., Hall, A., & Wiesenthal, D. L. (2013). Anger-provoking events in driving diaries: A content analysis. *Transportation Research Part F: Traffic Psychology & Behaviour, 19*, 108–120.

Wightman, C. S. (1936). The teacher's diary as an instrument of follow-up work. *The Journal of Educational Research, 30*(4), 237–240. http://dx.doi.org/10.1080/00220671.1936.10880666

Wild, F., & Macklin, A. H. (1923). *Shackleton's Last Voyage. The Story of the Quest.* London: Cassell.

Wildermuth, H. (1932). Schizophrenie von innen. *Zeitschrift für die gesamte Neurologie und Psychiatrie, 139*(1), 53–74. doi:10.1007/BF02864655

Wills, W. J., Dickinson, A. M., Meah, A., & Short, F. (2016). Reflections on the use of visual methods in a qualitative study of domestic kitchen practices. *Sociology, 50*(3), 470–485. doi:10.1177/0038038515587651

Wiseman, V., Conteh, L., & Matovu, F. (2005). Using diaries to collect data in resource-poor settings: Questions on design and implementation. *Health Policy & Planning, 20*(6), 394–404. https://doi.org/10.1093/heapol/czi042

Wood, D. (1991). Introduction: Interpreting the narrative. In D. Wood (Ed.), *On Paul Ricoeur: Narrative and Interpretation* (pp. 34–54). New York: Routledge.

Woodson, C. G. (2010). Benjamin Tucker Tanner (1835–1923) diary entry, December 24, 1860. In *Carter Godwin Woodson Papers, 1736–1974* (pp. 1–32). Washington, DC: Manuscript Division, Library of Congress.

Wragg, M. (1968). The leisure activities of boys and girls. *Educational Research, 10*(2), 139–144.

Yakel, E., Shaw, S., & Reynolds, P. (2007). Creating the next generation of archival finding aids. *D-lib Magazine, 13*(5/6), 2.

Yilmaz, K. (2013). Comparison of quantitative and qualitative research traditions: Epistemological, theoretical, and methodological differences. *European Journal of Education, 48*(2), 311–325. doi:10.1111/ejed.12014

Young, K., Ashby, D., Boaz, A., & Grayson, L. (2002). Social science and the evidence-based policy movement. *Social Policy & Society, 1*(3), 215–224. https://doi.org/10.1017/S1474746402003068

Zarantonello, L., & Luomala, H. T. (2011). Dear Mr Chocolate: Constructing a typology of contextualized chocolate consumption experiences through qualitative diary research. *Qualitative Market Research: An International Journal, 14*(1), 55–82. http://dx.doi.org/10.1108/13522751111099328

Zepeda, L., & Deal, D. (2008). Think before you eat: Photographic food diaries as intervention tools to change dietary decision making and attitudes. *International Journal of Consumer Studies, 32*(6), 692–698.

Zimmerman, D. H., & Wieder, D. L. (1977). The diary: Diary-interview method. *Journal of Contemporary Ethnography, 5*(4), 479–498.

Zinn, J. O. (2005). The biographical approach: A better way to understand behaviour in health and illness. *Health, Risk & Society, 7*(1), 1–9. http://dx.doi.org/10.1080/13698570500042348

Zundel, M., MacIntosh, R., & Mackay, D. (2016). The utility of video diaries for organizational research. *Organizational Research Methods.* doi:10.1177/1094428116665463

INDEX

Page numbers followed by *f* indicate figures; page numbers followed by *t* indicate tables

A

abstract of qualitative diary study, composing, 136–37
activist (qualitative) research projects, 48–49
Affleck, G., 64–65
African Americans, 5–7
ageism, 52
Agnew, V., 21
Allport, Gordon W., 18–19, 49, 150
Alzheimer's disease, diaries of caregivers for family members with, 82
ambiguous phenomena, 66–67
analysis, 101, 149
coding and, 113–31
Anderson, J., 15
anger diaries, 11, 121
animal behavior, 12–13
anonymity, 91, 92, 109, 132, 166
application (diary research), 163
applied diary research, 48–59

archival diaries. *See also specific topics*
approaches to reading, 35
rules for handling, 143–46
supporting documents for, 100–101
archival diary studies
"participants," 72–74
sourcing and accessing existing diaries for, 142
archival personal diaries, 72–73
archival research diaries, 73–74
archiving, data, 149–50
art and artists diaries, 10, 11, 45, 90, 100
artwork in diary entries, 90
Association for Autobiography and Autobiographical Heritage, 19
audience, 168
audio recorded entries, 30, 40, 58, 74, 87–92, 112, 121, 124, 152
auditing, 161
auto-ethnography, 40–41

autopsy principle/dead social scientist test, 21, 99–100
awareness. *See* reflexivity

B

Baddeley, J. L., 64
Ballantyne, R., 83
Barthes, Roland, 19–20
Bashkirtseff, Marie, 10–11
Beal, D. J., 58
behavior modification, 56
Beller, M., 122–23
Beresford, P., 52–53
big Q researchers, 135
Bingley, A., 29
biographical analysis, 122–24
biographical research, diaries in, 36–38, 37t
biographical structuring, 123
biographical turn, 36
blog posts. *See* online diaries
Blumer, H., 20
Boman, J. S., 75
Braun, V., 124–26
Briner, R. B., 66–67
Bruner, E., 39
Bühler, Charlotte, 12
Bunkers, S. L., 49–50
Burgess, Ernest, 14
Butrick, R., 5–6

C

cancer patient, diary of a, 55
Cantor, N., 150–51
Cardell, K., 30, 94–95
case studies, 36, 77
case study analysis. *See* biographical analysis
Cashmore, A., 92
Cassell, C., 63–64
category labels, naming the, 120
Chapman, Tracy, 89–90
Cherrington, J., 93
Chicago school (sociology), 13
child development, 11–13, 36, 70
chocolate consumption, 66, 115
Christianity and diaries, 3–4
chronological details, 64

citizen scientists, 2
Clark, C., 40–41
Clarke, V., 124–26
clinical and health diaries, 23–25, 47, 53, 55–57, 120
clinical research, diaries in, 54–57
codebook, 32, 128, 129t, 130, 132–33
coder's handbook/codebook, 128
elements of, 128
coding
analysis and, 103–4, 113–31
preparation of diaries for, 113
Cohen, D. J., 95
co-investigators, participants as, 75
commissioned diaries. *See* solicited diaries
confidentiality, 92, 109, 164, 166
confirmability, 163
constructionist diary research, 38–48
consumer research. *See* marketing and consumer research
Conteh, L., 150
content analysis, 32–33, 34t
steps of a, 118–21
types of, 118
contextual details, 66
contextualizing, 108
context units, 119
convenience sampling, 76
conventional content analysis coding, 118
Converse, J. M., 14
Conway, N., 66–67
Cook, S., 52
Cope, D. G., 161–62
counts, totaling/checking/tallying, 65–66
covert phenomena, 66–67
credibility of qualitative studies, 159–61. *See also* data credibility issues
critical theory. *See* post-colonial, anti-racist critical theory
cultural transformations that have facilitated diary writing, 3
culture, viii, 2, 3, 8, 19, 23, 25, 38, 63, 151, 152

cyber documentation, viii
cyber-tethered self, viii
Czerwinski, M., 70–71

D
daily diaries, 54, 95, 96
daily entries, 96
daily process study, 64–65
Daniel, G. R., 64
Darwin, Charles, 11–12
data archiving, 149–50
data collection phase (diary
    research), 142–49
  accessing diaries, 143–44
  design strengths and weaknesses in,
      154–55t
  guidelines for researchers during, 148
  locating diaries, 142–43
  seeking additional consent from
      collection holders:, 143
  sourcing and accessing existing
      diaries, 142
data credibility issues, 157–61
data organization (diary research),
    146, 148
dead social scientist, 99–100
debriefing (diary research), 148–49
de Haan, B., 123–24
descriptive diary research, 31–38
developmental phenomena, studies
    about, 115–16
developmental psychology, 11–13
Dewey, John, 151
diary articles by discipline over time,
    22f, 22–23
diary entries, 29–31. See also specific
    types of entries
  elements of, 47–48
  modes for making, 30. See also
      medium of diary entries
  subject content, 30
diary(ies), 1–2. See also specific topics
  contribution to new disciplines of
      human inquiry, 9–10
  endings in, 47
  features of, 46
  future of, 25–26
  generating and organizing new, 146

history of, 2–22
  the diary emerges in the literature
      of popular culture, 3–8
  the diary moves into the 21st
      century, 22–25
  from literary device to research
      tool, 2–3
  instructions for completing, 147
  nature of, 1–2
  secondary analysis of, 24, 26n
  side effects, 152
  ways they persuade readers of their
      authenticity while calling into
      doubt their veracity, 161
diary-interview method, 100–101
diary project planning and
    management, 140. See also data
    collection phase; post–data
    collection phase; pre–data
    collection phase
diary research, 152. See also
    specific topics
  future of, 25–26
  history of its role in social
      sciences, 2–3
  methodological strengths
      and weaknesses of,
      150–55t, 156–63
  prevalence over time, 22f, 22–23
diary researcher. See researcher(s)
diary research reports
  dimensions for which they can be
      evaluated, 162
  outlets for sharing, 104–6
diary research topics, 24
"diary rooms," online, 95
diary study. See also specific topics;
    specific types of studies
  nature of data one can obtain from
      a, 61–71
diary study participants, 28–29, 71.
    See also solicited diary study
    participants
  archival diary study
      "participants," 72–74
diary study publishing, 3, 8, 11,
    15, 23, 54, 55, 72, 73, 101,
    105, 106

diary style of thinking about one's life
    as a story to document, 25
Dickinson, A. M., 90–91
dictation software, 89
Diener, E., 114
digital anthropology and digital
    humanities, 39–40
digital diaries. *See* online diaries
digital narcissism, viii
digital technology, viii, 39–41, 58–59,
    74, 93–96
directive content analysis coding, 118
Discussion section of report, 106,
    108, 132
  composing, 109, 135–36
  contents and components of, 105,
    107–8, 132, 135–36
  goals of, 135
  literature review in, 108
documentation, society's increased, viii
Dollard, John, 19
Dostoyevsky, Fyodor, 11
dream diaries, 11
Drinker, Elizabeth, 7–8
Duff, W., 72
Duncan, E., 33
dynamic amorphous phenomena, 66

E
ecological momentary
    assessment, 24, 58
educational research, viii, 11, 14, 23,
    39, 40, 44, 45, 51, 53–54, 58,
    73, 75, 87, 94, 105, 142
emancipatory research, 19, 51
emic (inductive) approaches to data
    analysis, 31, 33, 38, 39, 43
emic themes (thematic analysis), 124
empiricism, 10, 16, 17, 21, 49
ephemera, 28, 70
epistemological orientations of diary
    studies, 31
epistemological reflexivity, 107, 110,
    136, 141
ethical considerations in qualitative
    diary research, 164–68. *See also*
    psychological research, ethics in

ethnographic diary studies, 38–41
etic (deductive) approaches to data
    analysis, 31, 33
etic themes (thematic analysis), 124
event-contingent diary studies, 97–98
everyday events, 62–63
Experimental Sampling Method, 97

F
Faustine Kowalska, Saint, 42
feminism and feminist diary
    studies, 49–51
feminist research, 51, 114
feminist theory, ix, 18, 19, 49, 50
feminist values, 50
field notes, 39, 40, 101. *See also*
    "research diaries"
filming. *See also* video diaries
    tips for, 91–92
Fincher, S., 46–48
Findings. *See* Results section of report
Finkel, Irving, 22, 73
Fisher, C. D., 57
Foddy, W., 86
Frank, Anne, 21
French narrative biographical efforts,
    19–20. *See also* Lee, Vernon;
    Lejeune, Philippe
frequencies, totaling/checking/
    tallying, 65–66
Freud, Sigmund, 11
friendship pyramid sampling, 76–77

G
Garfield, S., 62
Gatrell, A., 29
Geertz, Clifford, 2, 20
gender roles, 7, 21, 49, 50, 58, 65,
    68–69, 77, 101, 152. *See also*
    feminism and feminist diary
    studies
Gergen, K. J., 18
Gilgun, J., 136
Gill, J., 62–63
Gilman, E., 12–13
Gläser, J., 116
goal setting, 65, 75

Grazzani-Gavazzi, I., 33
Great Diary Project, 1
Green, P., 92
grounded theory coding, 124, 126
   levels of coding for, 126–28
grounded theory studies, 77
Grupa, P., 40–41

H
Hall, A., 121–22
Hall, G. Stanley, 11
handwritten entries, 87–88
Hansford, B., 83
Harding, D. J., 41
Harmsma, J., 123–24
health diaries. *See* clinical and health
   diaries
hermeneutic circle, 43
hermeneutic diary studies, 41, 43–44
hermeneutics, 43
Hesse, Herman, 5
Hill, I., 21
historical records, 10
historical research, diaries in, 35–36
Holden, Edith, 2
Horvitz, E., 70–71
Huberman, A. M., 113
human science discourse, trends in
   the sensibilities of, viii–ix
humor diaries, 15, 23, 67
Hyers, Lauri L., ix, 23, 49, 51, 58, 65,
   69, 83–85, 99, 116, 128, 129
Hynes, Samuel, 62

I
implications of study, expected, 112
incarcerated women, diaries from, 1,
   6, 114–15. *See also* Prison
industrial and organizational research,
   diaries in, 15, 23, 57–59
informants, participants as, 75
informed consent from participants,
   seeking, 147
institutional approvals, seeking, 142, 147
"interactionist mandate," 150–51
intercoder reliability, 161. *See also*
   inter-rater reliability

interdisciplinary use of diaries, 14–15,
   25, 31–59
Internet. *See* online diaries
interpretive validity, 162
inter-rater reliability, 121, 128, 130,
   132. *See also* intercoder
   reliability
interval/timed entries, 97
interviews with diarists, 100–101
Introduction section of report, 106,
   109, 137
   composing, 109, 133–35
   composing an outline of, 142
   contents and components of, 107–
   11, 121, 133–35
   shorter, 107
introspection, 9, 16, 17, 69, 75, 152

J
Jackson, A. Y., 117
Jackson, S., 91
James, William, 10, 16–17
Jerome, W. S., 4, 10, 63
Johnson, P., 158
Jones, R. K., 55
journals, professional. *See* diary
   articles by discipline over time
journals of conscience, 3

K
Kambouropoulou, P., 15–16
Kamler, B., 92–93
Kandler, R., 42
Kaun, A., 94
Kierkegaard, Søren, 69–70
Kiffin-Petersen, S., 67
Klein, P. D., 75
Krueger, E. T., 13

L
LaLonde, S., 160
Langford, R., 1, 56
language and linguistics, 12, 18, 23,
   31, 35, 37, 38, 40, 41, 43–45,
   51, 54, 89, 108, 117, 118, 124,
   133, 134
Laudel, G., 116

Ledger, K., 52
Lee, Vernon, 11
Lejeune, Philippe, 19, 48
Lempert, L. B., 114–15
Le Page, Michael, 78
Lewin, Kurt, 20, 48, 49
Liamputtong, P., 62–63
life as a story, diary style of thinking
    about, 25
life-history vs. archival methods, 13
linguistics. *See* language and
    linguistics
literacy, 3, 5, 8, 72, 93, 108
literature review
    background literature review in
        Introduction section of report,
        110, 133–34
    in Discussion section of
        report, 108
Locke, Edwin A., 65
logical positivism, 117. *See also*
    positivism
longitudinal details, 64
Lundgren, I., 43–44

M
Mackrill, T., 55–57
marketing and consumer research, 23,
    57–59, 67
Markwell, K. W., 44
Mass Observation Project, 14, 36, 73
Materials section of report, 112, 131
Matovu, F., 150
McGartland, M., 115
McIntosh, A., 91
McIver, S., 115
Meah, A., 90–91
meaning, identifying units of, 114
medium of diary entries, 29, 30, 87–96
member checking, 130, 159, 161
memoirs, 36
memory(ies), 9, 10, 33, 34t, 93, 113,
    159, 161
mental health and mental illness, 11,
    52–53, 55, 115
mental health benefits of diary
    keeping, 152

methodological reflexivity, 107, 141,
    158. *See also* reflexivity
Methods section of report, 106
    combining the Results section
        and, 108
    composing, 109, 131–32, 142
    contents and components of, 107,
        111, 121
    length, 107
"Metropolitan Diary" column
    (*New York Times*), 21
micro-, meso-, and macro-level
    phenomena, 30
Miles, M. B., 113
Milligan, C., 29
Millim, A. M., 21
mixed-methods
    studies, 14, 66, 83, 97, 100,
        124, 134, 140, 151
mixed-method structured
    diaries, 84–85
monthly entries, 97
Moran, J., 8, 10
Morawski, C. M., 75–76
Morisano, Dominique, 65
Morrison, Toni, 160
Morse, J. M., 162
multimodal/multimedia diary data,
    23, 30, 40
Murphy, S. A., 67
Murthy, D., 39–40

N
naïve realism, 38, 117, 124, 130
narrative analysis, 48, 123
narrative analysis coding, 128
narrative inquiry with
    diaries, 48–50
narrative movement, reinvigoration of
    the diary by, 18–22
narrative turn in social science, 71
narratology, 48
Native Americans, 5–6
naturalistic inquiry, 20, 32, 38, 49, 93,
    97, 99, 100, 165
non-storied narrative, 46
Noyes, A., 54

O

objectivity, 33, 49, 50
O'Halloran, P., 115
1000 Journals Project, 81–82, 95
Ong, Walter J., 8–9
ongoing recruitment, 73, 77
online diaries, 74, 93–95
    privately posted, 95
    reasons for soliciting, 94
opportunity sampling, 76
oral expression, 8, 30, 35, 40, 90, 152
organizational research. *See* industrial
    and organizational research
outreach (diary research), 146–47.
    See also recruitment

P

Packer, J., 83
Palen, L., 89
Palmer, Vivian, 13
participants. *See* diary study
    participants
Participants section of report, 108,
    112, 131
participatory action research (PAR)/
    participatory inquiry, 52
Patterson, A., 31, 58–59
Pedhazur, E. J., 130
Pennebaker, J. W., 64
personality, 20, 123, 124, 150, 151
Personal Mobile Digital Technology
    (PMDT), 95–96
phases, diary studies on, 64–65
phenomenological diary
    studies, 41–43
photographing diaries, 95, 143
photography in diary entries, 30, 35,
    39–40, 82, 90, 91, 104, 145
Picasso, Pablo, 90
pictures, 91. *See also* visual entries
Pietilä, A. M., 82, 86
Plowman, P. J., 68
Plummer, K., 17
Pocock, N., 91
Polkinghorne, D. E., 46
Popkin, J., 19
popular culture

the diary's emergence in the
    literature of, 3–8
trends in the sensibilities of, viii–ix
positivism, 16, 23. *See also*
    post-positivism
the diary as conflicting with, 16–18
grounded theory and, 126
qualitative research and, 38, 48, 109,
    111, 117, 133–35, 137, 140, 153
validity and, 117, 158
positivist assumptions, 28
positivistic science, 2, 16, 17, 23, 48,
    106. *See also* positivism
positivist quantitative empiricism,
    reductionism of, 20–21
positivist scientific framework,
    making a qualitative research
    report fit a, 106–9
post-colonial, anti-racist critical
    theory, 19, 51
post–data collection phase (diary
    research), 149–50
    design strengths and weaknesses
    in, 155*t*
post-positivism, 16, 38, 71, 106
Potter, J., 32
pre–data collection phase (diary
    research), 140–42, 153
    conceptualizing, 140
    design strengths and weaknesses
    in, 154*t*
    seeking institutional approvals, 142
    writing the basic study outline or
    proposal, 141–42
pre-diary phase (diary
    research), 154*t*
    guidelines for researchers
    during, 147–48
prejudice, ix, 23, 51, 65, 80, 98, 116,
    128, 129
Prieto, C. K., 114
Prince, M. P., 75
prison, women serving life
    sentences in, 1, 6, 114–15.
    See also incarcerated women
privacy, 25
private diary keeping, 3, 7

Procedure section of report, 112, 131–32
process studies/studies on process, 64–65
psychiatry, 52–53, 55
psychobiography, 123
psychodynamic biography, 123
psychological applications of diary research, 10–16
psychological research, ethics in, 49, 139, 142, 164–68
psychology, 19
  diary research in, 10–12, 15, 22f, 22–24, 150, 151
  medical model in, 49, 55
  narrative research and, 18–20
  research methodology in, 16, 17, 55
publishing diaries. *See* diary study publishing
purposive sampling, 24, 79

Q
qualitative method, diary as. *See also specific topics*
  overview of, 27–28
qualitative methodological devices that conflict with traditional social science writing, 106
  contextualizing, 108
  informal language, 108
  lengthier manuscript, 106–7
  overlap of writing and analysis, 109
  reflexivity, 106–8. *See also* reflexivity
  shorter Introduction section, 107
  unconventional organization of sections, 108
qualitative (diary) research, 103, 137–38. *See also specific topics*
  applied diary research, 48–59
  constructionist diary research, 38–48
  descriptive diary research, 31–38
  design issues and strengths in, 153, 154–55t, 156–59
  epistemological orientations of diary studies, 31

ethical considerations in, 164–68. *See also* psychological research, ethics in
  evaluative terminology applied to, 159–63
  overview, 27–28
  strengths of the diary method as a qualitative research method, 150–51
  weaknesses of the diary method as a qualitative research method, 151–52
  writing
    for applied consulting projects, 105
    for non-academic outlets, 104
    for scholarly outlets, 105–6
qualitative (diary) research reports, 137–38. *See also specific sections of reports*
  collective copyediting and proofreading, 137
  composing the title and abstract, 136–37
  making them fit a positivist scientific framework, 106–9
  preparing a pre-study project report outline, 110–12
queer theory, 18, 49, 68
quota sampling, 77

R
Radcliffe, L. S., 63–64, 67, 85
random assignment, 77
random selection, 77
rapport, 80, 157, 167
realism, naïve, 38, 117, 124, 130
recipient of an intervention, 75
recording units, 119
record keeping, viii, 10
records, society's concern about, viii
recruitment (diary research), 77–78, 146–47
  types of, 77
reflections, 69. *See also* reflexivity
reflexive process, 159
reflexive statements, 136

reflexivity, 47, 50, 51, 54, 80,
106–12, 131, 133. *See also*
methodological reflexivity;
researcher reflexivity
in biographical analysis, 123
defined, 106, 107, 136
personal, 107, 110, 136,
140–41, 158
Reflexivity section of report,
108, 135–36
registry card, 144
Reichmann, C. L., 51
Reis, H. T., 20, 56
relationships, interpersonal, 24
religion and diaries, 3–4, 10, 36, 42,
87, 129
Renders, H., 123–24
reporting, 101
reports. *See* qualitative (diary)
research reports
"research diaries," 39, 146. *See also*
archival research diaries;
field notes
researcher-diarist, 75
researcher reflexivity, 136, 154*t*,
158–59. *See also* reflexivity
researcher(s), diary, 28, 79
diaries becoming a researcher's
tool, 10–16
as an overlooked participant in
solicited diary studies, 79–81
rules and guidelines
for, 143–49
research questions, 134–35
responsible speaking, 166
Results section of report, 106,
109, 132–33
retention of participants, 77
Rice, Tilly, 62
Richardson, M. R., 67–68
risk-reduction diary
studies, 55–56
Roberts, B., 95–96
rolling recruitment, 77
Roseborough, J. E., 121–22
Rottmann, J., 75–76
ruminations, private, 69

S
Sacks, Oliver, 160
safe space provided by diary, 160
Saldaña, Johnny, 137
Salzman, M., 89
sample size, 79
sampling, 76–77
sampling units, 118
Sandelowski, M., 162
Schlaeger, J., 8
Schmelkin, L. P., 130
Schoppa, R. K., 35
scientific method, viii–ix
Scollon, C. N., 114
Scott, J., 92
scriptotherapy, 87
seasonal entries, 97
secretive nature of diary keeping, 152
Sedaris, David, 168
self-absorption, 16, 160–61
self-awareness, 8, 53, 57, 107, 152
self-consciousness, diaries as stirring a
self-reflective, 8–9
self-discovery, diary keeping as a form
of personal, 25
self-focus, technologically-assisted, 6
self-objectification, 8, 9
self-reflection, 9, 52, 54
research participants' capacity
for, 74
self-reflective self-consciousness,
diaries as stirring a, 8–9
self-reflexivity, 50. *See also* reflexivity
self-report (methodology), 16, 17
self-understanding, 45
semiotics, 44
semiotics diary studies, 41, 44–45
Serfaty, V., 94
sexism, 68–69
Shackleton, Ernest, 4–5
Shank, G., 80
Sheble, L., 1–2
Shiffman, S., 24
Shogagon, Sei, 7
Short, F., 90–91
Singer, M., 57, 166
singing, 89–90

situated meaning, 41
slaves and slavery, 5, 7
slow knowledge movement, ix
slow science, ix
Smith, L., 100, 122
snowball sampling, 76–77
social constructionism, ix, 19, 20, 117, 157
social constructivism, 49, 59
social gospel, Washington Gladden's, 49
social justice, xi, 48–49
social justice diary research, 48–53
social media, viii, 25, 29–30
social sciences
    history of role of the diary and diary research in, 2–3
    narrative turn in, 71
sociological applications of diary research, 10, 13–14
sociology, 17–20
    diary research in, 13, 17, 18, 22f, 22–24
    qualitative (vs. quantitative) research in, 14, 38, 49
solicited diaries. See also specific topics
    emergence as a primary research tool, 14
    vs. secondhand (unsolicited) diaries, 14–15
    supporting documents for, 100–101
solicited diarist's actual or presumed audience, variations in the, 98–100
solicited diary entry format, 81
    example, 83–85, 84f
    medium of communication of entries, 87–96
    timing of entries, 96–98
    variations in degree of structure in entries, 81–87
solicited diary studies, 23–24
    generating and organizing new diaries in, 146
solicited diary study participants, 74
    diverse vs. homogeneous samples, 75

participant selection criteria, 74–75
recruiting, rewarding, and retaining, 77–78
the researcher as an overlooked participant, 79–81
role in solicited diary studies, 75–76
sample size, 79
sampling, 76–77
Sorapure, M., 8
Soutar, G., 67
spillover effect, 66
Squires, P. C., 11
St. Pierre, E. A., 117
stakeholders, 52, 76, 80, 105, 141, 142, 149, 154, 156, 161
standpoint feminism, 49, 50
state vs. trait phenomena, ix, 20
Still, William, 5
Stopka, T. J., 87
story
    in diary, 5, 8, 15, 18, 22, 25, 45–48, 62, 66, 80, 82, 90, 100, 101, 103, 119, 122–25, 127, 128, 166
    diary style of thinking about one's life as a, 25
    features of, 46
stratified sampling, 77
stream of consciousness, 87
stress, daily, 24
structured and semi-structured diaries, 81–85
subtle phenomena, 66–67
suicidal ideation and suicide prevention, 64
summative content analysis coding, 118
symbolic interactionism, 20
systematic coding, 124
systems, diary studies on, 64–65

T
Tanner, Benjamin Tucker, 6–7
technology. See digital technology
Terman, L. M., 150
testimonies, personal, 62
thematic analysis, 124, 126
    phases in, 124–26

theoretical sampling, 77
theoretical validity, 162
therapeutic effects of diary keeping
    and scriptotherapy, 11, 87,
    152, 160
thick description, 2, 31, 66, 166
Thompson, C., 89
Thousand Journals Project. *See* 1000
    Journals Project
timed/interval entries, 97
time-use/time-budget diaries, 15, 23,
    24, 41, 54, 58, 63, 65, 96
title of qualitative diary study,
    composing, 136–37
To, M. L., 57
Tolstoy, Leo, 160
Toms, E. G., 72
Trail of Tears, 5–6
trait vs. state phenomena, ix, 20
transition to the unknown, 44
transparency of research, 162–63
travel diaries, 4–5
Travers, Cheryl J., 65
Tuchman, G., 35
Turner, Edith, 159
Twine, F. W., 90

U
utility (diary research), 163

V
validity, 32, 130, 158–59
    positivism and, 117, 158
    types of, 162
Välimäki, T., 82, 86
van Dijck, José, 25
Vares, T., 91
Vehviläinen-Julkunen, K., 82, 86
Victorian Era, 3
video cameras, 59, 91
video diaries, 54, 58, 91–94
video entries, 30, 147
virtual spaces, 40

visual data, 33, 41, 44, 90, 91, 112–13
visual diaries, 40, 90, 92, 119, 124
visual entries, 87, 90–92
visual images, 30, 58. *See also*
    photography in diary entries
visual methods, 152
voicemail method, 89

W
Waddington, K., 97
Wahlberg, V., 43–44
Wallcraft, J., 52–53
Ward, Samuel, 3–4
wartime diaries, 7, 14, 21, 46,
    62, 67, 69
Watson, B., 93
Watson, C., 25, 161
Watson, John B., 17
webblogs. *See* online diaries
weekly entries, 96–97
Weiss, H. M., 58
West, R., 1, 56
Wheeler, L., 20, 56
Wickens, C. M., 121–22
Wieder, D. L., 100
Wiesenthal, D. L., 121–22
Wildemuth, B., 1–2
Wilhite, S., 70–71
Wills, W. J., 90–91
Wiseman, V., 150
work–life balance, 42–43, 58,
    63–64, 85
workplace, viii, 23, 58, 66, 76, 101, 150
World Diary Project, 21–22,
    36, 65, 73
wrap-up (diary research), 148–49
writing about one's experiences,
    capacity for, 74
Wundt, Wilhelm, 16

Z
Zahra, A., 91
Zimmerman, D. H., 100